Preface

INTRODUCTION TO THE COURSE

The Second World War provided the impetus for the application of mathematical techniques to the planning of military operations, so that the limited resources of men, materials and equipment might be deployed to maximum advantage. The problems facing military planners are no different, in principle, from the problems facing business and government planners, and since the war there has been a rapid growth in the use of mathematical techniques, by business and government, to solve problems and aid decision-making. A knowledge of 'quantitative methods' (the term by which these techniques are now known) is today regarded as essential by the Business Education Council and by examining bodies for professional courses, and BEC has incorporated parts of the subject into the compulsory core modules of its National awards.

The areas of mathematics from which these techniques are drawn are algebra, probability theory and statistics, and we have found it convenient in this text to develop the subject under these broad headings. Part I ('Numerical methods') develops the mathematical foundations on which the remainder of the course is built, and should be of particular value to students taking the BEC National Common Core Module 2. The largest section of the text, Part II, describes the methods of statistics, and covers the requirements of the BEC Applied Statistics Option Module as well as those of the statistics examinations of a number of professional bodies (including the Institute of Cost and Management Accountants, the Institute of Certified Accountants, the Chartered Institute of Public Finance and Accountancy, and the Institute of Chartered Secretaries and Administrators). The arrangement of material will also make Part II suitable for students taking the BEC National Common Core Module 2 and Business Studies Board Core Module 5.

A number of the techniques described in Part III ('Algebraic methods') and Part IV ('Probabilistic methods') belong to that part of quantitative methods known as 'operations research' (so-called because these techniques were first applied to military operations). Students taking an operations research course, or studying quantitative methods for BEC awards or professional examinations (including those of the Institute of Cost and Management Accountants), should find these parts useful. In addition, students taking the BEC Applied Statistics course will find Chapter 14, 'Growth and decay', relevant to their studies.

The Appendices include a number of suggested assignments and simulations, and these should prove especially useful to those taking BEC courses. Also included are answers to the end-of-chapter questions (answers to non-numerical questions or parts of questions are not given).

SCOPE AND APPLICATIONS OF QUANTITATIVE METHODS

Most of what is now known as quantitative methods has been developed within the traditional subject-areas of statistics and operations research, and it is appropriate to outline at the outset of this course the scope and applications of these two subjects.

The first recorded use of the word 'statistics' was in the late eighteenth century, when it was defined as 'the science that teaches us what is the political arrangement of all the modern states of the known world'. At that time verbal methods were used to describe the characteristics of nations and states, but by the early nineteenth century the science of statistics was dominated by numerical methods. By the beginning of the twentieth century statistics was firmly entrenched as a branch of mathematics, and it has come to be applied not just to analysing the characteristics of states but to gathering and analysing data on any subject, from archaeology to zoology.

During the second half of the nineteenth century the word 'statistics' took on a second meaning — it came to refer to the data on which the analyses were based, so that one spoke of population statistics, transport statistics, etc. However, the word primarily refers to the science of collecting and analysing data.

Some of the applications of statistics in business are as follows:

1. Various measures of economic activity; an example of such a measure is the Retail Price Index — changes in this may have a considerable influence on the strategies of government, businesses, and unions
2. Market research: the study of markets using statistical techniques enables the businessman to decide what type, quality, and quantity of goods to produce and sell
3. The analysis of trends: knowledge of sales trends, population trends, etc., is essential for the formulation of business strategy
4. The determination of relationships: for example, between sales revenue and advertising expenditure — this is a further aid to decision-making
5. Production control and stock control: statistical techniques are widely used in these areas of business
6. The design and analysis of experiments, especially agricultural experiments.

Operations research (O.R.) was developed during the war by teams of scientists and mathematicians attached to a number of military headquarters. Their task was to analyse projected operations in order to determine, on a scientific basis, the best plan of action. After the war O.R. was developed further and applied to business operations, the main applications being:

1. Determining the optimum allocation of resources (of men, materials, capital, equipment, transport, etc.)
2. Deciding between alternative strategies
3. Solving problems involving queueing situations.

The basic O.R. method is the construction of a mathematical model (for example, a series of equations) to represent the problem being studied, and the manipulation of this model to obtain the optimum solution, that is the solution which, for instance, maximizes profits, or minimizes costs.

O.R. is now regarded as an important decision-making tool by both business managers in the West and state planners in the communist world.

High Wycombe   *Roger Carter*

Quantitative Methods for Business Students

Quantitative Methods for Business Students

Roger Carter BSc (Hons)

Lecturer in Numeracy and Quantitative Methods
Buckinghamshire College of Higher Education

Heinemann Professional Publishing: London

Heinemann Professional Publishing Ltd
22 Bedford Square, London WC1B 3HH

LONDON   MELBOURNE
JOHANNESBURG   AUCKLAND

First published 1980
Reprinted 1982, 1984, 1986, 1987
ISBN 0 434 90218 7

Typeset by
Reproduction Drawings Ltd,
Sutton, Surrey

Printed in Great Britain by
Redwood Burn Limited,
Trowbridge, Wiltshire

Contents

Part One

Numerical Methods

One

Arithmetical Calculations

English and mathematics are alike in one essential respect: they are both languages. The former uses words to represent concepts, the latter uses mathematical symbols and numbers. By applying the rules of English, extremely complex ideas can be formulated by combining words to form phrases and sentences, and the language has become far more than just a vehicle for communicating ideas: it actually assists the processes of thought and facilitates the solution of problems. Mathematics likewise is far more than just a convenient tool for expressing the values of goods or the profits of businesses: the numerate person, that is the person trained in the language so that he has a thorough grasp of the rules for manipulating mathematical symbols, is able to think clearly about and solve problems which leave the non-numerate person baffled.

The purpose of Part I of this course is to enable the student to master the basic rules governing that part of mathematics which is used in business. If this mastery is achieved, little difficulty will be experienced with the remainder of the course. We begin in this first chapter by reviewing the rules for dealing with arithmetical problems. It is assumed that the student is familiar with the operations of multiplication, division, addition and subtraction as applied to whole numbers, decimals and fractions.

THE NUMBER SYSTEM

The word 'decimal' (derived from the Latin word for 'tenth') is applied to our number system because that system uses ten as its base. The numbers zero to nine are denoted by the digits 0, 1, 2, . . . , 9. To represent numbers ten times as large, these digits are shifted one position to the left, the digit 0 being used as position indicator: 10, 20, . . . , 90. Further increases by a factor of 10 are indicated by further shifts in position: 100, 200, etc. Position is counted from the decimal point which, although not shown in the above examples, is nevertheless there; the number one could, in theory, be written 1., ten could be written 10., and so on.

A decrease by a factor of ten is shown by shifting the digits one position to the right, the digit 0 again being used, when necessary, to indicate position: one-tenth is .1, one-hundredth is .01, one-thousandth is .001. It is conventional to prefix the decimal point in these instances with the digit 0 (so that one-tenth is written 0.1), but this has no mathematical significance.

The number 73.092 therefore means 70 + 3 + .09 (nine-hundredths) + .002 (two-thousandths). Multiplying this number by ten results in all the digits being shifted one position to the left: 730.92; dividing this number by one hundred results in all the digits being shifted two positions to the right: .73092; and so on.

Although the decimal system is almost universally used, systems based upon numbers other than ten are possible. For example, the binary system, used in computing, has a base of two. In this system there are just two digits, 0 and 1, and any number can be represented by locating these digits in appropriate positions: zero is 0, one is 1, two is 10, three is 11, four is 100, five is 101, six is 110, seven is 111, eight is 1000, and so on. Under this system, an increase in a number by a factor of two (that is, doubling it) is shown by shifting the digits one position to the left, 0 being used to indicate position. A decrease by a factor of two (halving the number) is shown by shifting the digits one position to the right.

COMPARING NUMBERS: FRACTIONS, DECIMALS AND PERCENTAGES

It is frequently necessary to make comparisons between numbers. If we wish to compare the number 3 with the number 4, there are several methods from which to choose. We could state the comparison by means of:

a ratio	$3 : 4$
a fraction	$\frac{3}{4}$
a decimal	0.75
a percentage	75%

Ratios (considered in the next section) are most conveniently used when we wish to compare the size of one part of a total with another part of that total (for example, the ratio of males to females in a class). Fractions, decimals and percentages are used when it is required to compare the size of one part of a total with the total itself (for example, the percentage of males in a class).

If there are 10 cakes on the table and Billy eats one of them, then he has eaten one-tenth of the total. Written as a fraction this is $\frac{1}{10}$ —

the number eaten divided by the total. As a decimal number this is 0.1 — we say that Billy has eaten 0.1 of the cakes. To express this as a percentage (literally 'per hundred'), it is necessary to multiply either the fraction by 100

$$\frac{1}{10} \times 100 = 10\%$$

or the decimal by 100

$$0.1 \times 100 = 10\%$$

10% means 10 divided by 100

i.e $\frac{1}{10}$ or 0.1

If there are 15 sandwiches on the table and Billy eats one-fifth of them, then to find the number he has eaten it is necessary to multiply the total by the fraction

$$\text{the number eaten} = \frac{1}{5} \times 15 = 3$$

A similar calculation is carried out if we say that Billy eats 0.2 of the cakes

$$0.2 \times 15 = 3$$

or 20% of the cakes

$$\frac{20}{100} \times 15 = 3$$

Let us now turn the example around, and suppose that Billy eats 6 of the jam tarts, this being 12% of the total. In this case the total number is unknown, but the result of multiplying that total by a given percentage is known. At first sight the problem of determining the unknown total seems rather tricky, but there is a mathematical technique which can be applied to all problems involving operations on unknown quantities which reduces the method of solution to a series of routine steps:

1. Denote the unknown by a symbol, e.g. x
2. Write down a mathematical model (i.e. an equation) representing the given situation
3. Manipulate the model to determine what value x must take in order to satisfy it.

So in this example we begin by calling the unknown total number of tarts x. Next, we use the fact that 12% of x is equal to 6 to construct our model:

$$\frac{12}{100} x = 6$$

i.e. $0.12 \, x = 6$

Finally, we determine x by rearranging the equation so that the 0.12 is removed from the left hand side, leaving 'x = required answer'. The rule for manipulating equations to achieve this end is simple and obvious: whatever is done to one side of the equation must also be done to the other. (For example, if 2 is added to one side, then 2 must also be added to the other. If one side is multiplied by 3, then the other side must also be multiplied by 3.)

In order to find x in the above equation we must divide both sides by 0.12:

$$\frac{0.12}{0.12} x = \frac{6}{0.12}$$

$$\therefore \quad x = \frac{6}{0.12} = \frac{600}{12} = 50$$

One of the hallmarks of a numerate person is that he can normally tell if the answer to a numerical problem looks about right. This is an ability which is born of long practice of carrying out rough checks. In the above problem 12% is a little more than one-tenth, so 6 tarts comprise a little over one-tenth of the total. 6 is one-tenth of 60, and so the total must be rather less than 60. If we had obtained as our answer 20 tarts, or 80 tarts, these would obviously be wrong. 50 looks about right. A precise check in the above problem is obtained by working backwards from the answer: 12% of 50 = 6, the required number of tarts.

EXAMPLE

By selling an article for £80 a dealer makes a profit of 25% on his cost price.

(a) What is his cost price?
(b) Express the profit as (i) a fraction of the selling price, (ii) a percentage of the selling price.

ANSWER

(a) Call the cost price x.

Then the profit $= \frac{25}{100} x = 0.25x$

Selling price = cost price + profit = x + $0.25x = 1.25x$

Hence £80 = $1.25x$

$$\therefore \quad x = \frac{80}{1.25} = \text{£}64$$

(b)

Profit $= \frac{25}{100} \times 64 = \frac{1}{4} \times 64 = \text{£}16$

So profit as a fraction of the selling price

$$= \frac{16}{80} = \frac{1}{5}$$

Hence profit as a percentage of the selling price

$$= \frac{1}{5} \times 100 = 20\%$$

COMPARING NUMBERS: RATIOS

If there are 10 sausage rolls on the table and Billy eats 2 of them, the ratio of the number eaten to the number left is 2 : 8. Ratios can be cancelled in the same way as fractions: 2 : 8 = 1 : 4. Ratios can be used to show the relative sizes of any number of parts of a total: if there are 14 mince pies on the table, and Fred eats 2 of them, Billy eats 4 and Fatima eats the remaining 8, then the ratio of the number eaten by Fred to the number eaten by Billy to the number eaten by Fatima is 2 : 4 : 8 = 1 : 2 : 4.

The ratio 1 : 2 : 4 can be regarded as comprising 1 + 2 + 4 = 7 parts — Fred has 1 part, Billy has 2 and Fatima has 4. So Fred has 1/7 of the total number of parts (i.e. he has eaten 1/7 of the cakes), Billy has 2/7, and Fatima has 4/7.

EXAMPLE

A, B, and C enter into partnership, A providing £15,000 capital, B providing £9000, and C providing £12,000. The profit is to be divided among the partners in the ratio of their capital. In a year when the profit amounts to £15,000, how much does each receive?

ANSWER

Ratio of A's capital to B's capital to C's capital

$= 15{,}000 : 9000 : 12{,}000 = 15 : 9 : 12$

$= 5 : 3 : 4$

There are 12 parts in total : A has 5/12, B has 3/12 = 1/4, and C has 4/12 = 1/3. Hence A has 5/12 of the profits

i.e. $\frac{5}{12} \times 15{,}000 = £6250$

B has $\frac{1}{4} \times 15{,}000 = £3750$

and

C has $\frac{1}{3} \times 15{,}000 = £5000$. (Check: 6250 + 3750 + 5000 = 15,000.)

EXPONENTS

Mathematical calculations often involve powers of numbers (such as squares or cubes) and roots of numbers (such as square roots or cube roots). The rules for carrying out these calculations given below hold for all numbers, positive, negative or decimal. In stating these rules it is necessary to use letters to represent numbers: a, m and n can be *any* numbers; but to illustrate the rules we shall replace m and n by the numbers 4 and 2. Note that when letters are used instead of numbers it is conventional to either omit the multiplication sign '×' or replace it by a dot, ' . '.

1. a^m means 'a to the power m', i.e. a multiplied by itself m times. For example, 3^4 means $3 \times 3 \times 3 \times 3 = 81$. m is called the 'exponent' (or 'index').

2. $a^m . a^n = a^{m+n}$
   (*Proof* for $m = 4$ and $n = 2$:
   $a^4 . a^2 = (a.a.a.a)(a.a) = a.a.a.a.a.a$
   $= a^6 = a^{4+2}$)

3. $a^1 = a$
   ($a^4 . a = a.a.a.a.a = a^5 = a^{4+1} = a^4 . a^1$. Dividing both sides of this equation by a^4 gives $a = a^1$)

4. $a^0 = 1$
   ($a^4 = a^{4+0} = a^4 . a^0$. Dividing both sides by a^4 gives $1 = a^0$)

5. $a^m / a^n = a^{m-n}$
   ($a^4 / a^2 = \dfrac{a.a.a.a}{a.a} = a.a = a^2 = a^{4-2}$)

6. $a^{-m} = 1/a^m$
   ($a^{-m} = a^{0-m} = a^0/a^m = 1/a^m$)

7. The nth root of a is $a^{1/n}$ (This is the number which, when multiplied by itself n times, gives a)
   (e.g. $a^{1/2} . a^{1/2} = a^{1/2+1/2} = a^1 = a$. Hence the square root of a is $a^{1/2}$. Similarly for the 4th root: $a^{1/4} . a^{1/4} . a^{1/4} . a^{1/4} = a^{1/4+1/4+1/4} = a^1 = a$)

8. $(a^m)^n = a^{mn}$ ($(a^m)^n$ means a^m multiplied by itself n times.)
   ($(a^4)^2 = a^4 . a^4 = a^{4+4} = a^{4 \times 2}$)

EXAMPLE

Evaluate $(2^{-6})^{1/2} . (2^3)^{-2} . 2^9$

ANSWER

$(2^{-6})^{1/2} = 2^{-6 . 1/2}$ (by rule 8)

$= 2^{-3}$.

$$(2^3)^{-2} = 2^{3.(-2)} = 2^{-6}.$$

Hence the required value is

$$2^{-3}.2^{-6}.2^9 = 2^{-3-6+9} \text{ (by rule 2)}$$

$$= 2^0$$

$$= 1 \text{ (by rule 4)}$$

LOGARITHMS

Although logarithms have been superseded by pocket calculators as aids to multiplication and division, they have, as we shall see in Chapter 2, other important applications, and the student should be familiar with their use.

It is clear from the rules given in the previous section that $10^0 = 1$, $10^1 = 10$, and $10^2 = 100$. But the value of a number with a decimal exponent, such as $10^{0.1234}$, or $10^{1.1234}$, is far from obvious. The former number must lie somewhere between the values of 10^0 and 10^1, and the latter between the values of 10^1 and 10^2 — but what are their exact values?

Let us turn the question around, and ask, 'to what power must 10 be raised to give a certain result, say 1.246?' (A mathematician would express this question thus: 'What value of x satisfies the equation $10^x = 1.246$?'). x obviously lies between 0 and 1, since $10^0 = 1$ (which is less than 1.246), and $10^1 = 10$ (which is greater than 1.246), but to get an accurate value it is necessary to use tables of common logarithms. If 1.246 is looked up in the tables, the value of x will be seen to be 0.09555.

0.09555 is said to be the logarithm to the base 10 of 1.246 — this means that $10^{0.09555}$ is equal to 1.246. Bases other than 10 are possible, of course. If 1.246 is looked up in a table of 'natural logarithms' (which use a base of 2.71828), then the value found will be 0.21991, and this tells us that $2.71828^{0.21991} = 1.246$. We shall only be concerned with common logarithms (which use a base of 10).

These tables are restricted to logarithms of numbers lying between 1 and 10. To determine the logarithm of a number lying outside this range it is necessary to (a) shift the decimal point the number of places required to bring the number within the range of the tables, and (b) compensate for this shift by multiplying the result by the corresponding power of 10. For example, let us find the logarithm of 222.2:

$$222.2 = 10^2 \times 2.222$$

and

$$\log 2.222 = 0.34674 \text{ (from the tables)}$$

so

$$2.222 = 10^{0.34674}$$

and therefore

$$222.2 = 10^2 \times 10^{0.34674}$$

$$= 10^{2.34674}$$

Hence

$$\log 222.2 = 2.34674$$

The number that precedes the decimal point in the logarithm (2 in this example) is called the 'characteristic', the number that follows the decimal point (34674) is called the 'mantissa'.

The above procedure for determining the logarithm of a number can be reduced to the following simple rule. The mantissa is determined by looking up the number in the log tables; the characteristic is equal to the number of places that the decimal point has to be shifted to bring the number within the range of the tables. If the point has to be shifted to the left (as in the above example), then the characteristic is positive; if the point has to be shifted to the right (as in the following example), then the characteristic is negative.

0.2222 is a number for which the decimal point has to be shifted one place to the right. The characteristic is therefore equal to −1, and the mantissa equals $\log 2.222 = 0.34674$:

$$0.2222 = \tfrac{1}{10} \times 2.222$$

$$= 10^{-1} \times 10^{0.34674}$$

$$= 10^{-1+0.34674}$$

and therefore

$$\log 0.2222 = -1 + 0.34674.$$

A negative characteristic should not normally be subtracted from the mantissa, but should be located in front of the decimal point with the minus sign written above it:

$$\log 0.222 = \overline{1}.34674$$

This shows that the characteristic is negative but the mantissa is positive.

The table of antilogarithms reverses the above process: it gives the result of raising 10 to a specified power. Note that only powers of 10 lying between 0 and 1 can be looked up in this table, and the answers given (i.e. the antilogs) therefore lie between 1 and 10. The rule for finding antilogs is the converse of the rule for finding logs: the table gives the antilog of the mantissa, the decimal point being located after the first digit; the point is then shifted the number of places indicated by the characteristic — to the right if the characteristic is positive, and to the left if the characteristic is negative.

For example, let us find the antilog of 2.34674: the antilog of 0.34674 is 2.2220, and the value of the characteristic indicates that the point has to be shifted two places to the right. The answer is therefore 222.2. Note that in carrying out this operation we have determined the value of $10^{2.34674}$:

$$10^{2.34674} = 10^2 \times 10^{0.34674}$$
$$= 100 \times 2.2220$$
$$= 222.2.$$

Since the logarithm of a number is an exponent (10 raised to a certain power), then, as the following example shows, the rules for handling exponents can be applied: if numbers are multiplied together, their logarithms are added, and if one number is divided by another, the logarithm of the denominator is subtracted from the logarithm of the numerator.

EXAMPLE

Calculate using logarithms:

(a) 26.34×0.006863

(b) $26.34 \div 0.006863$

(c) $1.624^{68.79}$

ANSWER

(a) Log $26.34 = 1.42062$

   $\log 0.006863 = \overline{3}.83651$

   so $26.34 \times 0.006863 = 10^{1.42062} \times 10^{\overline{3}.83651}$

By rule 2 of the previous section, multiplication is carried out by adding exponents:

$$\begin{array}{r} 1.42062 \\ \overline{3}.83651 \\ \hline \overline{1}.25713 \end{array}$$

Hence the answer is $10^{\overline{1}.25713}$. The value of this number is found, from the antilog table, to be 0.18077.

(b) The logs are as in (a), but here we are dividing, so by rule 5 of the previous section the second exponent must be subtracted from the first:

$$\begin{array}{r} 1.42062 \\ \overline{3}.83651 \\ \hline 3.58411 \end{array}$$

The answer is antilog $3.58411 = 3838.0$.

(c) Log $1.624 = 0.21058$

   So

$$1.624 = 10^{0.21058}$$

   and therefore

$$1.624^{68.79} = (10^{0.21058})^{68.79}$$
$$= 10^{0.21058 \times 68.79}$$

(by rule 4 of the previous section). Now

$0.21058 \times 68.79 = 14.4858$

and therefore

$1.624^{68.79} = $ antilog 14.4858

$= 306{,}050{,}000{,}000{,}000.$

This illustrates the general method for determining a power of any number: multiply the logarithm of the number by the exponent, and find the antilog of the answer.

SEQUENCE OF OPERATIONS

When carrying out arithmetical calculations it is essential that the operations of multiplication, division, addition, and subtraction be undertaken in the correct sequence. When asked to calculate $5 + 2 \times 3$, many students arrive at an answer of 21. The correct answer, however, is 11; the operation of multiplication (or division) must be carried out first, then the operation of addition (or subtraction). If it is required to carry out the operations of addition or subtraction first, then this must be indicated by the use of brackets:

$(5 + 2) \times 3 = 7 \times 3 = 21.$

The operation of calculating powers must precede multiplication or division:

$2 \times 3^2 = 2 \times 9 = 18.$

Again, operations within brackets take precedence:

$(2 \times 3)^2 = 6^2 = 36.$

The mnemonic BEDMAS summarizes these rules:

Brackets first
Exponents next
Division and
Multiplication next, then
Addition and
Subtraction

The following example illustrates the use of this rule:

$2 \times 3^2 - (1 + 2 \times 2^2)^2 \div 3 =$

$2 \times 9 - (1 + 2 \times 4)^2 \div 3$

$= 18 - 9^2 \div 3 = 18 - 27 = -9$

MULTIPLICATION AND DIVISION INVOLVING NEGATIVE NUMBERS

The rule here is 'two negatives make a positive, a negative and a positive make a negative. This rule is illustrated in the following examples:

$(-2) \times (-3) = 6$

$(-2) \times 3 = -6$

$\dfrac{(-4) \times (-3)}{-2} = \dfrac{12}{-2} = -6.$

A negative sign preceding brackets operates on all the terms inside the brackets in accordance with the above rule:

$-(-2) = 2$

$-(a - b) = -a + b$

$-2(a + b) = -2a - 2b.$

SUMMATIONS

Many problems in statistics involve calculations on columns of figures. The following simple example illustrates the procedure for carrying out this type of calculation.

Billy buys 6 doughnuts at 7p each, 4 chocolate bars at 9p each, 8 liquorice sticks at 2p each, and 2 lollipops at 3p each. How many items does he buy and how much does he spend?

The way to lay out this calculation is shown in the first three columns of Table 1.1. In this table 'price' is denoted by the symbol p (though any other symbol, such as x, would serve equally well), and the quantity bought is denoted by q.

The number of items bought is obviously the sum of the values entered in the q-column

Table 1.1 Summation calculations

Price (pence) (p)	Quantity (q)	Price × Quantity (pq)	q^2	pq^2
7	6	42	36	252
9	4	36	16	144
2	8	16	64	128
3	2	6	4	12
	$\Sigma q = 20$	$\Sigma pq = 100$	$\Sigma q^2 = 120$	$\Sigma pq^2 = 536$

(we shall refer to these as '*q*-values'), i.e.
6 + 4 + 8 + 2 = 20. This sum is labelled Σq.
'Σ' is the Greek capital sigma (equivalent to
the English *S*), and it is an instruction to sum
all the values of the variable which follows it.
Σq means 'sum of the *q*-values'.

To obtain the total amount spent we must
obviously multiply each *p*-value by the corresponding *q*-value to obtain the *pq*-values
listed in column 3 (6 doughnuts @ 7p each =
42 p, 4 chocolate bars @ 9p each = 36p, etc.).
The results are summed to give the required
total, namely $\Sigma pq = 100$ pence.

By way of emphasis we repeat that the
correct sequence of operations to obtain Σpq
is (1) multiply each *p*-value by the corresponding *q*-value, (2) sum the results (cf. the
BEDMAS rule given earlier). A common error
is to attempt to compute Σpq by calculating
Σp (= 21 in this example) and Σq (= 20) and
multiplying the results. This does not give
Σpq, but $\Sigma p \Sigma q = 21 \times 20 = 420$; nobody, of
course, works out their grocery bills in this
way.

Let us complicate the example slightly by
supposing that Billy wishes to lay in large
stocks for Christmas, and determines the
quantities to buy by squaring the *q*-values in
Table 1.1. The total number of items bought
is obtained by computing $\Sigma q^2 = 120$ (see
column 4). (Note that Σq^2 is *not* equal to
$(\Sigma q)^2 = 20 \times 20 = 400$.)

To obtain the total amount spent it is
necessary to compute Σpq^2, shown in column
5. The pq^2-values can be obtained either by
multiplying the *p*-values by the q^2-values, or

by multiplying the *q*-values by the *pq*-values.

The memories provided on most pocket
calculators are very useful for summation calculations. To obtain Σpq, for example, the
steps are:

7 × 6 M+, 9 × 4 M+, 2 × 8 M+, 3 × 2 M+.

Pressing the MR (memory recall) key will give
the required result (100) on the display.

APPROXIMATIONS AND ERRORS

Many numbers used in business are not entirely accurate but are approximations and
therefore subject to error. The 'error' referred
to here does not arise from mistakes in calculation, but from the fact that completely
accurate figures are either unnecessary or else
impractical, impossible, or too expensive to
obtain. In this section we discuss the ways in
which approximate numbers and their associated errors are derived and manipulated.
Notes on the sources of error are given in
Chapter 4.

We shall use the example of a small business
whose assets are being revalued at the end of
an accounting year, and we shall suppose that
the value put on the premises is £25,000, to
the nearest thousand pounds. This number is
said to be accurate to 'two significant figures',
meaning that the first two digits only are
accurately known, the remaining digits being
unknown. The zeros which follow the significant figures serve merely to indicate the position of the decimal point.

This number might have been arrived at by taking the average of three independent estimates, say £24,500, £25,150, and £24,800. Adding these estimates and dividing by 3 gives as the average £24,816.67. A frequently-made mistake is to quote a number such as this as it stands, thus implying a higher degree of accuracy than actually exists — in this case the impression given is that the value of the premises is known to the nearest penny. To avoid this problem of spurious accuracy, the value should be 'rounded' to an appropriate number of significant figures.

To illustrate the procedure let us round this value to six significant figures, i.e. to one decimal place: 24,816.7 (note that this is closer to 24,816.67 than is any other 6-digit number). The accuracy implied by this number is still spurious, however, as the value of the premises cannot be known to the nearest 10p. If we round to five significant figures we obtain 24,817, but the implied degree of accuracy is still spurious, as this figure is accurate to the nearest pound. If we round to three significant figures we obtain 24,800, which looks more reasonable — but a glance at the three estimates shows that the value cannot be known even to the nearest one hundred pounds. The lowest estimate is £24,500, and the highest is £25,150, and these indicate that the value should be quoted to two significant figures, i.e. £25,000.

We stated at the outset that this value was reckoned to be accurate to the nearest £1000, thus implying that the actual value is closer to £25,000 than to £24,000 or £26,000. The actual value must therefore lie between £24,500 and £25,500, that is, it cannot lie more than £500 below or above the approximate value. The approximate value is therefore subject to a maximum error of £500, and this can be indicated by writing it thus:

£25,000 ± £500

This error gives the greatest difference that can exist between the approximate value and the actual value, and it is referred to as the 'absolute' error ('absolute' because the differ-ence can be negative or positive).

The procedure for rounding a number lying midway between two adjacent approximate values should be noted. For example, suppose that 185 is to be rounded to two significant figures, i.e. either to 180 or 190. If we adopt the policy of always rounding such numbers down (in this case to 180), then we shall tend, on the whole, to round numbers down rather than up, and the approximate values obtained will exhibit a consistent tendency, or 'bias', to be less than the actual values. If, on the other hand, we adopt the policy of always rounding such numbers up (in this case to 190), then a bias in the opposite direction will be introduced, and the approximate values will tend, on the whole, to be larger than the actual values. Any approximating procedure should be unbiased, and the convention adopted to achieve this is to round such a number so that the digit preceding the final zeros in the approximate value is even, not odd. So 185 should be rounded down to 180, and 155, for example, should be rounded up to 160.

An approximating procedure which is adopted in certain situations is 'truncation', i.e. the omission of the unwanted final digits (thus 18.329 truncated to four figures becomes 18.32). Banks, for example, ignore any halfpence that occur in transactions, and pocket calculators truncate any digits lying outside their display capacity. This procedure, although simple, obviously introduces a downward bias into the results obtained, and rounding is generally preferred. (For a class exercise on rounding and truncation, see Appendix IV, Assignment C3.)

To return to our example of the business premises valued at £25,000, we have shown that the absolute error in this figure is £500. The disadvantage of an error quoted in this way is that its importance is not made apparent. An error of £500 is insignificant in a relatively large figure such as £255,000, but very important in a relatively small figure such as £2000. This disadvantage is overcome if relative errors rather than absolute errors are quoted.

A relative error expresses the absolute error as a percentage of the approximate value. The relative error in the value quoted for the business premises is

$$\frac{500}{25{,}000} \times 100 = 2\%$$

The value can therefore be written:

£25,000 ± 2%

It is often necessary to undertake calculations involving approximate numbers, and so the rules for determining the size of the maximum error in the final result should be noted:

1. If one approximate value is added to or subtracted from another, the absolute error in the result is obtained by adding their absolute errors
2. If one approximate value is multiplied or divided by another, the relative error in the result is obtained by adding their relative errors.

To illustrate rule 1, let us suppose that the other assets of the business are the equipment, stock, and cash, and that the values put on these are as shown in Table 1.2. (The equipment is accurate to the nearest £100, the stock to the nearest £10, and cash to the nearest £1.) The absolute errors have been calculated and entered in the table. Also entered in the table are the lowest and highest values that each asset can take, and it is clear that the sum of the lowest values (£38,557.50) must equal the lowest value that the total assets can take, and the sum of the highest values (£39,668.50) must equal the highest value that the total assets can take. The total

of the approximate values is £39,113, which is £555.50 more than the total of the lowest values, and £555.50 less than the total of the highest values. So the figure of £39,113 is subject to an absolute error of £555.50, which, from the table, can be seen to be the sum of the absolute errors of the individual assets.

Note that maximum errors should normally be quoted to one significant figure, and that the approximate value should be given to the same degreee of accuracy that then exists in the error. In this case the error should be quoted as ± £600, and since this is accurate to the nearest £100 the total value of the assets should also be quoted to the nearest £100: £39,100 ± £600.

To illustrate rule 2, suppose that a company estimates that it has 100 tons of chemical which it values at £20 per ton (it believes the former figure to be accurate to within 10%, and the latter to within 5%). Since the relative error in the weight is 10%, the lowest and highest weights must be 90 tons and 110 tons, and since the relative error in the value per ton is 5%, the lowest and highest values are £19 and £21. Hence the lowest total value of the chemical is 90 × £19 = £1,710, and the highest total value is 110 × £21 = £2310. Now the approximate total value is 100 × £20 = £2000; the lowest total value is £290 less than this, and the highest total value is £310 more than this. According to rule 2, the relative error in the approximate total must be 10% + 5% = 15%, and the absolute error is therefore 15% of £2000, i.e. £300. Comparing this figure with the maximum errors of −£290 and +£310 calculated above, it can be seen that rule 2 gives a good (but not completely accurate) estimate of the error in the approximate total.

Finally, the symbol for 'approximately equal to' should be noted. 'x is approximately equal to 200' is written $x \simeq 200$.

Table 1.2   Asset values (£s)

Asset	Approximate value	Absolute error	Lowest value	Highest value
Premises	25 000	500	24 500	25 500
Equipment	12 600	50	12 550	12 650
Stock	1 460	5	1 455	1 465
Cash	53	0.50	52.50	53.50
Totals	39 113	555.50	38 557.50	39 668.50

EXERCISES

1. The table below shows a dealer's prices

and profits for various articles. Calculate the missing figures.

	Cost price (£)	Profit (£)	Profit as % of cost price	Selling price (£)	Profit as % of selling price
(a)	80	?	?	100	?
(b)	?	?	?	150	20
(c)	?	30	20	?	?
(d)	?	20	?	?	12½
(e)	100	?	?	?	25
(f)	?	?	15	70	?

2. (a) *A, B, C,* and *D* enter into a partnership, contributing capital in the ratio 7 : 4 : 5 : 6. If *D*'s capital is £7500, calculate the amounts contributed by the partners.

   (b) The profit in a certain year amounts to £23,100 and this is to be divided among the partners in the ratio of their capital. How much does each receive?

3. Calculate $\dfrac{(4^{-12})^{1/3}.4^{0.25}}{(\sqrt{2}).4^{-2}}$

4. Prove that $a^{m-n}.(a^{-n})^m.a^{m/2}.(a^m)^{n-1}$ $a^{n-m/2} = 1$

5. Using log tables calculate:
   (a) $10^{0.1234}$
   (b) $2.462^{1.357} \times 0.5678^{0.36} \div 248^{1.08}$

6. Calculate to two decimal places:
   $\dfrac{2.36}{3.42} (16.36 - 4.8^2) - 7.7(2.9 \times 9.2 - 11.98)$

7. Calculate to four significant figures:
   $9.1(8.7^2 + 5.42)^2 - \sqrt{(196 - 9.1)}$

8. In a remote valley of Central Asia lies the tiny village of Q'ow. In accordance with age-old tradition, the land of this village is divided up into rectangular holdings; each male of the village is granted a holding on attainment of manhood, the area of his holding being proportional to the esteem in which he is held by the village chief. There are six men in the village, and the sizes of their holdings, in metres, are as follows:

Man	Length (x)	Breadth (y)
A	12	8
B	15	9
C	20	12
D	14	7
E	10	9
F	10	8

Draw up a table with columns headed: x, y, $x + y$, $x - y$, $2x$, and $2y$, and answer the questions below:

(a) Using the above data, confirm that the following rules hold:
   (i) $\Sigma(x + y) = \Sigma x + \Sigma y$
   (ii) $\Sigma(x - y) = \Sigma x - \Sigma y$
   (iii) $\Sigma 2x = 2\Sigma x$ (This can be generalised to the rule $\Sigma ax = a\Sigma x$, where a is a constant.)
   (iv) Suppose the length of each man's holding is increased to 20 metres. Then it can be seen that $\Sigma 20 = 6 \times 20$. This illustrates the rule $\Sigma a = na$, where a is a constant and n is the number of times it has to be added.

(b) What is the total length of fencing if each man builds a fence around the entire perimeter of his holding (compute $2\Sigma x + 2\Sigma y$)?

(c) What is the total area of land so enclosed (compute Σxy)?

(d) The village chief (a woman) decrees that each man should have the length of his holding reduced by 1.5 metres. From the summations you have already worked out, deduce:
   (i) The new total length of fencing (use the relationship $\Sigma(x - a) = \Sigma x - \Sigma a = \Sigma x - na$)
   (ii) The new total area of enclosed land (use the relationship $\Sigma(x - a)y = \Sigma xy - \Sigma ay = \Sigma xy - a\Sigma y$).

9. A market gardener has 10 rows of cabbages, and he estimates that there are 80 cabbages in each row (± 10%), 15 rows of lettuces, with 140 lettuces per row (± 10%), and 5 rows of cauliflowers, with 65 cauliflowers per row (± 5%). He estimates that he can sell the cabbages for 20p each (± 3p), the lettuces for 10p each (± 1p), and the cauliflowers for 30p each (± 4p). Give the approximate value and the maximum error of the following:
   (a) The total number of plants
   (b) The total value of the plants.

Two

Equations and Graphs

DATA

Having briefly discussed in Chapter 1 the number system and the rules of arithmetic, we can now turn our attention to the nature of numerical data and the way in which elementary mathematics can assist in its analysis.

'Data', in the sense in which it is used on this course, means information expressed in numerical form — prices of goods, times taken to process orders, population statistics, and so on. Data is obtained either by *enumeration* (counting) or by *measurement*. If enumeration is used, then whole numbers only are possible, intermediate values being impossible, and the data obtained is called 'discrete'. One example is population statistics: there can be 10,365 people in a town, or 10,366, but not 10,365.47 people. The possible values that this data can take increase in 'jumps' from one whole number to the next. Another example of discrete data is prices of goods: there is a gap of 1/2p between one possible price and the next, no intermediate values being possible. (Money is counted, not measured, the smallest unit being 1/2p.)

Data obtained by measurement can take any value over a certain range. In this case there are no gaps between one possible value and the next, and so the data is said to be 'continuous'. One example of continuous data is heights of individuals: Billy's height, for example, might be 172.6309 . . . cm. Due to the inadequacies of our measuring instruments continuous data can only be measured to a limited number of significant figures. Billy's height, for example, might be measured to the nearest millimetre: 172.6 cm. This does not imply that his actual height equals 172.60000 . . . cm (written $172.6\dot{0}$ cm, the dot indicating that the final digit recurs indefinitely), but that his height lies somewhere in the continuous interval $172.55\dot{0}$ to $172.65\dot{0}$ cm.

Data is constantly being accumulated on prices, wages, television viewing habits, educational attainment, mortality — the list is endless. All of these countable or measurable things are called 'variables', for the data obtained may vary from one period of time to another, or from one individual to another, or from one country to another.

A variable cannot exist in isolation, but is related in some way to other variables. The variable 'Billy's height' is related to his age, his genetic make-up and his diet. An important part of quantitative methods is the construction of mathematical models to represent relationships between variables. In the next section we discuss graphical models, which use lengths drawn on graph paper to represent money in £s, time in years, or whatever other units have been used to count or measure in. Following that we describe modelling by means of equations using symbols such as 'x' and 'y' to represent the values taken by the variables.

GRAPHS

Suppose that Billy's height is recorded by his parents each year on his birthday. There is obviously a relationship between the variable 'Billy's height' and the variable 'Billy's age', and in Figure 2.1 this relationship is shown on a graph. Values taken by the variable 'Billy's age' are represented by a scale of lengths marked out on the horizontal axis, values taken by the variable 'Billy's height' are similarly represented on the vertical axis. The origin, that is the point where the two axes intersect, has the value zero on both axes.

The procedure for plotting the points on the graph is as follows. If at the age of 8 Billy attained a height of 123 cm, an (imaginary) vertical line is drawn through 8 on the horizontal axis, and an (imaginary) horizontal line is drawn through 123 on the vertical axis. The point representing

Billy's height at the age of 8 is located at the intersection of these two lines.

'Billy's height' is called the 'dependent variable', because the values taken by it are dependent upon Billy's age. 'Billy's age', on the other hand, does not depend upon his height but upon factors outside the scope of the example, and so it is called the 'independent variable'. (It should, however, be emphasized that in many cases the 'dependency' of one variable upon the other is more apparent than real.) The dependent variable should be represented by a scale marked along the vertical axis, the independent variable by a scale along the horizontal axis.

Many of the graphs met with on this course are 'time graphs'. In these 'time', whether measured in years, months, hours, or seconds, is the independent variable (and is therefore plotted along the horizontal axis). All moments in time, represented by all the possible points on the horizontal axis, actually

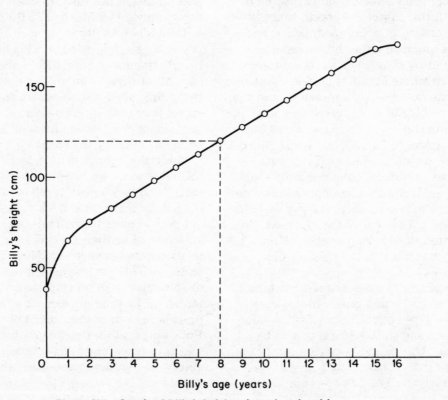

Figure 2.1   Graph of Billy's height plotted against his age

occurred, and it is therefore theoretically possible to record all the values taken by the dependent variable at all these moments and to plot these values as points on the graph. If this were done the plotted points would merge to form a continuous line. In practice, of course, only a selection of the possible values are recorded, and so only a selection of the possible points are plotted on the graph. But in the time graph in Figure 2.1 we can make a pretty good guess from the plotted points where the other points would have

example of such a graph is given in Figure 2.2. (Note that although the vertical axis should normally start at zero, the horizontal axis frequently has no meaningful 'zero', and the origin can be located at any convenient time-value.)

Points intermediate to the plotted points in Figure 2.2 do exist (since the week over which sales are totalled could start at any instant in one calendar week and end at the corresponding instant in the next calendar week), and it is appropriate to indicate this by joining up

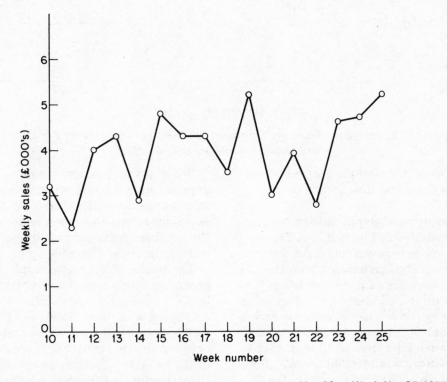

Figure 2.2   Weekly sales of XYZ Ltd for the period Week No. 10 to Week No. 25 1978

been located: Billy's height obviously increased smoothly rather than 'jerkily' as his age increased, and we can join up the plotted points by means of a smooth line. The values that Billy's height took at *any* age can be determined from this line by reversing the point location process described earlier.

Many time graphs describe data which varies in a 'jerky' manner, and in such cases the points do not lie on a smooth line. An

the plotted points by lines. However, the values taken by the variable 'weekly sales' change in an erratic manner, and it is not possible to predict what values the intermediate points take. Because of this straight lines should be used to join up successive plotted points, as indicated in the figure. Accurate predictions of the values of intermediate points cannot be made from these lines, but they do enable the eye to follow easily the

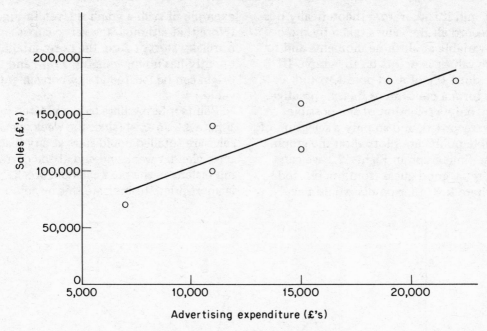

Figure 2.3   Scattergraph of sales plotted against advertising expenditure for 7 companies in a certain industry for the year 1978

successive values taken by the plotted points. (For further details on time graphs see Chapter 5.)

A different type of graph, called a 'scatter-graph', is illustrated in Figure 2.3. A fundamental difference between this graph and those described above is evident from the figure — a given value of one variable can have associated with it a number of different values of the other variable. When advertising expenditure was £11,000, sales were £100,000 and £140,000; when sales were £180,000, advertising expenditure was £19,000 and £22,000. The result is a scattering of points on the graph, and hence the name.

The scattergraph shown illustrates the relationship between sales and advertising expenditure of 7 companies in a certain industry in one particular year. The figures used are as follows:

Company:	A	B	C	D	E	F	G
Advertising (£000s):	15	7	22	15	11	11	19
Sales (£000s):	120	70	180	160	140	100	180

'Sales' is the dependent variable, since it depends upon (among other things) the amount spent on advertising. 'Advertising expenditure' depends upon factors external to the problem (such as company policy), and so is the independent variable.

The points of the scattergraph exhibit a general upward trend, indicating that higher levels of advertising expenditure tend to be associated with higher sales, and there therefore appears to be some sort of relationship between the two variables. Since any value of the variable 'advertising expenditure' is theoretically possible, this relationship can be represented on the graph by a continuous line: this is the 'line of best fit' (shown in Figure 2.3), the straight line which appears to the eye to best indicate the trend of the points. To insert this line on a scattergraph, a transparent ruler should be used, and the line drawn so that the deviations from the line of the points lying above it appear to cancel out the deviations from the line of the points lying below it.

The line of best fit can be used to make predictions. From Figure 2.3, for example, it can be seen that a level of advertising expenditure of say £18,000 can be expected to result in sales of around £160,000. Such a prediction is, of course, subject to uncertainty, since other factors besides the level of advertising can affect sales. Further details on scattergraphs and on the science of making this type of prediction can be found in Chapter 12.

LINEAR EQUATIONS

The example that we shall use in this section is of a small firm manufacturing woolly bedsocks. It has fixed costs of £500 per month (these are costs which remain constant from month to month, and include rent, rates, interest charges, and other overheads). The variable costs are £0.40 per pair of socks produced (these are costs which vary according to the output of the firm, and include material costs, labour, and other direct costs). At the end of each month a wholesaler buys as many socks as the firm can produce, paying £0.60 per pair for them.

The variables in this example are (a) the monthly output, that is the number of pairs of socks produced each month; (b) the total costs that the firm has to meet each month; and (c) the sales revenue that the firm earns each month. Of these the output is the independent variable, for it does not depend upon either the total cost or the revenue but upon factors external to the problem (such as the availability of labour and materials, and the rate of machine breakdown). The total cost and the revenue depend upon the output, so these are the dependent variables.

We shall follow the usual practice of denoting the independent variable by the symbol x. If in a certain month the firm produced 100 pairs of socks, then this information can be expressed thus: $x = 100$.

The symbol y is normally used to denote the dependent variable, but since in this example there are two such variables we shall use other symbols to avoid confusion, namely C to represent monthly costs (in £s) and R to represent monthly revenue (also in £s).

Having labelled the variables, we can now construct equations to model the relationships between them:

1. The Cost Equation

The total monthly costs consist of the fixed costs (£500) plus the variable costs (£0.40 per pair of socks produced). For example, if in a certain month 100 pairs of socks are produced, then total cost is:

$$C = 500 + 0.40 \times 100$$
$$= 500 + 40$$
$$= £540$$

If the firm produces x pairs of socks in a month, then total cost is:

$$C = 500 + 0.4x$$

2. The Revenue Equation

Each pair of socks produced sells for £0.60. If the firm produces x pairs of socks in a month, then the revenue is:

$$R = 0.6x$$

Although these equations are very simple, they form a useful model of the situation facing the firm. We can, for example, derive from them an equation representing the monthly profit (P) by using the fact that profit is equal to revenue less cost:

$$P = R - C = 0.6x - (500 + 0.4x)$$
$$= 0.6x - 500 - 0.4x$$
$$= -500 + 0.2x$$

If the firm produces, say, 1000 pairs of socks in a certain month, then the profit for that month can be determined very easily by substituting $x = 1000$ in this equation:

$$P = -500 + 0.2 \times 1000$$
$$= -500 + 200$$
$$= -300$$

So the firm makes a negative profit (i.e. a loss) of £300.

Businesses often need to know their break-even output, that is the output that has to be achieved for revenue to exactly balance costs. (An output which is less than this results in a loss, an output which exceeds this results in a profit.) At the break-even output the profit is zero, and so that output can be determined by substituting $P = 0$ in the profit equation:

$$0 = -500 + 0.2x$$
$$\therefore 500 = 0.2x$$
$$\therefore \quad x = \frac{500}{0.2} = 2500$$

Hence the break-even output is 2500 pairs of socks per month.

The above equations are all examples of 'linear' equations, so-called because they can be represented by straight lines on a graph. Such equations take the form $y = a + bx$, where x and y are the variables and the symbols a and b represent constants. For the cost equation $a = 500$ and $b = 0.4$, for the revenue equation $a = 0$ and $b = 0.6$, and for the profit equation $a = -500$ and $b = 0.2$.

GRAPHS OF LINEAR EQUATIONS

The above equations are graphed in Figure 2.4. The output x is the independent variable, and so the x-values are measured (in numbers of pairs of socks) along the horizontal axis. The scale (in £s) for C, R, and P is marked on the vertical axis.

It should be noted that the value of the constant a gives the point where the line on the graph intersects the vertical axis. The value of the constant b gives the slope of the line (the steepness of the slope being related to the magnitude of b). If b is greater than zero (written $b > 0$) the line slopes upwards from left to right, if b is less than zero (i.e. $b < 0$) the line slopes downwards.

On this particular graph it can be seen that at the break-even point the revenue line intersects the cost line (at $x = 2500$). For x-values which are less than 2500 the profit is negative, for $x > 2500$ the profit is positive, and at $x = 2500$ the profit is zero. Note that since $P = R - C$, the profit at any x-value equals the vertical distance between the revenue line and the cost line at that value.

To construct the line representing a linear equation it is necessary to determine two

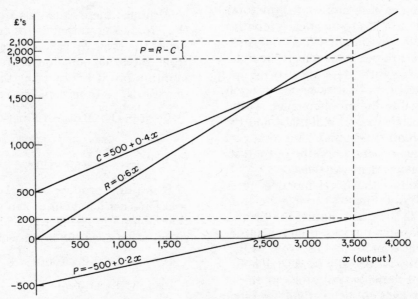

Figure 2.4   Graphs of the linear equations representing cost, revenue, and profit

points on the graph which satisfy the equation and then join them using a ruler. For the equation $C = 500 + 0.4x$, for example, choose two values of x reasonably far apart, say $x = 0$ and $x = 3000$, and calculate the corresponding values of C:

when $x = 0$, $C = 500 + 0.4 \times 0 = 500$

when $x = 3000$, $C = 500 + 0.4 \times 3000$

$= 1700$

One point is therefore located at $x = 0$ and $C = 500$ (this 'map reference' is written (0, 500)), the other at (3000, 1700), and the straight line through these points represents the equation. Using this line, the costs can be read off the graph for any value of x — for example, when $x = 3500$, $C = 1900$.

DETERMINATION OF THE EQUATION OF THE STRAIGHT LINE PASSING THROUGH TWO POINTS

The equation of a straight line invariably takes the form $y = a + bx$. To determine the equation it is necessary to calculate the values of the constants a and b, and this is done by substituting the x- and y-values of two points lying on the line in $y = a + bx$.

To illustrate the procedure, suppose that if the wholesaler in the above example sets the price at which he sells woolly bedsocks at £0.80 per pair, then he sells 4000 pairs a month, and if he sets the price at £1.00 per pair, then he sells 3000 pairs a month. He wishes to determine the demand equation, that is the equation relating price to quantity sold. He believes this equation to be approximately linear over the above range of values.

The first step is to label the variables x and y (or, if preferred, p for price and q for quantity). In this example the quantity sold is the dependent variable (for it depends upon the price charged). However, it is common practice in problems involving output or quantity to treat it as the independent variable (and thus to represent it by the horizontal axis on a graph). Any 'money' variables in

such problems (cost, revenue, price, etc.) are treated as dependent variables. We shall therefore denote 'quantity' by x and 'price' by y. The numbers used in this example can be simplified somewhat by measuring quantities in thousands: $x = 4$, for example, means 4000 pairs of socks. y will be in £s.

We are told that when $x = 4$, $y = 0.8$, and when $x = 3$, $y = 1$. The line on the graph representing the relationship between price and quantity therefore passes through the two points (4, 0.8) and (3, 1). To determine the equation of this line we substitute these x- and y-values in $y = a + bx$:

(1) $0.8 = a + 4b$ (substituting $x = 4$ and $y = 0.8$)

(2) $1 = a + 3b$ (substituting $x = 3$ and $y = 1$)

These are simultaneous equations that can be solved for a and b (in other words, the required values of a and b must satisfy both equation (1) and equation (2), and these values can be found by suitably manipulating (1) and (2)). The method is as follows:

(i)   Eliminate a by subtracting one equation from the other
(ii) Rearrange the resulting equation to find the value of b
(iii) Substitute this value of b in either (1) or (2) to find the value of a.

We begin by subtracting (2) from (1):

$0.8 - 1 = a - a + 4b - 3b$

$\therefore -0.2 = b$, i.e. $b = -0.2$.

We now substitute this value of b in (1):

$0.8 = a + 4(-0.2) = a - 0.8$

$\therefore a = 1.6$

Hence the required equation is:

$y = 1.6 - 0.2x$

Armed with this equation the wholesaler can determine the quantity he can expect to sell at any price over the relevant price range, or alternatively, the price he must charge to sell a specified monthly quantity. If, for example, he wishes to sell 3800 per month, the price is determined by substituting $x = 3.8$ in the equation:

Price $= y = 1.6 - 0.2 \times 3.8 = 1.6 - 0.76$

$= £0.84$

This equation must be regarded as an approximate model only of the real situation, and any conclusions derived from it — such as the above price — are subject to uncertainty. In the first place the underlying assumption — that the demand equation is linear — is unlikely to be exactly true. Secondly, other variables besides price affect demand, and this equation fails to take account of these. A more adequate model would be a non-linear equation in several variables — but the construction of such an equation is outside the scope of this course.

EXPONENTIAL EQUATIONS

Linear equations are very simple to handle, and many business situations can be adequately modelled by means of them. However, situations involving growth or decay are often encountered, and in these cases 'exponential equations' are required. These are equations of the form:

$$y = ab^x$$

where a and b are constants, and where x, the independent variable, normally represents the passage of time. A brief review only of this important topic is given here; for a detailed study see Chapter 14.

To graph an exponential equation it is necessary to determine the value of y for a number of values of x, plot the points so obtained on the graph, and join them with a smooth curve. As can be seen from Figure 2.5, the value of the constant a gives the intersection of the curve with the y-axis, the value of b determines the slope at a point. If $b > 1$ an upward-sloping curve is obtained which can be used to model growth situations (such as money earning compound interest, price inflation, population growth, or growth in a firm's sales). If $0 < b < 1$ a downward-sloping curve is obtained which can be used to model decay situations (such as depreciation in the value of plant and equipment). We shall not be concerned here with negative values of b.

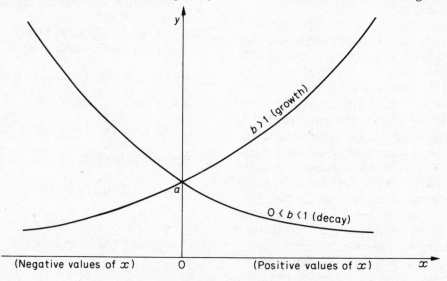

Figure 2.5   Graph of equations of the form $y = ab^x$

Exponential equations can be transformed to linear equations by taking logarithms, and this makes their analysis very easy. From the rules for logarithms given in Chapter 1 it can be seen that if $y = ab^x$, then $\log y = \log a + x \log b$. If now $\log y$ is plotted against x, a straight line will be obtained which intersects the $\log y$ axis at $\log a$ and which has a slope given by the value of $\log b$.

To avoid the need to take logarithms when graphing these equations, semi-logarithmic graph paper can be used. This has a logarithmic scale printed along the vertical axis, and an ordinary linear (or 'natural') scale printed along the horizontal axis. An example of such a graph is given in Figure 2.6. The x-axis is scaled in the usual way — a unit increase in length corresponds to the *addition* of a constant amount onto the value of x. A unit increase in length up the y-axis, however, corresponds to the *multiplication* of the y-value by a constant amount.

If it is required to give a visual comparison of growth rates, semi-logarithmic graph paper should always be used. For example, if the sales of Company A increase from £50,000 to £55,000 in a year, and those of Company B from £100,000 to £110,000, then both companies have achieved a rate of growth of 10%. If this data is plotted on semi-logarithmic paper, the line representing Company A's sales will be parallel to the line representing Company B's sales, indicating equal growth rates. If plotted on natural-scale graph paper, however, the line representing B's sales will increase more sharply than the line representing A's sales (since B's sales increased by £10,000, whereas A's increased by only £5000), and this will create the false impression of differing growth rates.

To illustrate the use of exponential equations, let us take the example of £100 invested at a fixed rate of compound interest (in other words, the interest is added to the investment as it accrues and earns further interest in subsequent periods of time). Suppose that at the end of three years the investment has grown to £150. What will it be worth after a further two years?

This is a straightforward growth situation that can be represented by the equation $y = ab^x$, where y is in £s and x is in years. When the £100 is first invested, $x = 0$; after three years (i.e. when $x = 3$) the investment equals £150. Two points satisfying the equation are therefore (0, 100) and (3, 150), and from these we can determine the values of the constants a and b by applying the method described in the last section.

First, we transform the exponential equation to a linear equation by taking logs:

$$\log y = \log a + x \log b.$$

We next substitute into this the above x- and y-values:

(1) $\log 100 = \log a + 0.\log b$
        (substituting $x = 0$ and $y = 100$)

$\therefore \log 100 = \log a$

$\therefore \qquad a = 100$

(2) $\log 150 = \log a + 3 \log b$
        (substituting $x = 3$ and $y = 150$)

In this example we do not have to subtract one equation from the other to obtain the value of a, for we have already found it in (1). To find b, we substitute this value of a in (2):

$$\log 150 = \log 100 + \log b$$

$$\therefore \log b = \frac{\log 150 - \log 100}{3}$$

$$= \frac{2.17609 - 2}{3} = 0.0587$$

$$\therefore \qquad b = \text{antilog } 0.0587 = 1.1447$$

Hence the equation is:

$$y = 100 \times 1.1447^x.$$

To find the value of the investment after any period of time we substitute the year number in this equation. After $x = 1$ year, the investment is worth $100 \times 1.1447 = £114.47$; after $x = 2$ years, it is worth $100 \times 1.1447^2 = £131.03$; after $x = 3$ years, it is worth $100 \times 1.1447^3 = £150$. Similarly, when $x = 4$, $y = £171.70$, when $x = 5$, $y = £196.54$, and so on. The value of the investment at the end of any year is obtained by multiplying its value at the end of the preceding year by 1.1447 — in other words, it is increasing by 14.47% over the previous year's figure. This percentage is the annual growth rate. Figure 2.6 shows the above *x*- and *y*-values plotted on semi-logarithmic graph paper, and it will be noted that the points lie on a straight line.

In this example we are told nothing about the rate at which compound interest is added to the investment — it might be monthly, quarterly, semi-annually, or annually — nor are we told the interest rate. However, if we know one, then we can deduce the other. For example, if the interest is added to the invest-ment once a year, then the interest rate is 14.47%. If interest is added every 6 months, then there are twice as many interest-earning periods, and it is convenient in this case to

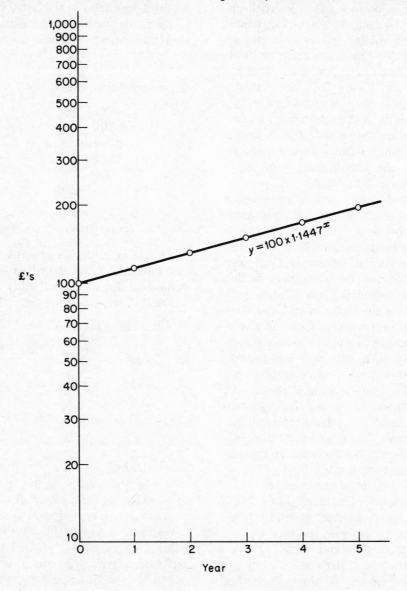

Figure 2.6   Semi-logarithmic graph showing the effect of compound interest on an investment of £100

rewrite the equation thus:

$$y = 100 \times 1.1447^x = 100(1.1447^{1/2})^{2x}$$
$$= 100 \times 1.0699^{2x}$$

(see the section on exponents in Chapter 1). After 6 months (i.e. $x = \frac{1}{2}$) the investment has increased to $100 \times 1.0699 = £106.99$, after 1 year (i.e. $x = 1$) it has increased to $100 \times 1.0699^2 = £114.47$, and so on. So if the interest is compounded semi-annually, then the interest rate is 6.99% per six months (i.e. $6.99 \times 2 = 13.98\%$ per annum). This has the same effect as interest compounded annually at the higher rate of 14.47% per annum, for the interest added halfway through each year itself earns further interest over the remainder of the year.

If interest is added quarterly, a convenient form of the equation is:

$$y = 100 \times 1.1447^x = 100(1.1447^{1/4})^{4x}$$
$$= 100 \times 1.0344^{4x}$$

In this case the interest rate is 3.44% per quarter, i.e. $3.44 \times 4 = 13.76\%$ per annum. This will have the same effect on the investment as compound interest at 14.47% p.a. added once a year, or 13.98% p.a. added twice a year.

Interest on loans is often calculated on a monthly basis, a typical interest rate being $1\frac{1}{2}\%$ per month. It will be clear from the above discussion that the equivalent rate, if interest is compounded annually instead of monthly, is not $1.5 \times 12 = 18\%$, but is calculated as follows:

$$1.015^{12} = 1.1956, \text{ i.e. } 19.56\% \text{ p.a.}$$

QUADRATIC EQUATIONS

Quadratic equations, so-called because they contain an x-squared term, take the form $y = a + bx + cx^2$, where x and y are variables, and a, b, and c are constants. The graph of such an equation is parabolic in shape, as shown in Figure 2.7. The turning point of the parabola is at the top if the constant c is

negative, and it is referred to as the 'maximum' (because at this point the value of y is greatest). If c is positive, the turning point is at the bottom and is referred to as the 'minimum' (y is minimized at this point). The intersections of the curve with the x-axis are called the 'roots'. As is clear from the figure, the x-value of the turning point is midway between the roots.

At the roots, the value of y is zero. Substituting $y = 0$ in the equation we obtain $0 = a + bx + cx^2$, and the two values of x which satisfy this (and which therefore locate the roots) are given by the formula:

$$x = \frac{-b \pm \sqrt{b^2 - 4ac}}{2c}$$

Quadratic equations can often be used to model situations in which, as x increases, y increases and then decreases (the revenue and the profit of a business may behave like this), or situations in which, as x increases, y decreases and then increases (the costs of a business often behave in this way). To illustrate the use of these equations we shall return to the woolly bedsock example referred to previously, and suppose that the wholesaler sells the socks at £1.00 a pair. I.C. Feet, a retailer, obtains his bedsocks from this wholesaler, and he finds that the fixed costs of this line of merchandise amount to £32 per month (these include an apportionment of the overheads, ordering costs, etc.). Each month he tops up his stocks to a predetermined level, so that he matches the number of pairs of socks he buys in to the number of pairs he sells. If we call this number x, then his monthly costs (C) are:

$$C = \text{fixed costs (£32)} + \text{variable costs (£1 per pair)}$$
$$= 32 + x$$

(All 'money' variables used here will be in £s.)

He finds that the number of pairs of socks that he sells in a month is related to the price that he charges, the equation which approximately models this relationship being:

$$\text{Price} = 2 - 0.005x$$

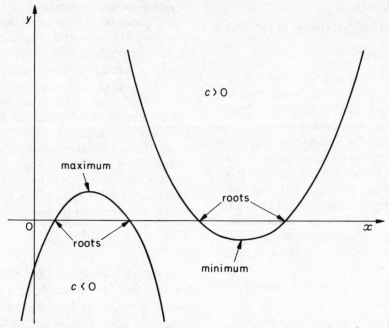

Figure 2.7   Graphs of equations of the form $y = a + bx + cx^2$

The revenue (R) that he obtains each month from his sales of socks is equal to the price charged per pair multiplied by the number of pairs sold:

R = price × quantity

$= (2 - 0.005x)x$

$= 2x - 0.005x^2$

His monthly profit (P) equals his revenue minus his costs:

$P = R - C$

$= (2x - 0.005x^2) - (32 + x)$

$= -32 + x - 0.005x^2$

This is a quadratic equation with $a = -32$, $b = 1$, and $c = -0.005$. To obtain the roots we substitute these values in the formula for x:

$$x = \frac{-b \pm \sqrt{b^2 - 4ac}}{2c}$$

$$= \frac{-1 \pm \sqrt{1^2 - 4(-32)(-0.005)}}{2(-0.005)}$$

$$= \frac{-1 \pm \sqrt{1 - 0.64}}{-0.01} = \frac{1 \pm \sqrt{0.36}}{0.01} = \frac{1 \pm 0.6}{0.01}$$

$$= \frac{0.4}{0.01} \quad \text{and} \quad \frac{1.6}{0.01}$$

= 40 and 160

The graph of the profit equation looks like the parabola at the left of Figure 2.7, with the roots at $x = 40$ and $x = 160$, and the maximum midway between them at $x = 100$. If I.C. Feet sells less than 40 pairs of socks in a month, or more than 160 pairs, he makes a loss. (If he sells less than 40, he is not covering his fixed costs, and to sell more than 160 he has to set his price too low to make any profit.) To maximize his profit he should sell $x = 100$ pairs of socks a month, and the price he should charge is found by substituting this value of x in the price equation:

Price = $2 - 0.005(100) = 2 - 0.5 = £1.50$

As an exercise the student should determine the values of C, R, and P for a number of values of x over the range $x = 0$ to x 400, and use the results to draw the cost line and the revenue and profit curves on a graph.

In this chapter we have discussed only the simplest types of equations that are used to model business situations. Some rather more complex equations are included in Chapters 16 and 18.

EXERCISES

1. (a) The annual profit in £000 of a company over the period 1970–78 was as follows:

Year:	1970	1971	1972	1973	1974
Profit:	24	25	32	41	36

Year:	1975	1976	1977	1978
Profit:	41	49	51	60

    (i) Draw a time-graph of these figures.
    (ii) Plot these figures on a scattergraph, and insert the line of best fit.

    (b) Let x represent the passage of time in years since 1970 (so that 1970 is $x = 0$, 1971 is $x = 1$, 1972 is $x = 2$, and so on), and let y represent annual profit in thousands of pounds (so that, for example, £25,000 is represented by $y = 25$). The line of best fit can be represented by an equation of the form: $y = a + bx$.

    (i) Determine the constants a and b by finding from the graph the x- and y-values of any two points lying on the line of best fit, substituting these values in the equations, and solving for a and b.
    (ii) Using this equation, estimate what the profit will be in 1979. Check your answer by the graph.

2. Jim keeps a careful record of his motor-bike costs and discovers that his fixed costs (tax, insurance, etc.) are £60 per year, and his variable costs (petrol, maintenance, etc.) are 2p per mile. There is public transport from his home to all the places he normally travels to by bike, the fare amounting to 5p per mile.

    (a) Using the symbol x to represent the number of miles travelled by Jim in a year, construct an equation relating the annual costs to x:
    (i) If he only travels by bike
    (ii) If he sells his bike and only travels by public transport.
    (b) From these equations determine what mileage he must exceed in a year to make owning a bike financially worth while.
    (c) Plot the two equations on a graph, and from it determine how much he saves in a year when $x = 1400$ if he sells his bike and travels instead by public transport.

3. An investment of £2000 earns compound interest at 12% per annum. What will the investment be worth after 10 years if the interest is compounded (a) annually; (b) semi-annually; (c) continuously?

4. The annual sales of a company increased approximately exponentially over the period 1970–78. They were:

Year:	1970	1971	1972	1973	1974
Sales: (£000s)	190	224	269	275	257

Year:	1975	1976	1977	1978
Sales: (£000s)	269	324	380	420

    (a) Construct a scattergraph of these figures using semi-logarithmic graph paper and insert the line of best fit.
    (b) Let x and y be as in question 1. The line of best fit can be represented by the equation $y = ab^x$, or, taking logs, $\log y = \log a + x \log b$. Determine the constants a and b by the method outlined in question 1(b)(i).

5. The annual sales of Company A are increasing at the rate of 10% p.a. from the figure of £100,000 in year 0 (so that in year 1 they were £110,000, in year 2 they

were £121,000, and so on). The annual sales of Company B are increasing at the rate of 20% p.a. from the figure of £50,000 in year 0.

(a) Derive equations which represent the sales of the two companies, and from them determine the year in which Company B catches up with Company A.

(b) Plot the two equations on semi-logarithmic graph paper and check the answer obtained to (a).

6. Determine the roots and the turning points of:
   (a) $y = 20 + 13x + 2x^2$
   (b) $y = 6 - x - x^2$.
   What are the y values of the turning points? Sketch the graphs of the equations.

7. A manufacturer makes a certain product for which his fixed costs are £800 per month and his variable costs are £1.20 per unit. His records show that he can increase the quantity sold per month by reducing the price, the relationship between price and quantity sold being as follows:

Price per unit (£s):	2.60	2.40	2.20	2.00	1.80	1.60
No. of units sold:	1000	1200	1400	1600	1800	2000

Calling the number of units sold per month x, you are required to:

(a) Show that the relationship between price and quantity sold is linear by plotting the above figures on a graph. By substituting any two pairs of values in the formula for linear equations ($y = a + bx$), and solving the simultaneous equations so obtained, determine the equation relating price to x.

(b) Determine the revenue equation from (a) by using the relationship: revenue = price × quantity sold.

(c) Determine the roots of the revenue equation and from them the value of x for which revenue is maximized. What is the maximum revenue?

(d) Determine the equation relating total costs to x.

(e) Using the relationship: profit = revenue − cost, determine the profit equation. Find the roots of this equation and hence the value of x which maximizes profit. What is the maximum profit?

(f) Draw the cost, revenue, and profit equation on a graph.

Three

Sets and Probability

CLASSIFICATION

In the last chapter it was observed that the collection of 'data', the raw material with which we have to work, involves the processes of counting and measuring. Before any quantitative investigation can take place, therefore, it is necessary to distinguish, or 'classify', the things which we wish to count. In order to measure and analyse unemployment, for example, it is necessary to state first exactly what is meant by the term. What conditions must an individual fulfil in order to be classified as 'unemployed'? British unemployment figures cannot be directly compared with those for the United States, because the two countries use different definitions, and some people who are classified as unemployed under the United States definition are not so classified under the British definition.

The process of classification is fundamental not just to quantitative analysis but to many areas of our lives, and we are constantly making unconscious classifications. An example of this process is afforded by the three totally different mental pictures that the following statements conjure up: 'She is a blonde who drives a pink sports car'; 'She owns several horses'; 'She is a housewife'. We subconsciously classify women into a number of different types, and our classification system imposes three different images upon our minds. If it is pointed out that these descriptions all apply to one individual, our mental picture becomes clouded, because this does not fit our rigid system.

SETS

The branch of mathematics dealing with classifications is called 'set theory'. A 'set' is a collection of things which can be classified, that is, distinguished from other things. In the above example there are three sets: the set of blondes who drive pink sports cars, the set of women who own horses, and the set of housewives.

Each of these sets has been defined by means of some characteristic or characteristics possessed by each of its members. Anything which does not possess those characteristics is not a member of the set. We could alternatively define a set by listing all its members. If Ms Smith, Ms Jones, and Ms Brown are the only blondes who drive pink sports cars, then this list of names defines the set. It is conventional to list the members defining a set within curly brackets: the above set is written {Ms Smith, Ms Jones, Ms Brown} .

Having defined a set we can carry out the process of counting the members of that set. The modulus symbol ‖ is used to denote the result of this process: $|A|$ means 'the number of members of the set A'. If P denotes the set of blondes who drive pink sports cars, then, since that set has three members, $|P| = 3$.

Another useful symbol is U, used to denote

the universal set of reference. In the above example, U is the set of all women. The three sets defined above, 'the set of blondes who drive pink sports cars' (P), 'the set of women who own horses' (which we will call Q), and 'the set of housewives' (which we will call R), are all 'subsets' of U. If a set A is a subset of a set B, then every member of A is also a member of B.

A set can be modelled by means of a Venn diagram. If each member is represented by a point marked on a piece of paper, and a boundary is drawn enclosing all the points, the space within the boundary represents the set. Figure 3.3 shows a Venn diagram representing the set of all the possible outcomes of a single roll of a die.

A Venn diagram representing the three sets defined previously (P, Q, and R) is shown in Figure 3.1. The three circles in that figure partially overlap, indicating that some women belong to P and Q, some belong to Q and R, and some belong to R and P. The overlapping space belonging to P and Q is called the 'intersection' of P and Q, and is denoted by $P \cap Q$. The members of $P \cap Q$ belong to both

P and Q, that is they are blondes who drive pink sports cars and own horses. The small space in the middle common to all three circles represents $P \cap Q \cap R$, namely the set of women who belong to P and Q and R (i.e. blonde housewives who drive pink sports cars and own horses).

The total space enclosed by the three circles represents the set known as the 'union' of P, Q, and R, denoted by $P \cup Q \cup R$. Its members are women who belong to P, or Q, or R. All blondes who drive pink sports cars, all women who own horses, and all housewives belong to $P \cup Q \cup R$.

As a further example consider a pack of 52 playing cards. The jacks, queens, and kings are referred to as face cards. The Venn diagram representing the set of 12 face cards (which we will call A) and the set of 13 heart cards (which we will call B) is shown in Figure 3.2. In this example $|U| = 52$, $|A| = 12$, and $|B| = 13$. $A \cap B$ is the set of cards common to both A and B, and consists of the jack of hearts, queen of hearts, and king of hearts. $|A \cap B| = 3$. $A \cup B$ is the set of cards belonging to A or B, and consists of the ace, 2, 3, . . . J, Q, K

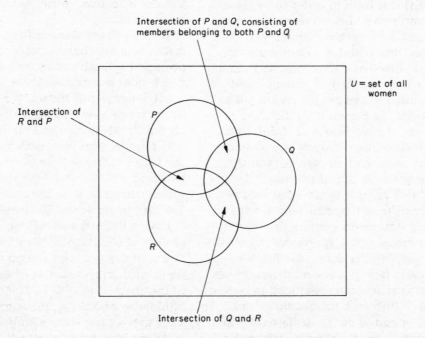

Figure 3.1   Venn diagram representing the three intersecting sets P, Q and R

of hearts, and also the jack, queen and king of spades, diamonds, and clubs. The number of members is 12 from *A plus* 13 from *B minus* the 3 members of $A \cap B$ (these three members have to be subtracted since they have been counted twice, once as members of *A* and once as members of *B*). Hence

$$|A \cup B| = |A| + |B| - |A \cap B| \qquad (1)$$

This equation is always true, provided *A* and

DEFINITION OF PROBABILITY

It is often observed that, like the punter who bets on horses, the businessman is a gambler. But whereas the activities of the former result merely in the shifting of wealth from one individual to another, the activities of the businessman actually create wealth. The prosperity of the western world is to a great extent due to businessmen risking capital on

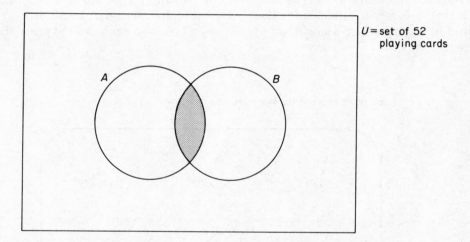

$U =$ set of 52 playing cards

Figure 3.2   Venn diagram representing the set of heart cards (A) and the intersecting set of face cards (B)

B are intersecting sets. As an exercise the student should prove, by inspection of Figure 3.1, that

$$|P \cup Q \cup R| = |P| + |Q| + |R| - |P \cap Q| -$$

$$|Q \cap R| - |R \cap P| + |P \cap Q \cap R| \qquad (2)$$

If two sets *A* and *B* have no members in common, they are called 'disjoint'. They do not intersect (and so are represented on a Venn diagram by non-overlapping circles), and $|A \cap B| = 0$. It follows from equation (1) above that in this case

$$|A \cup B| = |A| + |B| \qquad (3)$$

For example, if *U* is a pack of 52 cards, *A* is the set of spades, and *B* is the set of hearts, then $|A \cup B| = 13 + 13 = 26$.

uncertain business ventures. Probability theory was originally developed when mathematicians addressed themselves to the study of gambling situations, and it is best explained by considering simple examples involving throwing dice or drawing cards from a pack, but the principles involved apply equally well to the more complex and exciting world of business. Probability theory underlies much of statistics and operations research and it is therefore appropriate to introduce it at this point. More advanced ideas in probability are covered in Part IV.

We shall begin by considering the example of an ordinary die with faces numbered 1 to 6, but biased so that when it is rolled some faces are more likely than others to land uppermost. Suppose that we do not know what effect the bias will have on the way the die rolls, but we wish to determine the probability of scoring a 4 on a single roll. To determine this we shall have to roll the die a large number of times and count the number of times that a 4 is scored. If the die is rolled 1000 times, and 150 of these rolls results in a 4 being scored, then the proportion of rolls that result in a 4 is 150/1000 = 0.15. We would expect that roughly 0.15 of all subsequent rolls will result in a 4 being scored, and 0.15 is therefore our estimate for the probability of scoring a 4 on a single roll of this particular die.

The definition of probability that we have used to obtain the above probability estimate is

$$P(\text{success}) = \frac{\text{number of successes}}{\text{number of trials}}$$

The accuracy of a probability estimate increases as the number of trials increases.

The set of possible outcomes of a single roll of a die can be represented by a Venn diagram, as shown in Figure 3.3. The outcomes are 'mutually exclusive', that is the occurrence of one outcome excludes the possibility of any

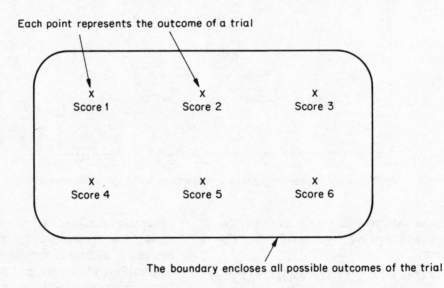

Figure 3.3 Venn diagram representing the possible outcomes of a single roll of a die

In the language of probability theory each roll of the die is called a 'trial', each result of a roll (score 1, score 2, score 3, score 4, score 5, or score 6) is called an 'outcome', and an outcome which gives the desired result (in this case 'score 4') is called a 'success'. The shorthand for 'probability of' is P: 'probability of success' is written P (success), 'probability of scoring a 4' is written P (score 4).

other outcome occurring. If we score a 4 then we cannot, in the same roll, also score 1, or 2, etc.

Let us change the example slightly, and assume now that the die is unbiased. In this case each face has an equal chance of landing uppermost, so each of the six possible outcomes is said to be 'equally likely'. Only one face out of the six faces is numbered 4, and we therefore conclude that the probability of scoring a 4 on a single roll of this particular die is $\frac{1}{6}$.

So if every outcome is equally likely, the probability of success is determined by using the definition:

$$P(\text{success}) = \frac{\text{number of successful outcomes}}{\text{number of possible outcomes}}$$

This definition gives an absolutely accurate measure of the probability of success.

In this chapter we shall explain the laws of probability using set theory. If the set of successful outcomes of a trial is denoted by A, and the universal set of all possible outcomes by U, then the above definition can be written:

$$P(\text{success}) = \frac{|A|}{|U|}$$

Note that $0 \leqslant |A| \leqslant |U|$ (since there can never be less than 0 successful outcomes, and there can never be more successful outcomes than the number of possible outcomes). It follows that

$$0 \leqslant \frac{|A|}{|U|} \leqslant 1$$

and therefore $P(\text{success})$ can never be less than 0 or greater than 1. If a result is impossible (for example, score 7 on a single roll of a die), then there are no successful outcomes, and therefore $|A| = 0$, and so $P(\text{success}) = 0$. If a result is certain (for example score 1 or score 2 or score 3 or score 4 or score 5 or score 6 on a single roll), then all possible outcomes are successful outcomes, and therefore $|A| = |U|$, and so $P(\text{success}) = 1$. If a result is unlikely to occur, then its probability will be close to 0; if a result is likely to occur, its probability will be close to 1.

Events
The outcomes of a trial are invariably mutually exclusive. This means that two such outcomes can never occur simultaneously — for example it is impossible to score 4 *and* 5 on a single

roll of a die. But it is possible to score 4 *or* 5 on a single roll, and it is by the use of the word 'or' that outcomes can be combined.

Any such combination of outcomes is called an 'event'. An event is a subset of U, the set of all possible outcomes of a trial. Note that a single outcome is also a subset of U (it is the subset containing that one outcome), and so it too can be called an event.

The event 'score 4 or score 5' is the subset containing the outcome 'score 4' and the outcome 'score 5', and it is represented by the indicated space in the Venn diagram in Figure 3.4. This subset does not contain any

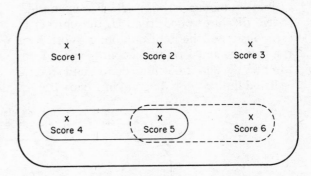

Figure 3.4   Venn diagram showing the subsets 'score 4 or score 5' and 'score 5 or score 6'

outcome other than these two — thus the event 'score 4 or score 5' and the event 'score 1' are mutually exclusive. However, the event 'score 4 or score 5' and the event 'score 5 or score 6' are not mutually exclusive, since they both contain the outcome 'score 5'. It is clear that mutually exclusive events are disjoint subsets of U, and are represented by non-overlapping spaces on a Venn diagram. Events which are not mutually exclusive are intersecting subsets of U, and are represented by overlapping spaces on a Venn diagram (see Figure 3.4).

Events are said to be independent if the occurrence of one of them has no influence upon the occurrence of the other. For example, if two dice are rolled, the score achieved by the first die does not affect the score achieved by the second die, and vice versa. If the first die scores 4, there is no magic mechanism which makes it less likely that the second die will also score 4. The events 'score 4 on the first die' and 'score 4 on the second die' are independent. Because they are independent they are not mutually exclusive, that is both events can occur together (as happens when both dice score 4). (Note that events may also be *dependent* and non-mutually exclusive — see the section on conditional probability in Chapter 17.)

If two independent events A and B occur together, then any outcome of A can occur with any outcome of B, and the total number of joint outcomes is $|A| \times |B|$. For example, if two dice are rolled, then U, the universal set, consists of the joint outcomes 'score 1 on the first die and 1 on the second', 'score 1 on the first die and 2 on the second', and so on, as listed in the Venn diagram in Figure 3.5.

U_1, the universal set of outcomes from rolling the first die, is the set $\{$ score 1, score 2, score 3, score 4, score 5, score 6 $\}$, and so $|U_1| = 6$. If U_2 is defined similarly for the second die, then $|U_2| = 6$. $|U| = |U_1| \times |U_2| = 6 \times 6 = 36$, and it will be observed that there are 36 possible joint outcomes listed in Figure 3.5.

Again, if A is the event 'score 4 on the first die', then $|A| = 1$. If B is the event 'score 4 on the second die', then $|B| = 1$. The event 'A and B' consists of the joint outcome 'score 4 on the first die and score 4 on the second die', and $|A$ and $B| = |A| \times |B| = 1 \times 1 = 1$. There is just one joint outcome which gives this event.

LAWS OF PROBABILITY

An event is simply a set of outcomes, and if we know the probabilities attaching to those

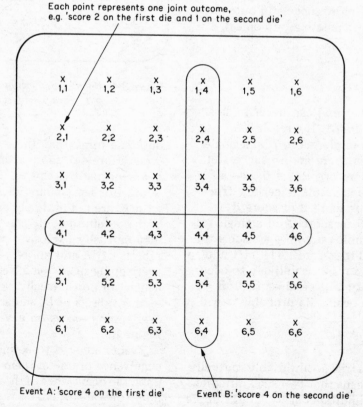

Each point represents one joint outcome, e.g. 'score 2 on the first die and 1 on the second die'

Event A: 'score 4 on the first die'   Event B: 'score 4 on the second die'

Figure 3.5 Venn diagram representing the possible outcomes if two dice are rolled

outcomes, then the laws of probability can be used to assign probabilities to events. In this section we derive these laws by using the second definition of probability, which assumes that the outcomes of a trial are all equally likely. The laws hold, however, even when the outcomes are not equally likely.

Addition law for mutually exclusive events

If A and B are mutually exclusive events, and U is the universal set of outcomes containing A and B, then the event 'A or B' consists of all the outcomes in A and all the outcomes in B, and is therefore the subset $A \cup B$. Hence

$$P(A \text{ or } B) = \frac{|A \cup B|}{|U|} \quad \text{(by the definition of probability)}$$

$$= \frac{|A| + |B|}{|U|} \quad \text{(by equation (3) on page 31)}$$

$$= \frac{|A|}{|U|} + \frac{|B|}{|U|}$$

$$= P(A) + P(B)$$

This law can be extended to cover any number of mutually exclusive events:

$$P(A \text{ or } B \text{ or } \ldots) = P(A) + P(B) + P(C) + \ldots$$

As an example of this law, suppose a fair die is rolled once, and A is the event 'score 4' and B is the event 'score 5'. Then P(score 4 or score 5) $= P$(score 4) $+ P$(score 5) $= \frac{1}{6} + \frac{1}{6} = \frac{1}{3}$.

Multiplication law for independent events

If A and B are independent events, and U_1 is the universal set of outcomes of the trial containing A, and U_2 is similarly defined for B, then the event 'A and B' is the subset $A \cap B$ of U, the universal set consisting of joint outcomes from U_1 and U_2. Hence

$$P(A \text{ and } B) = \frac{|A \cap B|}{|U|} \quad \text{(by the definition of probability)}$$

$$= \frac{|A| \times |B|}{|U_1| \times |U_2|} = \frac{|A|}{|U_1|} \times \frac{|B|}{|U_2|}$$

$$= P(A) \times P(B)$$

This law can be extended to cover any number of independent events:

$$P(A \text{ and } B \text{ and } C \text{ and } \ldots) =$$

$$P(A) \times P(B) \times P(C) \times \ldots$$

As an example of this law, suppose two fair dice are rolled, and A is the event 'score 4 on the first die' and B is the event 'score 4 on the second die'. Then P(score 4 on the first die and score 4 on the second die) $= \frac{1}{6} \times \frac{1}{6} = \frac{1}{36}$.

Addition law for independent events

If A and B are independent events, then the event 'A or B' consists of outcomes belonging to A or B (or both), and it is therefore the subset $A \cup B$ of U. Now $|A \cup B| = |A| + |B| - |A \cap B|$ (from equation (1), page 31), and it can be shown from this that

$$P(A \text{ or } B) = P(A) + P(B) - P(A \text{ and } B)$$

$$= P(A) + P(B) - P(A) \times P(B)$$

To extend this law to three independent events it is necessary to use equation (2) on page 31:

$$P(A \text{ or } B \text{ or } C) = P(A) + P(B) + P(C) -$$

$$P(A)P(B) - P(B)P(C) - P(C)P(A) +$$

$$P(A)P(B)P(C)$$

As an example of this law, suppose that A is the event 'score 4 on the first die' and B is the event 'score 4 on the second die', then

$$P(\text{score 4 on the first or second die})$$

$$= \frac{1}{6} + \frac{1}{6} - \frac{1}{6} \times \frac{1}{6}$$

$$= \frac{11}{36}$$

A further useful law is derived by considering the event 'not A', that is the subset of U which consists of all outcomes which do not belong to the event A. 'A' and 'not A' are clearly mutually exclusive, and therefore

$$P(A \text{ or not } A) = \frac{|A \text{ or not } A|}{|U|} = \frac{|U|}{|U|} = 1$$

It follows that $1 = P(A) + P(\text{not } A)$, and therefore

$$P(A) = 1 - P(\text{not } A)$$

EXAMPLE

Suppose three fair dice are rolled and we wish to determine the probability of achieving a total score of 4 or more. We approach this problem by considering the probability of *not* scoring 4 or more, that is the probability of scoring 3 or less. It is impossible to score less than 3 with three dice, and so we are left with the problem of determining the probability of scoring exactly 3. This score can be obtained in only one way: score 1 on the first die *and* 1 on the second die *and* 1 on the third die. So

$$P(\text{achieve a total score of } 3) = P(\text{score 1 on the first die}) \times P(\text{score 1 on the second die}) \times P(\text{score 1 on the third die})$$

$$= \tfrac{1}{6} \times \tfrac{1}{6} \times \tfrac{1}{6}$$

$$= \tfrac{1}{216}$$

Hence

$$P(\text{achieve a total score of 4 or more}) = 1 - P(\text{achieve a total score of 3})$$

$$= 1 - \tfrac{1}{216}$$

$$= \tfrac{215}{216}$$

EXERCISES

1. List all the subsets of the set $U = \{0, 1, 2, 3\}$ which contain the number 1.

2. Of the 220 employees of a company, 60 are females, and a quarter of these females are shift-workers. There are, in total, 120 shift-workers, Represent this situation by a Venn diagram, and from it deduce how many of the male employees are not shift-workers.

3. In a certain class there are 3 girls (Mary, Susan, and Jane), and 13 boys. During the course of the year 6 of the boys dated Mary, 7 dated Susan, and 6 dated Jane. One of the boys dated Mary and Susan but not Jane, and 3 of the boys dated Susan and Jane but not Mary. One of the boys dated all three girls, and one boy dated none of them. Represent this situation by a Venn diagram, and from it determine how many boys dated Mary and Jane but not Susan.

4. A fair coin is tossed three times. List all the outcomes as points on a Venn diagram (cf. Figure 3.5), and draw a boundary around the event A: 'score a head on the first toss and on the second toss'. Calculate $P(A)$. What is the probability of the event B: 'score a head on the third toss'? Calculate $P(A \text{ or } B)$.

5. A bowl contains 10 white balls, 5 red balls, and 5 blue balls. A ball is drawn at random, replaced, the balls stirred, and a second ball drawn. Find the probability that:
    (a) Both balls are red
    (b) The first ball is white and the second ball is blue
    (c) Both balls are white or blue
    (d) At least one ball is white
    (e) The first ball is red and the second ball is not red.

6. In a time of acute petrol shortage the probability that any filling station will have petrol for sale is 0.25. On a certain journey you pass four filling stations. On the assumption that you are dealing with independent events, calculate the probability that:
    (a) They will all have petrol
    (b) None will have petrol
    (c) At least one will have petrol

(d) The first one will have petrol, but none of the others will

(e) Just one will have petrol (i.e. either the first and no others, or the second and no others, etc.)

(f) At least two will have petrol.

7. Only half the seeds from a certain packet will germinate. A man plants three seeds in a pot. What is the probability that at least one will germinate?

Part Two

Statistical Methods

Four

Statistics and Statistical Data

THE SCIENCE OF STATISTICS

Statistics has been defined as the science of gathering and analysing numerical data, and it has earned its place among the sciences by virtue of the methodological manner in which statistical inquiries are conducted. As an example of statistical method, suppose that the management of a company is faced with a wage claim by its shop-floor workers and asks for information on their current earnings. The steps involved in finding this information and presenting it in a suitable form to management are as follows.

The first step is to obtain the relevant data — the week's payroll — but there is little point in presenting the figures in their original form to management. The human mind is unable to assimilate and make sense of such a mass of data. The next step, therefore, is to summarize the data by grouping the earnings into a small number of classes so that the management is presented with a 'frequency distribution', that is a brief list giving the number of workers earning between say £50 and £55 a week, the number earning between £55 and £60 a week, and so on.

Next the data is analysed by, for example, computing from the frequency distribution the average earnings and comparing this average with that obtained from previous pay-rolls (in order to determine the trend in earnings), and with the average earnings of other groups of workers in the same industry.

The final task is to present the salient facts and conclusions with the aid of suitably designed tables and charts so that the management can readily appreciate them and formulate policy on the basis of them.

This example illustrates some of the stages that any statistical inquiry must follow. A complete list of the main stages is as follows:

1. Define precisely the objectives of the inquiry and what information is required to meet those objectives. If there is any vagueness at this stage, it is possible that irrelevant data may be collected and analysed (which wastes money), or that essential data may be missed.

2. Check whether any or all of the information is already available in government or trade publications or in the internal records of the organization carrying out the inquiry. Information which has previously been collected and analysed, perhaps for some other inquiry, is called 'secondary data'. As with anything secondhand, it is inexpensive, but there are risks attached to its use. These risks arise from:

(a) The definitions used. For example, until recently the government defined and measured 'unemployment' by the number of insurance cards lodged at Employment Exchanges. The result was that many

many married women looking for work did not appear in the unemployment figures.

(b) The assumptions made. For example, some television ratings are based on calculations which assume a certain average number of viewers per set. This average may be highly inaccurate at certain times (for example, at Christmas).

(c) The fact that the data may be out of date.

3. If information is not already available, decide how it is to be collected. Decisions must be made on the method of data collection, and whether to carry out a census or a sample survey. If a sample is to be taken, the type and size of sample must be determined. Data which the investigator collects himself — called 'primary data' — is not subject to the pitfalls inherent in secondary data, but it is expensive.

4. If necessary, carry out a small-scale test survey, to discover and rectify any fault in the design of the questionnaires, and to ensure that the research personnel have been adequately briefed.

5. Carry out the inquiry, summarize and analyse the results, and present the conclusions using suitable tables and diagrams in a report.

In the remainder of this chapter we shall be considering the various sources of secondary data, the various ways of collecting primary data, and the methods of taking samples. Subsequent chapters deal with the methods of presenting, summarizing, and analysing data.

SOURCES OF SECONDARY DATA

The word 'statistics' is used not only to mean the branch of science concerned with the analysis of data, but also to mean the *data* on which the analyses are based. In advanced economies governments and businesses are dependent upon up-to-date statistics in order to formulate effective policies. Government measures designed to regulate the economy, such as the setting of tax levels, the formulation of wage guidelines, and the provision of subsidies to certain industries, are based upon the profile of the current situation provided by up-to-date statistics. A business needs to know, for instance, how it compares with its competitors in the national markets and in its wage rates, and what export possibilities exist for its products.

Statistics on these and a host of other aspects of our society and economy are published on a regular basis, but it is generally recognized that businesses make insufficient use of them. Part of the reason for this is ignorance on the part of the businessman of what is available and where to find particular items of information, and one of the purposes of a business statistics course is to indicate to the student how he can find his way through the maze of published statistics.

Most of the published statistics are produced by government departments, and are referred to as 'official statistics'. The statistical work of these departments is co-ordinated by the Central Statistical Office, which itself produces a number of monthly and annual digests which summarize and bring together statistics contained in the primary departmental publications. They also indicate the primary publications from which the summarized statistics are drawn. Consequently it is in these digests that any search for statistical data should begin.

The digests published by the Central Statistical Office include the following:

1. *The Annual Abstract of Statistics* which gives the yearly figures for the most important statistical series over the previous ten years. It is published annually, and the topics covered by it include: weather, population and vital statistics, social conditions, education,

labour, production, retailing and catering, transport and communications, overseas and home finance, national income and expenditure, banking, insurance, and prices.

2. *The Monthly Digest of Statistics* which covers roughly the same ground at (1), but gives monthly or quarterly figures for the previous two or three years, and is published monthly. Information on banking and finance is largely excluded from this publication, being covered instead in (3).

3. *Financial Statistics* (published monthly).

4. *Economic Trends* (published monthly) gives statistics which indicate the state of the economy (called 'economic indicators'). Monthly or quarterly figures are given for a period of just over a year. This publication is notable for the excellent charts which show changes in these statistics over the previous ten years.

5. *Social Trends* (published annually) has a similar format to *Economic Trends*, but covers indicators of the social condition of the nation.

Data is published earlier and in more detail in the primary departmental publications, some of which are listed below:

1. For population and vital statistics, see *Population Trends* and the report on the 1971 Census for Great Britain.

2. For social statistics, see the *General Household Survey* and the *Registrar General's Statistical Review of England and Wales*.

3. For manpower, earnings, personal expenditure, and retail prices, see the *Department of Employment Gazette*, the *New Earnings Survey*, and the *Family Expenditure Survey*.

4. For production and distribution, see the *Report on the Census of Production*, the *Report on the Census of Distribution, Trade and Industry*, and the Business Monitor series.

5. For national income and expenditure, see the *National Income and Expenditure 'Blue Book'* and *Inland Revenue Statistics*.

6. For external trade, see *Overseas Trade Statistics of the United Kingdom*.

The Central Statistical Office publishes a free booklet entitled *Government Statistics — a Brief Guide to Sources* which briefly describes the many government statistical publications. The student will find this a useful guide to what is available.

Familiarity with the main statistical publications will be gained only if time is spent browsing through them in the college library. Published statistics form a fruitful area for student assignments, and some are suggested in the exercises at the end of this chapter.

The Post Office Viewdata Service (Prestel)

The Post Office Viewdata Service, planned to come into operation in 1980, will provide a low-cost up-to-the-minute information service for business and private users. The information will be stored in regional computers linked into a national network, and transmission will be via the Post Office telephone system for display on the user's television set.

By operating a hand-held control unit (similar in size and appearance to a pocket calculator) the user will be able to access the following categories of information:
News and weather
Entertainments and sport
Travel and holidays
Hobbies and games
Market-place and buying advice
Community services and education
Jobs and careers

Facts and figures
Money
Stock Exchange and commodities
Company and market information
Manufacturing industry guide
Service industry guide
Reference information and government
    information
Calculations

To access information, the user calls the local viewdata centre by pressing the call button on the control unit and keying in his code number. The opening display on the television screen lists the main subject headings, and the required subject is selected by pressing the appropriately numbered button on the control unit. An index listing the subsections of the subject is then displayed, and again the required one is selected. The subdivisions of the selected subsection are then displayed, and the process is repeated until the required item of information is obtained. The system is flexible, and users can jump backwards or forwards to any information display for which they have the 'page' number.

The cost to the user will be just the charge for the telephone line (at local call rates) plus $\frac{1}{2}$p per 'page' of information.

The effect of the Viewdata Service on business in the 'eighties can be expected to be as revolutionary as the impact of the computer in the 'sixties. A by-product of this revolution is likely to be the demise of many traditional published sources of information.

PRIMARY DATA

If data on a certain topic is required but is not available, then it will have to be collected. In collecting primary data the researcher has to decide:

1. Which data collection method to use

2. Which sampling method to use, or

whether to take a census. The subsequent sections of this chapter are devoted to a description of the methods available.

In making his choice the researcher's prime concern is to achieve, with the limited resources available to him, the greatest possible accuracy — and therefore the least possible error — in the final result. A major preoccupation, therefore, is the avoidance of error. Because of the importance of error in statistical work we summarize here its principal causes and effects. The details will be found at the appropriate points in the sections that follow.

Errors can arise from:

1. Faulty data collection, caused by, for example, the researcher's questioning technique, or lack of co-operation on the part of those questioned, or insufficient time being available to ensure accurate results

2. The sample from which the data is collected being unrepresentative of the population.

Provided the sample is selected on a 'random' basis (see below), then any errors of type (2) arise through the operation of the laws of chance, and their effect on the final result can be calculated using probability theory. This type of error is unavoidable, and allowance can be made for it.

The other errors arise through lack of resources or human failings, and they are far more serious. Not only is it normally not possible to estimate their effect on the final result, but they frequently tend consistently in a certain direction. This consistent tendency, or 'bias', may seriously affect the validity of the result. Great care in the choice and training of interviewers, in the design of the questionnaire form, in the selection of the sample, and in all the other aspects of the data collection exercise, is essential if bias is to be avoided.

DATA-COLLECTION METHODS

Observation

This method is used, for example, in traffic censuses (in which automatic devices record the number of vehicles passing), or in surveys of seat-belt usage (in which observers count drivers and passengers wearing and not wearing seat-belts), or in the determination of a firm's stock levels (in which items of stock are counted).

Observation can be a relatively inexpensive method yielding accurate results. To interview people to obtain seat-belt usage, for example, would be extremely time-consuming and would lead to bias (since respondents would tend to state a higher usage than was actually the case). If questionning is used to collect data, it is sometimes supplemented by observation to check for bias.

Observation suffers from the disadvantage that it does not probe into the underlying reasons for the behaviour observed. If, in a traffic census, it is required to determine the reasons for the observed traffic flow, the vehicles must be stopped and the drivers asked for details of their journeys.

Experimentation

Much statistical work has been done on the design and analysis of agricultural experiments, to determine the effects on selected crops of various combinations of soils, fertilizers, etc. In recent years market researchers have carried out experiments on consumer behaviour to determine the effect on sales of new advertising methods, new packaging, alternative pricing policies, etc. A test market is chosen for the trials, and from the results conclusions are drawn about the whole market. New products are sometimes tested in a similar way.

Survey (i.e. questionning) methods

These methods have the advantage that they can be used for both recording behaviour and probing the reasons underlying that behaviour. They are, however, less objective than the methods described above, and therefore more prone to bias. They usually involve the completion of a printed questionnaire form, either by an interviewer or by the respondent, but in the case of inquiries covering very complex subjects, unstructured interviews are used.

Great care must be exercised in the design of questionnaires, for a poor design will lead to bias. The main points to be borne in mind are:

1. It should be as brief as possible while covering the object of the inquiry

2. The questions should be simple and unambiguous

3. Leading questions (such as 'Don't you agree that . . .?') and emotive words must be avoided

4. The questions should be capable of a precise, brief answer, if possible by means of a tick in a box

5. The questions should form a logical sequence.

An example of a questionnaire form is given in Appendix IV, Section A.

The main survey methods are as follows:

1. *Postal questionnaires* are an inexpensive and fast way of contacting a large number of people over a wide area. Interviewers are not required, but this carries the risk that questions may be misunderstood and answered incorrectly, and the response rate may be low — often less than 15% of people contacted bother to reply. The low response rate is a serious drawback because the people who complete and return the questionnaire will tend to be those who for some reason have an interest in the subject of the inquiry, and they will not

therefore form a representative sample. (It is possible to estimate the extent of the resulting bias — called 'non-response bias' — by interviewing a sample of those who do not return the questionnaire.) In the case of government questionnaires, the information is normally required by law, and the problem of low response is avoided.

2. *Personal interviews* are, in contrast, expensive to conduct, but they largely eliminate the problems of low response and incorrect completion of questionnaires, and they enable the subject of the inquiry to be investigated in greater depth. Provided the interviewers are well trained and highly skilled, this is for most purposes the best data-collection method. If poorly selected and trained interviewers are used, then bias will arise, for example, through the interviewer's manner, or because emotive words are used or leading questions asked. 'Interviewer bias', as it is called, is often the most serious source of error in a survey result.

3. If is is required to collect data on a continuous basis over a long period of time, a *panel* is used. Each member of the panel records his relevant actions (for example, television programmes watched, or goods purchased) on the form provided, which he submits at regular intervals (usually fortnightly). To encourage members to maintain records over a long period it is often necessary to offer money or gifts. This method is particularly useful when it is required to determine the changing patterns of consumer behaviour over time.

SAMPLE SURVEYS

In deciding which members, out of the population under investigation, to obtain the required data from, the researcher's first task is to define precisely the population, and possibly obtain a list of all its members. Such a list is called a 'sampling frame'. If the population under investigation consists of all the adults living in a certain area, then the electoral register for that area would be a suitable sampling frame. The telephone directory (or some other selective list) excludes many members of the designated population, and so would not be suitable. (The telephone directory would, however, form a suitable frame for a GPO survey of subscribers.)

It should be noted that in statistics the term 'population' applies to *any* universal set — so that one might speak of the population of lengths of bolts produced by a certain machine, or the population of sales made by a firm. A sampling frame for the latter would be the invoices on file.

It might be thought that the best sort of survey is a census, which involves collecting data from every member of the population. A census is necessary if it is required to find out the sizes of the various segments or classes within a population, but for most purposes it is far from ideal. The resources available for the survey have to be spread thinly over the entire population, so that a cursory investigation only of each member is possible, and the consequence of this is that the subject of the inquiry cannot be probed in any depth and there is a greater likelihood of bias arising.

Sample surveys do not suffer from these drawbacks, for the research personnel can spend sufficient time with each member of the sample to carry out a full and accurate investigation, and, if the survey is properly conducted, bias will be minimal. The problem is that the sample may not be representative of the population, not through any fault in the method of selecting the sample, but due to chance factors. Any survey results obtained by using sample data will therefore differ to some extent from the results that would be obtained if data from the entire population were available. These differences are called 'sampling errors', and an important part of statistics is concerned with the mathematical analysis of these errors. We shall deal with this analysis in Chapter 10 and 11, but some appreciation of sampling errors is essential at this stage of the course.

To illustrate what is meant by sampling errors, suppose that the height of each student enrolling for a certain class is measured, and the average height for the class determined. (The sort of average referred to here is the 'arithmetic mean', calculated by adding the heights and dividing by the number of students — see Chapter 6.) The average height of this year's intake of students to the class will not be exactly the same as the average last year, nor will it exactly equal the average next year. There might, for example, be more tall students in this year's intake, or more short students — each class will have a different selection of heights. A class is a sample drawn from the population of students, and there will be differences, however slight, between the average for one sample and the average for other samples, and no sample average will precisely equal the average for the population of students. It is random factors — such as an exceptional number of tall students in a class — which are the cause of these sampling errors.

The effect of sampling errors on a survey result can be reduced by increasing the size of the sample. If there are only two or three students in a class, they might all be tall, or short, and the sample average may differ markedly from the population average. If, however, there are fifty or sixty students in a class, the proportions of tall, medium, and short students will tend more closely to reflect the population proportions. The effect of sampling errors is, in fact, inversely proportional to the square root of the sample size, so that to halve the effect of sampling errors it is necessary to quadruple the size of the sample.

RANDOM SAMPLES

Random factors may not be the sole cause of a sample being unrepresentative of the population from which it is drawn. If class A is an engineering class, and class B is secretarial, then we would expect the average height of class A students to exceed the average height of class B students, for the classes are drawn mainly from different sections of the population of students — males in the case of class A, females in the case of class B. If we wished to determine the average height of the population, we should be foolish to base our results on either of these samples. Not only would our result be seriously in error, but, without additional information, we should be unable to determine the extent of the error.

Clearly we must not restrict membership of our sample to certain sections of the population, but we must allow every member of the population an equal chance of being selected. Samples selected on this basis are called 'random samples', and their importance in statistical work lies in the fact that the sample result, although subject to sampling errors arising from random influences, is *not* subject to incalculable errors arising from a non-random, or biased, selection method.

There are three ways of selecting a random sample, and we can illustrate these by considering the example of a survey being undertaken of the sales made by a firm, the sampling frame used being the invoices on file:

1. One way would be to remove the invoices from the file, place them in a large bowl, thoroughly stir, and remove the required number.

2. A more sophisticated procedure would be to select a random sample of invoice numbers using a table of random numbers, and remove the invoices so selected from the file. This is the most commonly used method.

3. The easiest method is known as 'systematic' or 'quasi-random' sampling, If there are 10,000 invoices on file, and a sample of size 200 is required, then the procedure would be to select every fiftieth invoice. The starting invoice number — between

1 and 50 — is chosen randomly, subsequent numbers increasing in jumps of 50. This method cannot be applied in many situations, for it is unbiased only if the population exhibits no periodicity. It would, for example, be inappropriate to use this method to sample houses on an estate — every fifth house might have four bedrooms, the remainder having three.

SAMPLING FROM HUMAN POPULATIONS

There is little difficulty in selecting a random sample of invoices on a file, but problems arise when human populations are sampled. The people selected may be scattered all over the country, some living in very inaccessible places, and, unless the data is collected by post, interviewers will spend the greater part of their time travelling. As a result the resources available will yield a relatively small sample.

Another problem is the large amount of variability in human populations. There are considerable differences in attitudes, habits, etc., from one social group to another. This will result in large sampling errors if a disproportionately large or small number of people from one section of the population is selected. Although the effect of these errors can be calculated, the results of the survey would be much improved if the sample could be selected in such a way that each section was represented in the correct proportion.

The following variants of random sampling overcome these difficulties, and they are used, either singly or in combination, in most sample surveys involving human populations:

1. In *multi-stage sampling* the country is divided into areas, and a random sample of these is chosen. The areas chosen are then subdivided into districts, and a random sample of these is taken. If required, further subdivisions can be made. Finally, a random sample of the population living in each district is selected and interviewed. The sample is thus confined to a number of small districts, and interviewer travelling is minimized. The amount of variability in this type of sample is higher than in a simple random sample of the same size, and this results in larger sampling errors. This is more than offset, however, by the fact that given resources will yield a much larger sample under this method than under simple random sampling.

2. *Stratified sampling* is used to reduce the effects of variability in the population. The method consists of taking random samples, not from the population as a whole, but from the various sections of the population. The results obtained from these samples are then combined in proportion to the sizes of the sections. The effect of this is to reduce the size of the sampling errors. A sample might be stratified in a number of ways, for example, into male and female, into young, middle-aged and old, and into the various social classes. Additional 'strata' in the population that might be reflected in the sample composition are urban and rural dwellers (for a survey for the leisure industry), native and immigrant (for a survey into attitudes towards the police), and so on.

Random samples, although ideal in theory, suffer from the practical difficulty that they involve the selection of individuals from a sampling frame and then the location of those selected. This is a time-consuming process, and for some surveys the population is not known and hence a sampling frame cannot be constructed — as in the case of an investigation into the health of smokers. The following methods overcome these difficulties, but because they are non-random, the results obtained will be biased to an unknown extent:

1. *Quota sampling* is a method favoured by market researchers, and if properly carried out can yield excellent results at a relatively low cost. Interviewers question members of the public in the street up to

a given quota. This quota will be stratified so that the correct proportions from the various sections of the population are represented, and the interviewing locations will be chosen by the multi-stage method. The selection of the sample depends upon the interviewer's judgement, but he must adhere to his quota — so many males, so many females, so many young, so many old, etc.

2. *Cluster sampling* is a useful method when the population is not known. A series of starting-points within the population is chosen (by the multi-stage method), and a specified number of the population interviewed in the vicinity of the starting-point. To carry out a survey of commuters travelling by rail, a random sample of trains might be chosen, and then a random sample of carriages of those trains, and then every fifth passenger, for example, in the selected carriages interviewed.

A brief description of a sample survey undertaken by students at the Buckinghamshire College of Higher Education is given in Appendix IV, Section A.

EXAMPLE OF A SAMPLE SURVEY: THE FAMILY EXPENDITURE SURVEY

We have chosen this as our example of a sample survey as the Index of Retail Prices, which is discussed in some detail in Chapter 7, is based upon its findings.

The Family Expenditure Survey is a continuous survey which was introduced by the government in 1957, and is conducted by the Office of Population Censuses and Surveys. Each year a sample of over 10,000 households is selected by the multi-stage method, as follows. The country is divided into 1800 areas, from which a stratified sample of 168 areas is chosen. The stratification is by region, by type of area (urban, rural, etc.), and by ratable value. The purpose of this is to ensure that the areas selected are representative of

the country as a whole. The selected areas are divided into districts, and four districts from each are selected by systematic sampling. From each chosen district 16 households are selected by taking a systematic sample from the register of electors. The total number of households selected is therefore $16 \times 4 \times 168 = 10,752$ and of these around three-quarters co-operate.

The selected households in an area are visited in rotation and each member over the age of 16 is asked to keep records covering a period of a fortnight of all payments made. In addition, the interviewers complete questionnaires covering such matters as items of regular expenditure such as gas and electricity bills, details of occupation, income, age, marital status, and so on. A payment of £1 is made to each member of the household involved in the survey. The documents are checked by survey officials and forwarded to the Department of Employment for analysis and publication.

EXERCISES

1. Write an account of the main statistics contained in a selection of the following publications: *Regional Statistics, Department of Employment Gazette, Trade and Industry, National Income and Expenditure 'Blue Book', Report on the Census of Distribution, Digest of U.K. Energy Statistics.*

2. Describe the main official sources of data on: transport, wages, manpower, production, distribution, and overseas trade, and indicate the type of data available.

3. Using the sources referred to in this chapter, write an account of trends in pollution (or any other suitable topic) in the U.K.

4. (a) Obtain from published sources the number of television licences held and the number of cinema admissions each

year for the last ten years, and illustrate the relationship between the two on a scattergraph. What conclusions can you draw?

(b) Compare the unemployment rates for the various regions of the country.

5. (a) Discuss the possible causes of bias in the collection of primary data.

(b) What methods of sampling and data collection would you suggest using in order to determine: (i) rates of pay in an industry which is composed of large and small firms; (ii) attitudes of college students to politics; (iii) the the incidence of dutch elm disease in the U.K.?

Five

Presentation of Data

The data gathered from sample surveys or other sources has to be presented in a form which makes it readily comprehensible to its various users. Many varieties of tables, charts and graphs are available for data-presentation — the choice will depend upon the nature of the data and the uses to which it is to be put. For example, if the management of a company requires a detailed analysis of the monthly sales over the past twelve months, then presentation by means of a table is most appropriate. If the company news-sheet wishes to portray the breakdown of sales by product or market, then some form of chart may be best. If it is required to highlight the way in which sales are changing over time, then a graph should be used.

To illustrate the principles involved in the construction of tables, charts and graphs, we shall use the example of a sole trader who owns two coin-operated launderettes, each of which has the following machines: a number of washers, a number of dryers and a drycleaner. The trader keeps records of the amounts earned by these three groups of machines, the figures over the period 1977–79 being as follows.

In 1977 the total takings from launderette A were £7850 (to the nearest £10), of which £3750 was earned by the washers, £2110 by the dryers, and £1990 by the drycleaner. The figures for launderette B were: total, £9130; washers, £3920; dryers, £2340; drycleaner, £2870. The corresponding figures for 1978

for launderette A were £8750, £4290, £2440, and £2020, and for launderette B they were £9470, £4360, £2470, and £2640. For 1979 the corresponding figures were £9960, £4970, £2970, and £2020 for launderette A, and £9810, £4770, £2870, and £2170 for launderette B.

TABLES

It is difficult to make sense of the above data when it is expressed in this narrative form. The performance of launderette A cannot be readily compared with that of launderette B, the earnings of one group of machines cannot be easily compared with the earnings of others, and trends in takings from one year to another are not apparent. These difficulties can be overcome by setting out the data in tabular form. A simple table containing just the annual takings for the two launderettes over the three-year period is given in Table 5.1.

Table 5.1 Annual takings of Launderette A and Launderette B over the period 1977–79 (in £'s).

	1977	1978	1979
Launderette A	7850	8750	9960
Launderette B	9130	9470	9810
Total	16,980	18,220	19,770

The data in the example has been classified not just by launderette and year, but also by type of machine. To incorporate this additional detail in the table it is necessary to give a break-down of the launderette takings, as shown in Table 5.2.

Table 5.2 Break-down of launderette takings

	1977		1978		1979	
	Takings (£)	%	Takings (£)	%	Takings (£)	%
Launderette *A*						
Washers	3750	22	4290	24	4970	25
Dryers	2110	12	2440	13	2970	15
Drycleaner	1990	12	2020	11	2020	10
Subtotal	7850	46	8750	48	9960	50
Launderette *B*						
Washers	3920	23	4360	24	4770	24
Dryers	2340	14	2470	14	2870	15
Drycleaner	2870	17	2640	14	2170	11
Subtotal	9130	54	9470	52	9810	50
Total	16,980	100	18,220	100	19,770	100

The principles underlying the design of these tables should be noted:

1. Any totals required are brought down vertically rather than carried across horizontally, the vertical presentation being the easiest to follow. If totals are required in both directions, then *time*, if it is one of the variables, should normally be listed horizontally (as in these tables). However, these are not hard and fast rules; if a large number of time periods are involved, it may be more convenient to list *time* vertically — see question 2 page 61).

2. Percentages have been included in Table 5.2, but these tend to clutter the table and should be inserted only if they are essential for the subsequent analysis of the data.

3. The tables are suitably titled, and the units used (in this case £s) are indicated. If necessary, the sources of the data should be stated, and also the degree of accuracy in the data.

Table 5.2 is the most detailed and useful of the two tables, and from it certain comparisons can be made:

1. Launderette *B*'s takings, although rising each year, comprise a steadily reducing percentage of the overall total. Launderette *A*'s takings are growing more rapidly.

2. The trend in drycleaning takings is much less healthy than the trend in washer and dryer takings. The takings of launderette *A*'s drycleaner are remaining almost static from year to year, but as a percentage of the total takings they are steadily falling. The takings of launderette *B*'s drycleaner are actually contracting, but in 1979 it was still earning more than launderette *A*'s drycleaner.

Knowledge of these trends is important for the following reasons:

1. The trends indicate what the volume of business will be in the near future, and they therefore facilitate planning — for example, the number of machines in launderette *A* may have to be increased to cater for the projected volume.

2. They indicate the areas of the business which require special attention. The sort of questions they raise are:

(a) Why are launderette *B*'s takings growing more slowly than those of launderette *A*? (Increased competition? Changing population? Inappropriate pricing policy? Inferior machines?)

(b) Why is the drycleaning trend so dismal, and how can it be improved? (Is a higher standard of finish required?)

The importance of questions of this sort is self-evident, but unless data is properly presented, they may never be formulated.

If a comparison between the takings of the various groups of machines is required, then a table similar to Table 5.2 should be constructed, but with 'Washers', 'Dryers' and

'Drycleaners' as the main side-headings, and 'Launderette *A*' and 'Launderette *B*' as subheadings under each of these side-headings. The sub-totals obtained would show by how much the total takings of the washers and the dryers had increased, and by how much the total takings of the drycleaners had decreased.

A very important type of table which has been omitted from the above discussion is a 'frequency table'. This and the associated chart (a 'histogram') are dealt with in Chapter 8.

CHARTS

The purpose of charts and graphs is to select relevant features from the data under consideration and present them in pictorial form, so that visual comparisons can be made. The main types of statistical chart are described below.

Bar charts

Bar charts are used for comparing the sizes of figures, the height of each bar representing the size of the corresponding figure. (The width of the bars, and the distance between each bar, is a matter of taste.) The bar chart shown in Figure 5.1 gives a visual indication of the growth in the total takings of the launderette business over the three-year period. It should be noted that an appropriate title has been given to this chart and that the axes have been suitably labelled.

Component bar charts

Figure 5.2 shows a component bar chart. In this, the bars are divided into sections to show the breakdown of totals into component

Figure 5.1 Bar chart showing the total takings of the launderette business for the period 1977–79

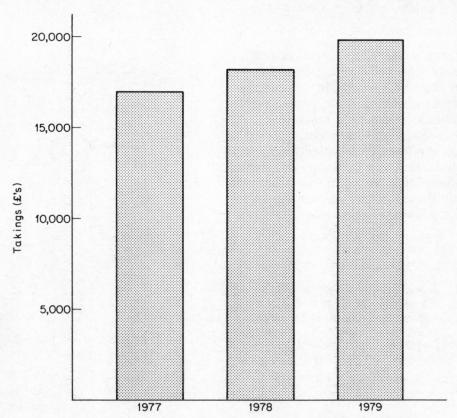

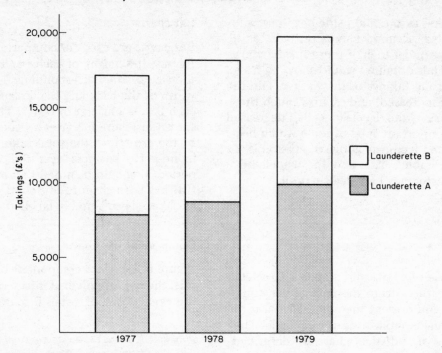

Figure 5.2   Component bar chart, with components representing the sizes of the takings of launderette A and launderette B for the period 1977-79

figures, the height of each section representing the size of the corresponding component. The sections should be suitably
coloured or shaded, and a key provided. In
this connexion it should be noted that
adjacent sections should be distinguished by
shadings of different intensities (black, white
grey, etc.) rather than by the use of hatching
lines which differ only in direction (horizontal, vertical etc.), as the eye can appreciate
intensity differences more easily.

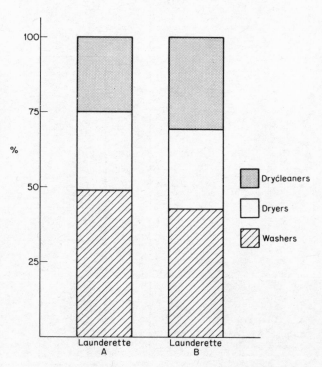

*Figure 5.3   Percentage component bar chart showing
the relative sizes of the takings of the
three groups of machines for the two
launderettes for 1977. (The percentages
are calculated as follows: launderette A
washers, $\frac{3750}{7850} \times 100 = 48\%$, launderette
A dryers, $\frac{2110}{7850} \times 100 = 27\%$, etc.)*

Percentage component bar charts

Percentages can be represented similarly by means of percentage component bar charts (see Figure 5.3). In this case the total height of the bar remains constant (at 100%), and the varying heights of the sections show the relative sizes of the component figures.

Pie charts

Pie charts can be used instead of percentage component bar charts to show relative sizes of figures. In this case the angle of each 'slice' of the pie is proportional to the size of the corresponding component figure (see Figure 5.4). The calculation of these angles differs

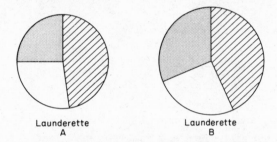

Launderette A   Launderette B

Figure 5.4 Pie charts showing the relative sizes of the takings of the three groups of machines for the two launderettes for 1977. (Key as for Figure 5.3.)

from percentage calculations only in that 360° instead of 100% has to be 'shared' between the components. For the launderette A pie shown in Figure 5.4 the calculations are:

Angle representing takings from washers

$$= \frac{3750}{7850} \times 360° = 172°$$

Angle representing takings from dryers

$$= \frac{2110}{7850} \times 360° = 97°$$

Angle representing takings from drycleaner

$$= \frac{1990}{7850} \times 360° = 91°$$

$$\text{Total} = 360°$$

The construction of these charts requires the use of a protractor and compass.

If desired, the size of the pie can be varied to enable the sizes of the total figures to be compared (this has been done in Figure 5.4). To do this the circle should be drawn with its radius proportional to the square root of the total. In the case of Figure 5.4, the total takings of launderette *A* in 1977 were £7850, and of launderette *B*, £9130, and the square roots of these numbers are 89 and 96. If 1 cm is chosen to represent 50, the radii of the two circles are:

$$\frac{89}{50} = 1.78 \text{ cm and } \frac{96}{50} = 1.92 \text{ cm.}$$

Pie charts are compact and attractive, and they require no scales. Furthermore, if there are more than 4 or 5 component figures, their relative sizes can be more readily appreciated from a pie chart than from a percentage component bar chart. However, if only a few components are involved, the eye can more easily compare the heights on a component bar chart than the angles of a pie chart.

Multiple bar charts

Multiple bar charts, illustrated in Figure 5.5, are a very effective means of comparing the sizes of component figures, but they have the disadvantage that the sizes of total figures are not shown.

Pictograms

Figure 5.6 is an example of a *pictogram*, a chart which consists of pictures of the data under consideration. A pictogram comparing the amount of bread consumed per head in different countries, for instance, might use pictures of loaves, each loaf representing so much bread. Such charts can be eye-catching and easily understood, but their use is limited to providing a visual comparison of total figures, since there is no way of including components in them. Note that it is incorrect to attempt to show changes in totals by changing the size of the picture — it is the

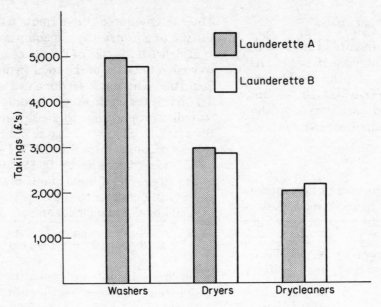

Figure 5.5 *Multiple bar chart showing the takings of the launderette machines for 1979*

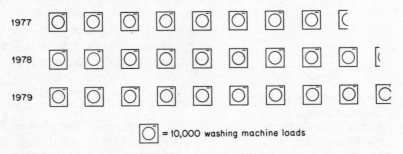

Figure 5.6 *Pictogram showing the total number of washing machine loads processed p.a. over the period 1977–79*

number of pictures, not the size, which must be made proportional to the size of the total figure.

GRAPHS

Graphs are often preferred to charts if it is required to show the way in which data changes over time. The principles of graph construction are explained in Chapter 2. Unlike charts, the horizontal axis of a graph must consist of a continuous scale. It would, for example, be impossible to represent the

data shown in Figure 5.3 on a graph. The data represented in Figure 5.1 — the total takings for the launderette business for 1977, 1978, and 1979 — is portrayed graphically in Figure 5.7. This type of graph is sometimes referred to as a 'line chart', in contrast to the 'band chart' shown in Figure 5.9. In constructing this graph we have assumed that the annual totals were calculated at 31 December each year — the points representing these totals are plotted against those dates.

For the purpose of obtaining annual totals, the year used could be 1 January to 31 December, or 2 January to 1 January, or 3 January to 2 January, and so on. Shifting in

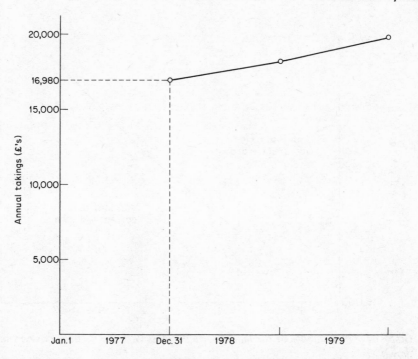

Figure 5.7   Graph showing the annual takings of the launderette business for the period 1977–79

this way the 365-day period over which the annual takings are measured gives rise to a series of 'moving annual totals', each one differing slightly from its predecessor, and these could be plotted as points on the graph and joined by a smoothly curved line. These intermediate moving annual totals are not available for insertion in figure 5.7, and so the three plotted points are joined by straight lines. These lines enable the trend of the graph to be more easily discerned, but they do *not* indicate the values of intermediate moving annual totals.

Care must be exercised in the design of graphs, otherwise they can give a distorted impression of trends, particularly if the vertical axis does not start at zero. Figure 5.8 shows a graph of the total launderette takings over the three-year period with the vertical axis starting at £16,000. The point representing the annual total for 1979 is four times as high as the point representing the 1977 annual total, and the immediate impression gained is that the annual takings

have increased fourfold in two years. To make it clear that in this graph the height of a point must *not* be equated by the eye with its value, the vertical axis should be drawn with a break in it. (A correctly constructed vertical axis is shown at the right of Figure 5.8). The advantage of omitting the lower portion of the vertical axis is that the part of the graph containing the plotted points is expanded in the vertical direction, and this has the effect of magnifying the trends. Thus it can be seen from Figure 5.8 that the takings are increasing more rapidly in 1979 than in 1978, a fact which is not apparent from Figure 5.7.

Graphs can be drawn to incorporate the sizes of component figures. An example of such a graph (called a 'band chart') is given in Figure 5.9. It is constructed in a similar way to the component bar chart shown in Figure 5.2. Percentage band charts (similar to percentage component bar charts) are drawn in a like manner.

Two or more sets of figures can be plotted on the same graph (if necessary using two

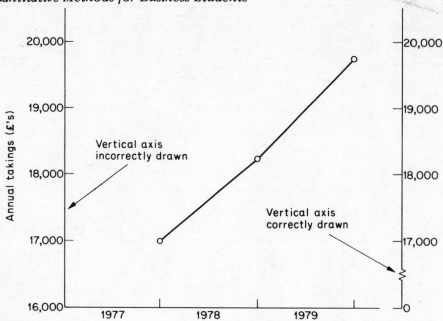

Figure 5.8 *Graph of annual takings of the launderette business with the vertical axis correctly and incorrectly drawn*

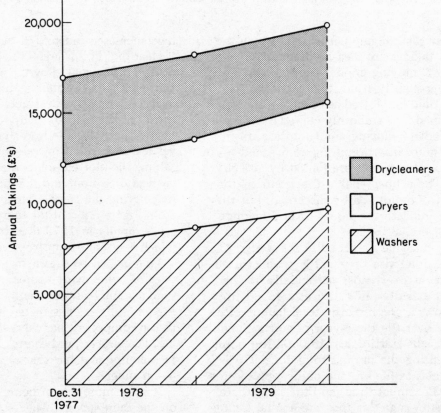

Figure 5.9 *Band chart showing the annual takings of the washers, dryers and drycleaners for the period 1977–79*

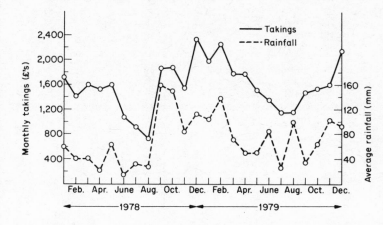

Figure 5.10 Graph with double vertical axis showing monthly takings and average monthly rainfall over the period January 1978– December 1979

vertical axes, one on the left of the graph and the other on the right), thus enabling trends to be compared. For example, the monthly takings of the launderette business (listed in Table 5.3) could be compared with the monthly rainfall figures, as shown in Figure 5.10. There does appear to be some degree of association between the two, though this is masked to some extent by seasonal factors such as peaks in the spring and at Christmas and a trough around August.

Z CHARTS

Z charts — so-called because they resemble the letter Z in appearance — are one-year time graphs incorporating three sets of figures:

Monthly sales or production figures (these form the lower arm of the Z)
Cumulative totals (these form the diagonal of the Z)
Moving annual totals (these form the upper arm of the Z).

Figure 5.11 shows the Z chart for the launderette business for 1979. It is based on the figures for monthly takings given in columns (2) and (3) of Table 5.3. (The 1978 figures in column (2) are included to enable the moving annual totals to be calculated.)

The cumulative totals for 1979 (column (4)) are calculated as follows. The takings that have accumulated by the end of January

1979 are just the January figures of £1990. The takings that have accumulated by the end of February are the January plus the February figures: £1990 + £2260 = £4250. The cumulative total at the end of March is £4250 + £1780 = £6030, and the other cumulative totals are calculated in a similar way.

The moving annual totals or M.A.T.s (column (5)) are found by summing the monthly takings for successive twelve-month periods. The M.A.T. at the end of December 1978 is the sum of the monthly takings from 1 January 1978 to 31 December 1978 (= £18,220). The M.A.T. at the end of January 1979 is the sum of the takings from 1 February 1978 to 31 January 1979. This is obtained most simply by subtracting the January 1978 takings from £18,220 and adding the January 1979 takings: £18,220 — £1680 + £1990 = £18,530. The M.A.T. at the end of February can be obtained similarly by subtracting the February 1978 takings from the M.A.T. for January and adding the February 1979 takings: £18,530 — £1410 + £2260 = £19,380. The remaining M.A.T.s are calculated similarly. It should be noted that for the month of December the cumulative total and the M.A.T. must come to the same figure.

The figures in columns (3), (4), and (5) are now plotted on the graph (Figure 5.11). To enable the fluctuations in the monthly figures to be more easily seen, these figures are usually plotted against an expanded scale

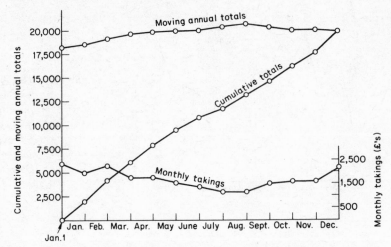

Figure 5.11   Z chart for launderette takings (1979). Note that the left-hand vertical axis is located at the date 31 December 1978/1 January 1979. So the monthly takings and M.A.T. at 31 December 1978 are plotted on this axis, as is the cumulative total (of £0) at 1 January.

Table 5.3   Z chart figures (in £s)

| | 1978 | | 1979 | |
| Month | Monthly takings | Monthly takings | Cumulative totals | M.A.T. |
(1)	(2)	(3)	(4)	(5)
Jan	1680	1990	1990	18530
Feb	1410	2260	4250	19380
Mar	1600	1780	6030	19560
Apr	1540	1780	7810	19800
May	1610	1530	9340	19720
June	1070	1360	10700	20010
July	920	1170	11870	20260
Aug	730	1140	13010	20670
Sept	1870	1480	14490	20280
Oct	1880	1530	16020	19930
Nov	1550	1590	17610	19970
Dec	2360	2160	19770	19770
	18220			

(shown on the right-hand side of Figure 5.11).

In practice Z charts are constructed during the course of the year as the monthly figures come in, and they give an up-to-date picture of the sales or production situation. They show the current month's figures, the total so far accumulated in the year, and the M.A.T. The moving annual totals are particularly valuable, for they indicate the long-term trend. The monthly figures are subject to seasonal fluctuations, but a moving annual total, since it spans a complete cycle of the seasons, is free of this sort of influence. For example, the seasonal drop in trade in the summer has caused the monthly figures for May to August to show a steady decline, but the long-term trend over this period (as indicated by the moving annual totals) is steadily rising. The converse is true for the period August to December: the monthly takings are rising in what might appear to be an encouraging manner, but the long-term trend is showing a depressing decline.

EXERCISES

1. In 1970 the number of people killed in road accidents in built-up areas during daylight hours was 2293, the number seriously injured was 37,153, and the number of severities of all types (killed, seriously injured, and slightly injured) was 175,972. During the hours of darkness the corresponding numbers for built-up areas were 1899, 22,802, and 86,386. In non built-up areas the numbers in daylight were 1935, 20,414, and 63,868, and in darkness they were 1357, 12,991, and 36,670. In 1976 the numbers for built-up areas in daylight were 1800, 30,286, and 159,912, and in darkness they were 1801,

21,227, and 86,370. In non built-up areas the numbers were 1561, 16,317, and 57,685 in daylight, and 1404, 11,619, and 35,276 in darkness. (Source: *Annual Abstract of Statistics*.)

Show the above data in tabular form, and construct suitable charts (including pie charts). Give reasons for your design of table and charts, and comment on the trends revealed by them.

2. The end-of-year stocks of coal in the UK in thousands of tons over the period 1968–77 are given in Table 5.4. Represent the data by means of a band chart, and draw a graph to show the changes in stocks held at gas-works. Comment on the trends revealed.

3. Plot the sets of figures shown in Table 5.5 on a graph using a double vertical axis, and comment on the trend.

4. The sales figures (in £s) in Table 5.6 relate to the toys department of a department store. Construct a Z chart and state what it shows.

Table 5.4

| Year | Distributed Stocks | | | | | Undistributed |
	Power stations	Gas-works	Coke ovens	Other	Total	Total
1968	12490	726	1107	231	14554	28000*
1969	11018	461	1231	225	12935	18500*
1970	9575	276	1434	342	11627	7102
1971	15712	72	1777	421	17982	10229
1972	16791	50	1890	314	19045	10934
1973	14537	27	1937	265	16766	10679
1974	13414	3	1822	338	15577	5885
1975	17668	2	2296	250	20216	10450
1976	19288	2	2642	170	22102	10490
1977	18826	2	2331	203	21362	9675

*To the nearest 100 thousand tons
(Sources: *Monthly Digest of Statistics; Energy Trends*)

Table 5.5

Radioactivity in Milk in the UK								
Year	1962	1964	1966	1968	1970	1972	1973	1974
Ratio of strontium 90 to calcium (picocuries/gm calcium)	11.7	28.0	12.1	7.6	6.1	4.5	4.1	3.3
Concentration of caesium 137 (picocuries per litre)	62	153	46	16	17	13	8	9

(Source: *Social Trends*)

Table 5.6

	Jan	Feb	Mar	Apr	May	June	July	Aug	Sept	Oct	Nov	Dec
1976:	5132	3648	4287	3615	4292	5577	5430	5143	6780	15480	20282	45478
1977:	13049	3535	5259	4678	3390	5809	6801	5445	6830	12062	28807	54823

Six

Summarization of Data (1) — Summary Measures

The mind is unable to assimilate the unending streams of data generated by every type of human activity. Even the daily takings record of the simple launderette business described in the last chapter would, at the end of the year, contain over 2000 entries! Some means of summarizing a mass of data such as this is required, so that its essential characteristics can be comprehended and analysed. The tables and charts discussed in the previous chapter provide one way of making sense of a collection of figures, but in order to carry out an exact statistical analysis, a more rigorous mathematical summarization procedure is required, the end result of which is one or two numbers which embody the principal features of the data.

To show the way in which these numbers, or 'summary measures', are derived, we shall use the data shown in Table 6.1, namely the prices of carrots, lettuces, and cauliflowers observed on a particular day in 15 greengrocer shops in a certain town. For simplicity it is assumed that the $\frac{1}{2}$p unit is not used in any of these shops.

The data listed in the table exhibits the following features:

(a) The average price charged for lettuces seems to be about the same as the average price charged for carrots, but the spread of prices charged for lettuces is greater than the spread of the carrot prices. On the other hand, the spread of the lettuce prices is about the same as the spread of the cauliflower prices, but the average prices are quite different.

(b) The lettuce prices bunch around the lower end of the price range, there being only a few dispersed prices at the upper end. In contrast, the carrot prices are evenly distributed about the middle value. The cauliflower prices bunch around two figures, 30p and 34p — the result, perhaps, of two different sizes of cauliflower being on sale, some shops selling one size, some the other.

This example shows that the essential distinguishing features of a set of values, which we must be able to quantify by means of summary measures, are:

1. The average, or *central tendency*, of the values

Table 6.1 Prices (in pence) observed in 15 shops, listed in order from cheapest to dearest

Carrots (per kg)	10	11	11	12	12	13	13	13	13	13	14	14	15	15	16
Lettuces (each)	10	10	10	10	11	11	11	12	13	13	14	15	17	18	20
Cauliflowers (each)	26	26	28	30	30	30	30	32	34	34	34	34	36	36	36

2. The spread, or *dispersion*, of the values
3. Any tendency to bunch towards the lower (or higher) values, that is the *skewness* of the values

This chapter deals with the main methods of measuring central tendency, dispersion, and skewness. Other measures (e.g. of features such as the tendency of the cauliflower prices to bunch around two values) are rarely used and are not discussed in this text.

CENTRAL TENDENCY

1. One measure of central tendency is the *mode*, which can be defined as the most frequently occurring value — 13p in the case of the carrot prices, 10p for lettuces, but (and here we run into difficulties) 30p *or* 34p for cauliflowers. A further problem is that if each value occurs only once, then there is no mode. Even apart from these difficulties, the mode is for most purposes an unsatisfactory measure of central tendency, for it does not take account of any values other than the most common one. To quote 10p as the average price of lettuces would be highly misleading. However, the mode has some uses, particularly in cases in which a large proportion of values are equal to it. Employers tend to pay the modal — most frequently occurring — wage-rate; most houses are designed with the modal family in view — they have three bedrooms.

2. A second way of measuring central tendency is by means of the *median*, which can be defined as the middle value — 13p for the carrots, 12p for the lettuces, and 32p for the cauliflowers. To determine the median, the values must be arranged in ascending order (as has been done in Table 6.1), and, if there are n values, the median is the value of the $\frac{n+1}{2}$ th one. In the case of the cauliflower prices, n = 15, so

$$\frac{n+1}{2} = 8$$

prices, n = 15, so

and hence the median is the value of the 8th price. If there were 16 cauliflower prices, then

$$\frac{n+1}{2} = 8.5$$

and the median would lie halfway between the 8th and 9th price — it would equal 33p.

The usefulness of the median is limited by the fact that it is unaffected by the extent to which other values depart from it. In the case of the lettuce prices, for example, the shop selling 20p lettuces could reduce the price by up to 8p without affecting the median. This characteristic of the median is, however, an advantage in cases when a few very low (or high) values, if taken into account, would result in a misleadingly low (or high) average value. In the case of the lettuce prices, the median is, in fact, the least misleading average.

3. For most purposes a measure of central tendency which takes into account all the values is required. The most commonly used measure of this type is the *arithmetic mean*, normally referred to simply as the *mean*. (It should be noted, however, that there are other types of mean; one is the 'weighted mean', discussed in the next chapter.) The arithmetic mean is the ordinary 'average' — though, strictly speaking, any measure of central tendency is an average — and it is calculated by summing the values and dividing the result by n, the number of values. If the symbol x is used to denote the values under consideration (so that in the case of the carrot prices the first value of x is 10p, the second value of x is 11p, and so on), then the mean is denoted $\overline{x}$, and its formula is:

$$\overline{x} = \frac{\Sigma x}{n}$$

For the carrot prices, $\Sigma x = 195$, $n = 15$, and so

$$\overline{x} = \frac{195}{15}$$

$$= 13p$$

The mean suffers from the disadvantage that it may not correspond to any actual value. The mean cauliflower price, for example, is 31.73p. More importantly, the mean can be greatly affected by a few very low (or high) values, and when this occurs it may not be a very representative measure of central tendency.

The main uses of the mode, median and mean can be summarized as follows. The *mode* can be usefully employed when a large proportion of the values are equal to it, an example being size of family. The *median* is often utilized when the data exhibits a pronounced 'skew', that is a bunching towards the lower values (as is often the case with incomes) or towards the higher values. The *mean*, the only measure of the three which takes into account all the data, is the most useful general purpose measure, with a wide application in statistical work.

So in applying the word 'average' to adult males, for example, one would normally use the mode if the subject is family size, the median if the subject is income, and the mean if the subject is weight.

DISPERSION

1. One measure of dispersion, or spread, is the *range*, which is simply the difference between the highest and the lowest values — 6p in the case of the carrot prices, 10p in the case of the lettuce prices, and 10p in the case of the cauliflower prices. The range is easy to calculate and understand, but it takes account of only the two extreme values. One exceptionally high (or low) value — such as the 20p lettuce price — will lead to a misleading result.

2. Another measure is the *quartile deviation*, which is half the range of the middle 50% of values. To calculate this the values must first be placed in ascending order (as was necessary in calculating the median), and the values

lying one-quarter and three-quarters of the way through the distribution (or list) determined. These values are referred to as the 'first quartile' and the 'third quartile', and are denoted Q_1 and Q_3 respectively. (The median, the value lying one half, or 'two-quarters', of the way through the distribution, is denoted Q_2.) The formula for the quartile deviation is:

$$Q.D. = \tfrac{1}{2}(Q_3 - Q_1)$$

In the case of the carrot prices, Q.D. = $\tfrac{1}{2}(14 - 12) = 1$p.

The formulae for determining which value is Q_1 and which is Q_3 are similar to that used for the median. Q_1 is the $\dfrac{n+1}{4}$th value, and Q_3 is the $\dfrac{3(n+1)}{4}$th value; in the case of the carrot prices, for which $n = 15$, Q_1 is the 4th value (= 12p) and Q_3 is the 12th value (= 14p).

The quartile deviation, like the median, is unaffected by extreme values, and so it is a useful measure when the values are skewed (as in the case of the lettuce prices).

3. The main disadvantage of the above two measures is that they do not take account of all the data. The most useful and widely applied measure of dispersion, the *standard deviation*, does not suffer from this defect, but it is more difficult to calculate and to understand.

To appreciate the construction of the standard deviation, consider the carrot prices. The first step in measuring the spread of these prices is to calculate the differences between each price and the mean. As in the calculation of the mean considered in the previous section, we denote the prices by x. The mean $(\bar{x})$ has been found to equal 13p, and the required differences are therefore:

$$x - \bar{x} = -3, -2, -2, -1, -1, 0, 0, 0, 0, 0,$$
$$1, 1, 2, 2, 3.$$

The mean of these differences or 'deviations', would form a suitable measure of dispersion. In calculating this the negative signs have to be ignored (otherwise the average will always equal zero, since the negative deviations about the mean always cancel the positive deviations). The modulus symbol $\|$ is used to show that negative signs are ignored, the formula for the mean deviation being

$$\frac{\Sigma |x - \overline{x}|}{n}$$

In the case of the carrot prices

the mean deviation

$$= \frac{3+2+2+1+1+0+0+0+0+0+1+1+2+2+3}{15}$$

$$= 1.2\text{p}.$$

Another way of eliminating the negative signs is to square the differences. A squared number is easier to handle mathematically than a modulus, and the resulting measure of dispersion has properties which make it greatly superior to the mean deviation. Squaring the above deviations we obtain:

$$(x - \overline{x})^2 = 9, 4, 4, 1, 1, 0, 0, 0, 0, 0,$$

$$1, 1, 4, 4, 9.$$

The mean of these squared deviations is:

$$\frac{\Sigma(x - \overline{x})^2}{n}$$

$$= \frac{9+4+4+1+1+0+0+0+0+0+1+1+4+4+9}{15}$$

$$= \frac{38}{15}$$

$$= 2.5\dot{3}$$

This measure of dispersion is known as the 'variance'.

Since the differences have been squared, this measure is in squared units ('squared pence' in this case). It is much more convenient to use a measure of dispersion which is expressed in the same units as the mean, and to achieve this it is necessary to calculate the square root of the variance. The resulting measure is called the 'standard deviation', the formula being:

$$\text{S.D.} = \sqrt{\frac{\Sigma(x - \overline{x})^2}{n}}$$

For the carrot prices

the standard deviation $= \sqrt{2.5\dot{3}} \simeq 1.6\text{p}$

Students are always left slightly aghast when they first encounter this formula, and it is admittedly difficult to form a concept of the standard deviation. It is perhaps of some help to realize that in very many cases two-thirds of the values lie within one standard deviation of the mean, 95% of the values lie within two standard deviations of the mean, and virtually all of the values lie within three standard deviations of the mean. In the case of the carrot prices, one standard deviation below the mean to one standard deviation above the mean covers the price range 11.4p to 14.6p, which includes 9 out of the 15 listed prices, or almost two-thirds.

The calculation of the standard deviation is simplified by the use of a short-cut method described at the end of this chapter. The formula given above is not very easy to work with in practice (since if $\overline{x}$ is not a whole number, the squared differences can be cumbersome), and the following formula is normally used:

$$\text{S.D.} = \sqrt{\frac{\Sigma x^2}{n} - \overline{x}^2}$$

$$= \sqrt{\frac{\Sigma x^2}{n} - \left(\frac{\Sigma x}{n}\right)^2}$$

(This can be simply derived from the original formula by expanding the $(x - \overline{x})^2$ term and manipulating the summations.)

The enormous value of the standard deviation will be appreciated when sampling theory is studied (Chapters 10 and 11). It is conventional in sampling theory to use English letters when speaking of sample summary measures (referred to as sample 'statistics') and Greek letters when speaking of population summary measures (referred to as population 'parameters'). When referring to sample data, the symbol for the mean is $\overline{x}$ and the symbol for the standard deviation is s; when referring to population data, the symbol for the mean is μ ('mu', equivalent to the lower-case 'm') and the symbol for the standard deviation is σ ('sigma', equivalent to the lower-case 's'). Outside the context of sampling theory, S.D. is often used to denote standard deviation.

THE COEFFICIENT OF VARIATION

This summary measure is used to indicate the amount of variability present in the data. It is calculated by expressing the standard deviation as a percentage of the mean:

$$\text{Coefficient of variation} = \frac{\text{S.D.}}{\bar{x}} \times 100$$

It is apparent from Table 6.1 that there is more variability in the lettuce prices than in the carrot prices; the coefficient of variation enables an exact comparison to be made. In the case of the carrot prices, the coefficient of variation = $1.6/13 \times 100 = 12.3$, and for the lettuce prices it is 23.8.

If the median and the quartile deviation are used as measures of central tendency and dispersion, the 'quartile coefficient of dispersion' can be used to measure variability. This is calculated in a similar way, by expressing the quartile deviation as a percentage of the median.

THE COEFFICIENT OF SKEWNESS

'Skewness' denotes the tendency for values to bunch at one end of a distribution, the values at the other end being relatively dispersed. The mode is the value at which the greatest amount of bunching occurs, and skewness is measured by calculating the extent to which the mode departs from the mean. If the mode is located towards the lower values, the skewness is said to be positive; if it is located towards the higher values, the skewness is negative. The formula for the coefficient of skewness is:

$$\text{Sk} = \frac{\text{mean} - \text{mode}}{\text{S.D.}}$$

For the lettuce prices (for which $\bar{x} = 13$ and S.D. = 3.1)

$$\text{Sk} = \frac{13 - 10}{3.1} \simeq +1.0$$

In contrast, the symmetrically distributed carrot prices have a coefficient of skewness of

$$\frac{13 - 13}{1.6} = 0$$

The difference between the mean and the mode is generally about three times as great as the difference between the mean and the median. An alternative formula for the coefficient of skewness (and the one which is generally used, owing to the difficulties which are often involved in calculating the mode) is therefore:

$$\text{Sk} = \frac{3(\text{mean} - \text{median})}{\text{S.D.}}$$

If the median and quartile deviation are used as measures of central tendency and dispersion, then the 'quartile coefficient of skewness' can be used to measure skewness. This employs the fact that the difference between the first quartile and the median on the one hand, and the difference between the median and the third quartile on the other, become progressively more unequal as skewness increases. The formula is:

$$\text{Sk}_q = \frac{(Q_3 - \text{median}) - (\text{median} - Q_1)}{\text{quartile deviation}}$$

CALCULATING THE MEAN AND STANDARD DEVIATION BY THE METHOD OF ASSUMED MEANS

The mean and standard deviation are the two most frequently used summary measures, and the student should be able to calculate them accurately and rapidly. The calculations can be arduous and prone to error; however, unlike the calculations of the mode, median, etc., it is not necessary first to list the values in ascending order. In the case of the carrot prices, the calculations were in fact quite simple, for easy numbers were involved (the mean, for example, was a whole number, which greatly simplified the standard deviation calculations). The calculations will not normally work out as conveniently as this, but the labour can be much reduced by applying what is known as the method of assumed means. The technique is to transform the values to simpler numbers, calculate the mean and standard deviation of these simpler numbers, and then apply the transformation in reverse to arrive at the mean and standard deviation of the original values.

In this text we shall use lower-case letters to denote original values, and upper-case letters to denote transformed values. In the calculation of the mean and standard deviation of the cauliflower prices which follows, x denotes the original values, and X denotes the transformed values. The mean and standard deviation of the transformed values are denoted $\overline{X}$ and S.D.$_X$ respectively.

The x-values, then, are as given in Table 6.1 (26, 26, 28, etc.). The first step is to simplify these by subtracting a suitable number (called the 'assumed mean') from each. To gain the greatest amount of simplification, the assumed mean should be an x-value which occurs relatively frequently and which lies towards the middle of the distribution. In this case 30 is the best candidate. Subtracting 30 from each x-value results in the following numbers:

$$-4, -4, -2, 0, 0, 0, 0, 2, 4, 4, 4, 4, 6, 6, 6$$

The mean of these values will be exactly 30 less than the mean of the original x-values. Notice, however, that the spread of the values has not been altered, and so the standard deviation of these values will equal the standard deviation of the original x-values.

It is sometimes possible to effect a further

simplification by dividing by a suitable factor. In this case it is possible to divide by 2, the resulting X-values being:

$$-2, -2, -1, 0, 0, 0, 0, 1, 2, 2, 2, 2, 3, 3, 3$$

The spread of the value has now been halved, and so the standard deviation has been halved.

Table 6.2 The method of assumed means — the cauliflower prices

x	X $= \frac{1}{2}(\overline{x} - 30)$	X^2
26	−2	4
26	−2	4
28	−1	1
30	0	0
30	0	0
30	0	0
30	0	0
32	1	1
34	2	4
34	2	4
34	2	4
34	2	4
36	3	9
36	3	9
36	3	9
Totals	13	53

Mean of the X values $= \overline{X}$

$$= \frac{\Sigma X}{n}$$

$$= \frac{13}{15}$$

$$= 0.867$$

Standard deviation of the X-values

$$= \text{S.D.}_X$$

$$= \sqrt{\frac{\Sigma X^2}{n} - \left(\frac{\Sigma X}{n}\right)^2}$$

$$= \sqrt{\frac{53}{15} - \left(\frac{13}{15}\right)^2}$$

$$= \sqrt{3.53 - 0.751}$$

$$= 1.668$$

We have therefore arrived at the X-values in this example by subtracting 30 from each x-value, and dividing the remainders by 2. Written as an equation, the transformation is:

$$X = \frac{x - 30}{2}$$

The way in which this transformation should be laid out, and the way in which the mean and standard deviation calculations should be laid out, are shown in Table 6.2. From this table it can be seen that $\overline{X} = 0.867$, and S.D.$_X$ = 1.668.

To obtain the mean of the original x-values it is necessary to reverse the transformation. The last step in the transformation was to divide by 2, and so the first step now is to multiply by 2:

$$0.867 \times 2 \simeq 1.73$$

The transformation process began with the subtraction of 30 from each value — and so the reversal is completed by adding on 30:

$$\overline{x} = 1.73 + 30 = 31.73\text{p}$$

To obtain the standard deviation of the x-values, the only step required is to multiply S.D.$_X$ by 2. (As was pointed out above, subtracting the assumed mean from the x-values does not affect the standard deviation.)

$$\text{S.D.} = 1.668 \times 2 = 3.34\text{p}.$$

If the assumed mean is denoted by A.M., and if the factor by which the remainders are divided is denoted by c, then the formulae for calculating the mean and standard deviation by the method of assumed means are:

$$\overline{x} = \text{A.M.} + c(\overline{X})$$

$$\text{S.D.} = c(\text{S.D.}_X)$$

EXERCISES

1. Eight components produced by an experimental process are tested to destruction. Their lifetimes in hours, to the nearest hour, are as follows:

   22, 13, 16, 13, 7, 22, 10, 25

   Calculate the mean and the standard deviation of these lifetimes (a) without transforming these numbers, and (b) by making the transformation: subtract 13 from each number, and divide the remainders by 3.

2. The weekly wages of the 12 male and 8 female employees of a certain firm are as follows (to the nearest £):

   Males (£s): 40, 55, 40, 65, 50, 30, 60 40, 35, 40, 65, 50

   Females (£s): 31, 37, 36, 42, 39, 30, 36, 34

   (a) For each sex calculate:
     (i) The mode, median, range, and quartile deviation. (To carry out these calculations put the numbers in ascending order.)
     (ii) The mean and the standard deviation. (Make suitable transformations.)
     (iii) The coefficient of variation and the coefficient of skewness.
   (b) Using the measures calculated in (a), comment briefly on the differences in the wages paid to the males and the females.

3. The weekly wages of the two groups of employees of question 2 are found, two years later, to be as follows:

   Males (£s): 43, 59, 47, 71, 59, 35, 67, 43, 39, 51, 75, 71

   Females (£s): 43, 48, 68, 53, 63, 38, 48, 63

By calculating suitable summary measures contrast these wages with those given in question 2.

4. For the lettuce prices given in Table 6.1 calculate (a) the mean and the standard deviation, and (b) the quartile coefficient of dispersion and the quartile coefficient of skewness.

Seven

Index Numbers

INTRODUCTION

Many statistics are published as index numbers, and it is therefore necessary to understand how these numbers are constructed and how they are to be interpreted.

Index numbers show how the average price or the average quantity of a group of items is changing over time. They express the current price or quantity level as a percentage of the level at some reference point in the past, called the base date. The index number of the base-date level is 100. If the index number at a subsequent date is 110, this indicates a 10% increase on the base-date level.

An example which will be referred to later in this chapter is the index of production for the timber and furniture industry. The base year in this case is 1975, the index numbers for the period 1966 to 1977 being as follows:

Year:	1966	1967	1968	1969	1970	1971
Index number:	86.6	89.2	96.2	90.1	90.3	93.0

Year:	1972	1973	1974	1975	1976	1977
Index number:	102.5	117.6	101.5	100.0	100.9	97.9

It can be seen from this series that the average level of production in the industry for 1966, for example, was 13.6% below the base-year level, and the average for 1973 was 17.6% above the base-year level. There was a steady increase in production from 1966 to 1973 (with a slight peak in 1968), followed by a decline from 1973 onwards.

This particular index number, therefore, provides a thumbnail sketch of trends in the output of the timber and furniture industry over the period under review. Some of its uses are as follows:

1. It enables individual furniture companies to compare their output record with that of the industry as a whole

2. Trends in the output of the industry can be compared with other trends, both within the industry and in other sectors of the economy

3. Projections can be made to ascertain likely future levels of output (see the chapter on time series analysis).

These comparisons and projections facilitate decision-making at company, industry and government level.

To illustrate the way in which index numbers are constructed, we shall suppose that our employer, who leases his business cars from a car-hire firm, has received notice of an increase in the rental from £40 to £43 per week. We shall also suppose that his only other car cost is petrol, and that this has recently risen from £1.60 to £1.66 per gallon. Our employer asks us to examine what effect these increases will have on his car costs.

RELATIVES

To show the effect of a price change such as this we must begin by expressing the new prices as percentages of the old prices. These percentages are called 'price relatives', and in this example they are:

Rental $\dfrac{43}{40} \times 100 = 107.5$

Petrol $\dfrac{1.66}{1.60} \times 100 = 103.75$

These relatives show that the rental has increased by 7.5%, and the petrol has increased by 3.75%.

If the old price of an item is denoted by p_o and the new price is denoted by p_1, then the formula for the price relative is:

$$\frac{p_1}{p_o} \times 100$$

If it is required to show changes in quantities of items produced or sold, then 'quantity relatives' must be used. If q_o denotes the old quantity and q_1 denotes the new quantity, then the formula for the quantity relative is:

$$\frac{q_1}{q_o} \times 100$$

WEIGHTED AVERAGES

Having calculated the price relatives for rental and petrol, the next task is to determine their combined effect on our employer's car costs. We cannot determine this by means of the ordinary arithmetic mean

$(= \dfrac{107.5 + 103.75}{2} = 105.625)$, because

rental and petrol do not form equal proportions of the total car costs. The rental forms the major part of the costs, and therefore a rental increase has a larger effect than an equivalent petrol increase. In order to give due weight to an item's importance, it is necessary to calculate what is known as the 'weighted arithmetic mean' (usually called the 'weighted average'). The formula is:

Weighted arithmetic mean

$$= \frac{\Sigma wx}{\Sigma w}$$

$$= \frac{w_1 x_1 + w_2 x_2 + \cdots + w_n x_n}{w_1 + w_2 \cdots + w_n}$$

where w_1 is the weight assigned to the value x_1, w_2 is the weight assigned to the value x_2, and so on. If the items are all weighted equally, then this formula reduces to the ordinary arithmetic mean.

In this example the importance of the items 'rental' and 'petrol' can be measured by how much they actually cost per week: if 5 cars are hired, the weekly car rental is $5 \times £40 = £200$; if 25 gallons of petrol are bought per week, the weekly petrol cost is $25 \times £1.60 = £40$. The weighted average of price relatives is therefore:

$$\frac{200 \times 107.5 + 40 \times 103.75}{200 + 40} = 106.875$$

Our employer's car costs have therefore increased by 6.875 per cent.

A weighted average of relatives is an index number, and by its use changes in a number of items of differing importance can be brought together into a single figure for the purpose of showing their average change. The above weighted average of price relatives is a price index, and this shows how the general level of prices in the 'basket' of items included in the index has changed. A weighted average of quantity relatives would give a quantity index, and this would show how the general level of quantities of the items in the basket has changed.

PRICE INDICES

The above price-index calculation was based on the weighted average formula, the weights being the quantities (q) multiplied by the old prices (p_o), and the values being the price relatives. The price-index formula is therefore:

Price index = weighted average of price relatives

$$= \frac{\Sigma wx}{\Sigma w}$$

$$= \frac{\Sigma qp_o(\frac{p_1}{p_o} \times 100)}{\Sigma qp_o}$$

$$= \frac{\Sigma p_1 q}{\Sigma p_o q} \times 100$$

By applying this formula in price-index calculations the preliminary step of computing price relatives is avoided — it is necessary merely to weight the prices by the quantities (by calculating $p_1 q$ and $p_o q$).

When the prices of items alter, the quantities sold generally alter also. In calculating price indices a choice has therefore to be made between using the original quantities (q_o) as weights or the current quantities (q_1). If the original quantities are used, then the index is called a 'base-weighted' or 'Laspeyre' price index, and the formula is:

Laspeyre price index $= \dfrac{\Sigma p_1 q_o}{\Sigma p_o q_o} \times 100$

If the current quantities are used as weights, then the index is called a 'current-weighted' or 'Paasche' price index, the formula being:

Paasche price index $= \dfrac{\Sigma p_1 q_1}{\Sigma p_o q_1} \times 100$

It is not always practicable to determine the quantities involved, and it is not then possible to calculate Laspeyre or Paasche price indices. The weights have to be assigned on some other basis, and a weighted average of price relatives calculated.

QUANTITY INDICES

Quantity index numbers are used to indicate the average change in quantities of a group of items, and they are derived in the same way as price index numbers. Prices are often used as the weighting factors (since a change in the quantity of a high-priced item is more important than a similar change in the quantity of a low-priced item). Laspeyre indices use the original prices as weights (base-weighting), Paasche indices use the current prices as weights (current-weighting):

Laspeyre quantity index $= \dfrac{\Sigma p_o q_1}{\Sigma p_o q_o} \times 100$

Paasche quantity index $= \dfrac{\Sigma p_1 q_1}{\Sigma p_1 q_o} \times 100$

If it is not practicable to weight by prices, then the weights have to be assigned on some other basis, and a weighted average of quantity relatives calculated.

BASE AND CURRENT WEIGHTING COMPARED

Current-weighting has one great advantage over base-weighting: each item is weighted in accordance with its current importance, and there is therefore no danger of producing a misleading index number through the use of outmoded weights. Current-weighting is therefore preferred in situations in which the progressive outmoding of the weights used will seriously affect the validity of the index. Current-weighting is also preferred in many accounting contexts (because of the increasing emphasis on the use of current rather than historical purchasing prices in accounting).

In many situations, however, base-weighting is preferred to current-weighting, for the following reasons:

1. There is a close association between price and quantity — a relatively large increase in the price of one item, for example, will generally be accompanied by a decrease in the quantity sold — and this has the effect of reducing the impact of price changes in the case of a current-weighted price

index or of quantity changes in the case of a quantity index. Base-weighting does not mask the effect of changes in this way.

2. The calculation of weights can be time-consuming and expensive, and base-weighted index numbers (for which this calculation is carried out only once) are often preferred for this reason.

3. If an index number series is base-weighted, then one year in the series can be compared with any other year. If current-weighting is used, then, due to the changing weights, valid comparisons can be made only with the base year. This limits the usefulness of the series.

THE BASE YEAR

The period over which the initial prices (p_o) and quantities (q_o) are measured is called the 'base year' of an index. The base prices and quantities are often collected over a full year in order to eliminate the effect of seasonal and other short-term influences and thus to make the figures obtained as representative as possible.

If business activity during the base period is abnormal (as would be the case if there was at that time a general strike, a prolonged drought, or an outbreak of war), then index numbers for subsequent years (which are calculated by comparing the subsequent prices or quantities with the base prices and quantities) will be misleading. Laspeyre index numbers will be particularly affected, as the weights used for subsequent years will be the (abnormal) base-year weights. An index number series should therefore be based upon a reasonably normal year. The index number for the base year is always 100.

EXAMPLE

I. Kneeman Ltd make three products — Thingum, E-jigs, and Sew-ons. The output and

Table 7.1 Prices and output of I. Kneeman Ltd

Product	PRICES (£s)			OUTPUT (000s)		
	1975	1976	1977	1975	1976	1977
Thingum	2.50	2.70	3.00	69	70	72
E-jigs	4.00	4.50	5.00	43	39	33
Sew-ons	1.60	1.80	2.00	50	55	56

prices for the period 1975 to 1977 are given in Table 7.1. We shall compute a Laspeyre price index and a Paasche quantity index using 1975 as base year.

The base year (1975) prices and quantities are denoted p_o, q_o, the 1976 prices and quantities are denoted p_1, q_1, and the 1977 prices and quantities are denoted p_2, q_2.

To obtain the Laspeyre price indices, we have to compute the following:

for 1976: $\dfrac{\Sigma p_1 q_o}{\Sigma p_o q_o} \times 100$

for 1977: $\dfrac{\Sigma p_2 q_o}{\Sigma p_o q_o} \times 100$

To obtain the Paasche quantity indices, we need to compute:

for 1976: $\dfrac{\Sigma p_1 q_1}{\Sigma p_1 q_o} \times 100$

for 1977: $\dfrac{\Sigma p_2 q_2}{\Sigma p_2 q_o} \times 100$

The calculations of the numerators and denominators of these fractions are shown in Table 7.2. The required index numbers are:

Laspeyre price index:

$\dfrac{469.8}{424.5} \times 100 = 110.7$ (1976)

$\dfrac{522}{424.5} \times 100 = 123.0$ (1977)

Paasche quantity index:

$$\frac{463.5}{469.8} \times 100 = 98.7 \quad (1976)$$

$$\frac{493}{522} \times 100 = 94.4 \quad (1977)$$

(The index numbers for the base year are, of course, 100)
indicating an increase of 11.1% over the 1976 level.

An ordinary fixed base index number can be converted to a chain base number by expressing each year's number as a percentage

Table 7.2   Index number calculations

p_0	p_1	p_2	q_0	q_1	q_2	$p_0 q_0$	$p_1 q_0$	$p_2 q_0$	$p_1 q_1$	$p_2 q_2$
2.50	2.70	3.00	69	70	72	172.5	186.3	207	189	216
4.00	4.50	5.00	43	39	33	172	193.5	215	175.5	165
1.60	1.80	2.00	50	55	56	80	90	100	99	112
					Totals	424.5	469.8	522	463.5	493

The Laspeyre price index shows that the company increased its general level of prices in 1976 by 10.7% over the 1975 level, and in 1977 by 23.0% over the 1975 level. The Paasche quantity index shows that the general level of output of the company in 1976 decreased by 1.3% from its 1975 level, and in 1977 it decreased by 5.6% from its 1975 level.

CHAIN INDEX NUMBERS

If it is required to compare one year's prices or quantities with the prices or quantities for the previous year (rather than with the base-year prices or quantities), then it is necessary to calculate what is known as a 'chain index number'. In the case of a Laspeyre price index, for example, the chain index will use the base-year quantities as weights, but will compare the current year's prices with the previous year's prices. In the example given above, the chain price index for 1977 will have the formula

$$\frac{\Sigma p_2 q_0}{\Sigma p_1 q_0} \times 100$$

and its value will be

$$\frac{522}{469.8} \times 100 = 111.1$$

of the previous year's. The method is illustrated in Table 7.3, where the fixed base quantity index for the output of the timber and furniture industry referred to earlier is converted to a chain base index. This table shows that the annual rate of increase was 3% in 1967, 7.8% in 1968, −6.4% (i.e. a decrease) in 1969, and so on.

Besides providing a direct comparison between each year and its predecessor, a chain index has the advantage that revised weightings or new items can be introduced into the index from time to time. Some index numbers revise the weightings each year. If this were done for the Laspeyre price index in the I. Kneeman example above, the index for 1977 would have the formula

$$\frac{\Sigma p_2 q_1}{\Sigma p_1 q_1} \times 100$$

the index for 1978 would have the formula

$$\frac{\Sigma p_3 q_2}{\Sigma p_2 q_2} \times 100$$

and so on — each year in the series is using the previous year as base. Like the Paasche index, this avoids the problem of outmoded weights, but the disadvantage is that valid comparisons can only be made with the previous year, and comparisons with earlier years in the series may be highly misleading.

Table 7.3 Chain-base calculations

Year	Fixed-base index no.	Chain-base index no.
1966	86.6	—
1967	89.2	$\dfrac{89.2}{86.6} \times 100 = 103.0$
1968	96.2	$\dfrac{96.2}{89.2} \times 100 = 107.8$
1969	90.1	$\dfrac{90.1}{96.2} \times 100 = 93.6$
1970	90.3	$\dfrac{90.3}{90.1} \times 100 = 100.2$
1971	93.0	$\dfrac{93.0}{90.3} \times 100 = 103.0$
1972	102.5	$\dfrac{102.5}{93.0} \times 100 = 110.2$
1973	117.6	$\dfrac{117.6}{102.5} \times 100 = 114.7$
1974	101.5	$\dfrac{101.5}{117.6} \times 100 = 86.3$
1975	100.0	$\dfrac{100.0}{101.5} \times 100 = 98.5$
1976	100.9	$\dfrac{100.9}{100.0} \times 100 = 100.9$
1977	97.9	$\dfrac{97.9}{100.9} \times 100 = 97.0$

CHANGING THE BASE OF FIXED-BASE INDEX NUMBERS

One index number series can only be compared with another if both have the same base year. The example is given in question 4 at the end of this chapter of a furniture manufacturing company which wishes to compare its production index (for which the base year is 1972) with the production index for the timber and furniture industry (for which the base year is 1975). In order to compare the two series it is necessary to re-base one of them, and the company decides to re-base its own series on 1975. The procedure, illustrated in the answer to question 4, is to express each year's index as a percentage of the 1975 index. Although the base year of the series is now 1975, the weights used are those prevailing in 1972.

THE RETAIL PRICE INDEX

The General Index of Retail Prices is a good example of an official index number, and it is instructive to consider briefly its history and method of construction.

The original cost of living index was introduced in order to measure the cost of maintaining the standard of living of working-class households at the 1914 level. July 1914 was fixed as the base, and a 'basket' of goods and services consumed by the typical working-class family of the time was selected and weightings allocated. The index was (and still is) constructed by calculating a weighted average of price relatives.

The index was base-weighted, and 1914 was used as the base for over thirty years — in spite of the fact that by the 1930s the items in the basket and the weightings used were so out-of-date that the index underestimated the true position by over 20%.

The successor to the cost of living index was the 'Interim Index of Retail Prices'. This had June 1947 as base, and used weightings which were established by a survey made of 10,000 households shortly before the second World War and modified by the results of a small-scale survey undertaken in 1947. A further survey of family expenditure was carried out in 1953–54, and the results were used to determine weightings for the 'Index of Retail Prices'. This was established in 1956, and it used the January of that year as base.

The index was subsequently re-based on January 1962, and from that date the weights have been revised annually on the basis of the results of the continuous Family Expenditure Survey (see page 49). The index for each month is calculated by the chain-base method, using the previous January as base, and the index number obtained is linked back to January 1962 = 100 by the re-basing procedure outlined in the previous section. The current index uses January 1974 as base, but is otherwise little changed.

Changes in the Retail Price Index give an indication (though not a precise indication) of changes in the value of money, and they are therefore used, for example, as a basis for establishing wages policies at national level and negotiating wage settlements at local level. The index is, however, an average taken over the whole country, and it does not give an accurate indication of changes for specific areas or specific groups of workers.

OTHER OFFICIAL INDEX NUMBERS

It is impossible to give an account of all the official index numbers which are to be found in publications such as the *Annual Abstract of Statistics*. They include, for example, wages indices (which show trends in wages and salaries), retail sales indices (which show sales trends in various categories of shops), indices of retail stocks (which show stock-holding changes), and indices of imports and exports (which show prices and volume changes of imports and exports). Important economic indicators are the Index of Industrial Production and the various Index Numbers of Wholesale Prices, and these are described briefly below.

The Index of Industrial Production

Production indices are compiled for individual industries and groups of industries (one example being the index for the timber and furniture industry considered earlier), and, in the case of the Index of Industrial Production, for the whole of industry in the manufacturing, mining, construction, and energy sectors. There are, in total, 880 industries in these sectors, classified into 20 groups in accordance with the Standard Industrial Classification 1968. The index measures changes in the general level of output of this part of industry, and it can therefore be used as an indicator of the country's industrial performance.

The index is a weighted average of quantity relatives. Each of the 20 groups of industries is assigned a weight which is proportional to the value of its net output (and therfore to its importance), this value being obtained, up to the mid-1970s, from the *Report on the Census of Production*. (For example, the weight of the mining and quarrying group is

56, that of the food, drink, and tobacco group is 84, that of coal and petroleum products is 7. The sum of the weights of all 20 groups is 1000.) The quantities used are, where possible, the actual output figures of each group. The index is base-weighted, and it uses a fixed base (in contrast to the Retail Price Index, which is chained).

The date of the first Census of Production was 1907, and the index of production was first produced in 1928. Subsequent censuses have been taken at five-yearly intervals from 1948 on, the last census being that taken in 1968. As the results of each census became available the weights used in the index were revised and the index rebased. These censuses have been replaced by a system of quarterly returns by manufacturing establishments of production, orders, and sales, and the weights used in the index are now derived from these. At the time of writing 1975 is the base year.

The index numbers of wholesale prices

These consist of some 8,000 price relatives which are combined in various groups to show changes in prices of raw materials for particular industries (see the relevant table in the *Annual Abstract of Statistics*). Each group index is a weighted average of the relevant price relatives, the weights used being derived from a number of sources, including the quarterly production returns referred to above. The group indices are base-weighted.

Wholesale price index numbers are generally thought to be better indicators of changing money values than the Retail Price Index, and a number of private bodies produce their own indices. One example is Reuter's Daily Index of U.K. Staple Commodity Prices, which gives a day-to-day indication of price fluctuations.

EXERCISES

1. Using the data in the table below you are required to:

(a) Calculate price relatives for each year for each product, using 1974 as base
(b) Construct a base-weighted index number by calculating a weighted average of price relatives for each year
(c) Convert the index numbers obtained in (b) to a chain-base series
(d) Re-base the index numbers obtained in (b) on 1977.

| | | *Prices (pence)* | | | |
	Weight	1974 (p_o)	1975 (p_1)	1976 (p_2)	1977 (p_3)
Butter	2	17	19	25	22
Milk	4	8	9	10	11
Cheese	1	45	50	60	70

2. A company employs four grades of manual workers, M1, M2, M3, and M4. The number of workers in each grade and the hourly rates of pay over the period 1972–78 were as follows:

| | 1972 | | 1974 | | 1976 | | 1978 | |
Grade	No.	Rate	No.	Rate	No.	Rate	No.	Rate
M1	120	0.80	165	1.10	130	1.40	115	1.65
M2	105	0.70	142	1.00	123	1.25	120	1.50
M3	105	0.62	125	0.86	107	1.05	92	1.25
M4	92	0.50	110	0.70	70	0.90	55	1.10

Using 1972 as base, you are required to:
(a) Construct a Laspeyre wages index
(b) Construct a Laspeyre quantity index to show manpower changes.

3. The production index of a furniture manufacturer is as follows (base year = 1972):

Year:	1968	1969	1970	1971	1972
Index:	81.6	83.8	87.2	91.5	100.0

Year:	1973	1974	1975	1976	1977
Index:	126.6	120.1	124.9	129.8	136.0

    (a) Compare this series with that for the furniture industry (given on page 70) by re-basing it on 1975. State what the comparison shows.

    (b) Convert this series to a chain index and comment on the results.

4. You are informed that a certain price index had the value 130 in 1977. What do you need to know about the method of construction of this index before you can use this information?

5. The following table gives the production and prices for the products made by a certain company for the period 1975–78:

    (a) Using 1975 as base, calculate for the period:
       (i) a Laspeyre price index
      (ii) a Paasche price index

    (b) Construct a chain price index for the period, weighting each year's prices by the previous year's quantities

    (c) State what the results of your calculations show.

Product	Production (000s)				Prices (£s)			
	1975	1976	1977	1978	1975	1976	1977	1978
A	65	60	55	55	2.00	2.50	3.20	3.50
B	50	55	55	65	1.30	1.50	1.90	2.10
C	80	90	95	120	0.90	1.20	1.55	1.65

Eight

Summarization of Data (2) — Frequency Distributions

FREQUENCY DISTRIBUTIONS

The calculation of the mean, standard deviation, and other summary measures considered in Chapter 6 presents little problem when the number of values to be summarized is small. Imagine the task, however, if the number of carrot or lettuce prices (Table 6.1) were not 15, but several hundred or even thousand. The amount of data would be unmanageable, and it would then be necessary to reduce the number of values to around 15 or less by constructing a 'frequency distribution'.

To illustrate the method, frequency distributions of the carrot and lettuce prices are shown in Table 8.1. Only seven different carrot prices were observed in the 15 shops

Table 8.1 Frequency distributions of the carrot and lettuce prices

Carrots		Lettuces	
Price (pence) (x)	Frequency (f)	Price (pence) (x)	Frequency (f)
10	1	10	4
11	2	11	3
12	2	12	1
13	5	13	2
14	2	14	1
15	2	15	1
16	1	16–20	3
	15		15

(see Table 6.1): one shop charged 10p, two shops charged 11p, two shops charged 12p, five shops charged 13p. etc. The *frequency* with which 10p occurs is 1, the frequency with which 11p occurs is 2, the frequency with which 12p occurs is 2, and so on, as shown in the table.

By constructing a frequency distribution we have, in this example, converted 15 individual values to 7 frequencies — not a great reduction, but if applied to cases involving hundreds or thousands of values, the reduction would be very great indeed.

Note that in Table 8.1 the highest lettuce prices have been grouped together in a single 'class', covering the price range 16p–20p. Since only three prices occur in this range, grouping them in this way reduces the amount of data that has to be handled without too much loss of accuracy.

HISTOGRAMS

A frequency distribution can be represented diagrammatically by means of a 'histogram'. Histograms representing the carrot price and lettuce price distributions are shown in Figures 8.1 and 8.2. These look like ordinary bar charts, but in fact they differ from them in three essential respects:

1. The horizontal axis of a histogram must be continuous (as on a graph).

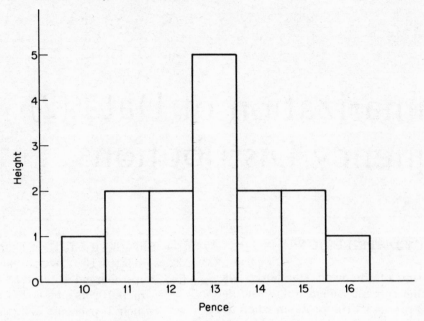

Figure 8.1 Histogram of carrot prices

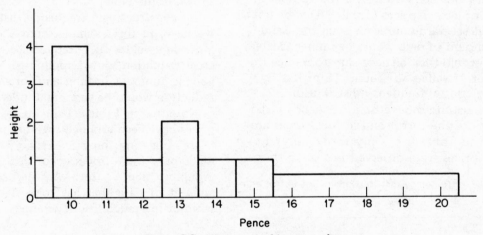

Figure 8.2 Histogram of lettuce prices

2. The *area* of each bar (not the height) represents the frequency.

3. There must be no gaps between adjacent bars, except where gaps occur in the data (such as the gaps in the cauliflower prices, see Table 6.1). Any gaps between adjacent bars are, in effect, bars of zero area, representing values that occur with zero frequency.

To show the method of construction, consider the lettuce price frequency distribution. The horizontal axis of the histogram must cover the range of lettuce prices, namely 10p to 20p. To draw bars representing each frequency, we first determine the breadths and then the heights. Since there are to be no gaps between adjacent bars, and since adjacent prices differ by 1p (remember that it was assumed for simplicity that the $\frac{1}{2}$p unit was not used), it follows that each bar must have a breadth equal to 1p on the horinzotal scale. In fact, the histogram should be drawn so that the limits of each bar are located mid-way between adjacent prices — so that the bar representing 10p extends from 9.5 to 10.5, the bar representing 11p extends from 10.5 to 11.5, and so on. The bar representing 16 to 20 should extend from 15.5 to 20.5. Note that if the $\frac{1}{2}$p unit were used, these limits would have to be more precisely defined, otherwise $10\frac{1}{2}$p, for example, would lie in both the first and the second bars. The limits of the first bar should then be 9.5 and *under* 10.5 ('under 10.5' means 10.4999 . . .), those of the second bar should be 10.5 and under 11.5, and so on.

To determine the height of each bar, the formula 'area = breadth × height' must be used. Area represents frequency, and so the height of a bar equals frequency divided by breadth. The height of the first bar is therefore $\frac{4}{1}$ = 4, that of the second bar is $\frac{3}{1}$ = 3, and so on. The height of the bar representing the class 16p to 20p (this bar is 20.5 − 15.5 = 5p wide) is $\frac{3}{5}$ = 0.6.

This histogram is typical of a positively skewed distribution: the highest bar (corresponding to the mode) is at the left, and there is a drawn-out 'tail' to the right. A negatively skewed distribution would have these features reversed. The symmetrically distributed carrot prices give rise to a symmetrical histogram; the cauliflower prices, with two modes, result in a 'bi-modal' histogram.

GROUPED FREQUENCY DISTRIBUTIONS

To demonstrate the value of frequency distributions in data summarization, we shall use an example consisting of not 15 but 100 values. The previous example was of discrete prices; in this case we shall use continuous data. The example is of a sample of 100 letters produced by a typing pool. The time taken to type each letter is measured to the nearest 0.01 of a minute, and this results in the list of 100 typing times shown in Table

8.2. (Note that these times are in minutes and decimals of a minute, *not* minutes and seconds.)

Table 8.2   Sample of 100 typing times (in minutes)

20.72	14.53	23.31	19.25	16.87	7.15	17.44	12.28
11.30	19.55	23.85	17.14	4.85	10.95	21.65	28.10
11.91	29.64	15.38	11.57	22.61	21.16	13.20	16.03
19.03	22.08	18.39	19.47	17.06	24.14	15.19	12.29
13.39	17.77	23.31	15.16	25.02	16.29	20.03	13.57
16.61	19.41	22.97	18.64	13.12	18.36	12.99	18.73
22.44	14.73	19.83	14.46	18.51	15.82	12.58	26.78
18.29	9.53	20.38	21.30	13.56	17.62	22.80	27.54
10.44	17.59	20.45	23.74	18.70	26.31	11.03	12.41
25.43	13.86	15.57	21.86	16.78	14.07	20.92	14.96
24.50	13.67	22.50	9.69	16.32	24.25	8.32	16.93
20.84	16.33	21.11	15.50	15.70	18.81	17.90	25.98
25.56	19.11	12.65	15.20				

No two typing times are the same, and we cannot therefore draw up a frequency distribution like that produced for the carrot prices. Just as the lettuce prices lying in the range 16p to 20p were grouped together, so it is necessary to devise some grouping system for the typing times.

To do this first scan the data to determine the range: the lowest time is 4.85 minutes, the highest is 29.64 minutes. We have therefore to divide up the interval 4 to 30 minutes into suitable classes. We could, for example, use the following classes: 4.00–4.99 minutes, 5.00–5.99 minutes, 6.00–6.99 minutes, and so on up to 29.99 minutes. This covers every possible recorded typing time, and it reduces the amount of data that has to be analysed — there would be 26 frequencies instead of 100 individual values. However, for ease of calculation, less than this number of frequencies is desirable.

The above classes have a 'class interval' of one minute. This is too small, so we could try a class interval of 10 minutes: 4.00–13.99, 14.00–23.99, 24.00–33.99 minutes. We now have only three classes and therefore three frequencies to deal with, so the calculations will be very simple. The problem now is that too much detail has been lost. If the various summary measures were calculated from these, the results would be wildly inaccurate.

A compromise has to be reached between too much data on the one hand, and unacceptable errors through loss of detail on the other. As a general rule there should be between 7 and 15 classes, depending on the degree of accuracy required in the subsequent analysis. To simplify the analysis, the class intervals should all be equal, but in the case of highly skewed distributions this is not possible, as the class intervals required to cover the tail of the distribution must be larger than those required in the vicinity of the mode (see Table 8.7). In the typing times example a class interval of 3 minutes is appropriate, the classes being 4.00-6.99, 7.00-9.99, and so on.

The figures bounding the classes (4.00, 6.99, 7.00, etc.) are called the 'class limits'. The subsequent analysis is simplified if there is no gap between the upper class limit of one class and the lower class limit of the class above. It would, of course, be incorrect to define the classes 4.00-7.00, 7.00-10.00, etc., since the values 7.00, 10.00, etc., could then belong to two classes. To avoid this the classes should be defined thus: 3.995-6.995, 6.995-9.995, and so on (cf. the discussion on the lettuce price classes). These limits are rather cumbersome, and the simplest definition is 4 and under 7, 7 and under 10, 10 and under 13, etc. This simple definition shifts the class limits upwards by 0.005 minutes, which results in a negligible inaccuracy in the calculation of the summary measures. As a general guide, this simple way of defining the classes is permissible if the data is continuous, but if the data is discrete the resulting inaccuracy may be significant and this simplification should not be made. For example, the correct way of defining the classes in question 4 (page 90) is 54.5-64.5, 64.5-74.5, etc. To use the definition 55 and under 65, 65 and under 75, etc., results in an upward shift of 0.5, which will be transmitted into the subsequent analysis, and which is not as insignificant as the error of 0.005 in the typing times example.

Having defined the classes, the next task is to determine the frequencies. The first typing time recorded in Table 8.2 is 20.72 minutes, and so a tally mark is recorded against the class 19 and under 22 (see Table 8.3). The second time is 11.30, and so a tally mark is recorded against the class 10 and under 13. This process is continued until all the typing times have been allocated to classes. The number of tallies in each class is the frequency of that class (Table 8.3).

The data is now greatly simplified, and a meaningful pattern is beginning to emerge. We can see, for example, that the average time is somewhere between 16 and 19 minutes, and it is clear that the amount of skewness in the distribution is negligible. The task of calculating the various summary measures is now quite easy, as we show below.

DETERMINATION OF THE MODE

The histogram of the frequency distribution of typing times is shown in Figure 8.3. (Note that since the class intervals are all equal, the bars can be drawn with height = frequency.) The highest bar represents the modal class, that is the class with the highest frequency. The procedure for determining an exact value for the mode is shown in the figure.

DETERMINATION OF THE MEAN AND STANDARD DEVIATION

To show how the formulae for the mean and standard deviation of a frequency distribution are derived, consider again the distribution of carrot prices shown in Table 8.1.

The mean of the carrot prices is obtained by:

1. Summing the carrot prices:

    $$1 \times 10 + 2 \times 11 + 2 \times 12 + 5 \times 13 +$$
    $$2 \times 14 + 2 \times 15 + 1 \times 16 = 195$$

    (i.e. calculating Σfx, where f denotes the frequency and x denotes the price)

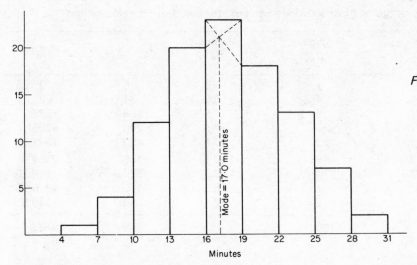

Figure 8.3 Histogram of typing times. To locate the mode, join the indicated corners on the highest bar by straight lines, and draw a vertical from the intersection of the lines to the horizontal axis.

2.   Dividing by the number of prices:

$$1 + 2 + 2 + 5 + 2 + 2 + 1 = 15$$

(i.e. by Σf).

The formula for the mean is therefore:

$$\bar{x} = \frac{\Sigma fx}{\Sigma f} \quad (= \frac{195}{15} = 13\text{p for the carrot prices})$$

As explained in Chapter 6, the standard deviation is obtained by:

1.   Subtracting the mean from each price and squaring the answers (i.e. calculating $(x-\bar{x})^2$ for each value of x)

2.   Summing the results of (1) (i.e. calculating $\Sigma f(x-\bar{x})^2$)

3.   Dividing by the number of prices (i.e. Σf) and taking the square root. The formula for the standard deviation is therefore:

$$\text{S.D.} = \sqrt{\frac{\Sigma f(x-\bar{x})^2}{\Sigma f}}$$

By expanding the $(x-\bar{x})^2$ term and manipulating the summations, it can be shown that this is equivalent to the following formula, which is easier to use in practice:

$$\text{S.D.} = \sqrt{\frac{\Sigma fx^2}{\Sigma f} - \bar{x}^2}$$

$$= \sqrt{\frac{\Sigma fx^2}{\Sigma f} - \left(\frac{\Sigma fx}{\Sigma f}\right)^2}$$

These formulae can be directly applied to the frequency distributions of the carrot and lettuce prices given in Table 8.1, for in these the values of x are precisely defined. In the grouped frequency distribution of typing times shown in Table 8.3, however, class limits are assigned to x, not exact values, and to apply the formulae it is necessary to assume that the typing times are evenly distributed through each class and that the class midpoints can be used as 'average' x-values. The calculation of the mean and standard deviation of the typing times using these midpoints as the x-values is shown in Table 8.3.

The calculations can be simplified by transforming these x-values by the method of assumed means (outlined in Chapter 6). The procedure is to choose an x-value (the assumed mean) lying towards the middle of the distribution, subtract it from each x-value and, provided the class intervals are all equal, to divide the remainders by the class interval. (If the class intervals are not all equal, a suitable divisor may be half the smallest class interval.) As in Chapter 6, the transformed x-values are denoted by the upper case X. The mean and standard deviation calculations are carried out using the X-values, and the transformation is applied in reverse to the results: to obtain the

Table 8.3 Frequency distribution of typing times showing mean and standard deviation calculations

Class (minutes)	Tally	Frequency (f)	Midpoint (x)	fx	fx²
4 and under 7	/	1	5.5	5.5	30.25
7 and under 10	////	4	8.5	34	289
10 and under 13	THH THH //	12	11.5	138	1587
13 and under 16	THH THH THH THH	20	14.5	290	4205
16 and under 19	THH THH THH THH ///	23	17.5	402.5	7043.75
19 and under 22	THH THH THH ///	18	20.5	369	7564.5
22 and under 25	THH THH ///	13	23.5	305.5	7179.25
25 and under 28	THH //	7	26.5	185.5	4915.75
28 and under 31	//	2	29.5	59	1740.5
Totals		100		1789	34555

$$\text{Mean} = \frac{\Sigma fx}{\Sigma f}$$

$$= \frac{1789}{100}$$

$$= 17.89 \simeq 17.9 \text{ minutes.}$$

$$\text{Standard deviation} = \sqrt{\frac{\Sigma fx^2}{\Sigma f} - \left(\frac{\Sigma fx}{\Sigma f}\right)^2}$$

$$= \sqrt{\frac{34,555}{100} - 17.89^2}$$

$$= \sqrt{345.55 - 320.0521}$$

$$= 5.0495 \simeq 5.0 \text{ minutes.}$$

mean of the original *x*-values, multiply by the class interval and add on the assumed mean, and to obtain the standard deviation, multiply by the class interval. The calculation of the mean and standard deviation of the typing times by this method is shown in Table 8.4.

Provided the class intervals are all equal, the procedure for obtaining the *X*-values is very simple: choose a class towards the middle of the distribution, assign it an *X*-value of zero, and count upwards using negative signs

Table 8.4 Mean and standard deviation calculations using the method of assumed means

Class (minutes)	Frequency (f)	Midpoint (x)	X	fX	fX²
4 and under 7	1	5.5	−4	−4	16
7 and under 10	4	8.5	−3	−12	36
10 and under 13	12	11.5	−2	−24	48
13 and under 16	20	14.5	−1	−20	20
16 and under 19	23	17.5	0	0	0
19 and under 22	18	20.5	1	18	18
22 and under 25	13	23.5	2	26	52
25 and under 28	7	26.5	3	21	63
28 and under 31	2	29.5	4	8	32
Totals	100			13	285

Assumed mean (A.M.) = midpoint of chosen class = 17.5.
Class interval (c) = 3.

$$\text{Mean} = \text{A.M.} + \frac{\Sigma fX}{\Sigma f} \times c$$

$$= 17.5 + \frac{13}{100} \times 3$$

$$= 17.5 + 0.39$$

$$= 17.89 \text{ minutes.}$$

$$\text{Standard deviation} = c \times \sqrt{\frac{\Sigma fX^2}{\Sigma f} - \left(\frac{\Sigma fX}{\Sigma f}\right)^2}$$

$$= 3 \times \sqrt{\frac{285}{100} - \left(\frac{13}{100}\right)^2}$$

$$= 3 \times \sqrt{(2.85 - 0.0169)}$$

$$= 5.0495 \text{ minutes}$$

and downwards using positive signs (see column 4 of Table 8.4). Note that the third column of the table listing the class midpoints can be omitted if this procedure is adopted.

DETERMINATION OF THE MEDIAN AND QUARTILE DEVIATION

The median is the x-value lying halfway through the distribution, the first quartile is the x-value lying one-quarter of the way through, and the third quartile is the x-value lying three-quarters of the way through. To determine these it is necessary to construct a cumulative frequency table, as shown in Table 8.5. The cumulative frequencies are calculated in the same way as the Z-chart cumulative totals (Chapter 5): the number of typing times which are less than 7 minutes is 1; the number of times which are less than 10 minutes is $1 + 4 = 5$; the number of times which are less than 13 minutes is $5 + 12 = 17$, and so on.

Table 8.5 Cumulative frequency distribution of typing times

Class (minutes)	Frequency (f)	Cumulative frequency (cum f)
4 and under 7	1	1
7 and under 10	4	5
10 and under 13	12	17
13 and under 16	20	37
16 and under 19	23	60
19 and under 22	18	78
22 and under 25	13	91
25 and under 28	7	98
28 and under 31	2	100

There are 100 typing times, so the median is the value of the 50th (or, more correctly, $50\frac{1}{2}$ — but the error resulting from omitting the fractional part of this number is negligible). From Table 8.5 it can be seen that the first 37 times are less than 16 minutes, and the first 60 times are less than 19 minutes. It follows that the 50th time lies in the class 16 and under 19 minutes — in fact it is the $50 - 37 = $ 13th x-value in the class. There are

23 x-values in this class, and it is assumed that they are evenly distributed through it. It follows that the median lies 13/23 rds of the way through the class, and, since the class interval is 3 minutes, it must therefore lie $13/23 \times 3$ minutes into the class. The lower class limit is 16 minutes, and so the value of the median is

$$16 + \frac{13}{23} \times 3 = 16 + 1.6956 \simeq 17.7 \text{ minutes.}$$

The first quartile is determined similarly: it is the 25th typing time, that is the 8th x-value in the class 13 and under 16

$$= 13 + \frac{8}{20} \times 3 = 14.2 \text{ minutes.}$$

The third quartile is the 75th typing time, that is the 15th x-value in the class 19 and under 22

$$= 19 + \frac{15}{18} \times 3 = 21.5 \text{ minutes}$$

Hence the quartile deviation is

$$\tfrac{1}{2}(21.5 - 14.2) = 3.65 \text{ minutes}$$

CUMULATIVE FREQUENCY CURVES

Figure 8.4 shows the cumulative frequency curve of the distribution of typing times. It is constructed by plotting the cumulative frequencies of Table 8.5 against the upper class limits. (A common error is to plot the cumulative frequencies against the class midpoints; it should be remembered, however, that the accumulation is made at the upper limits — the number of typing times which are less than 7 minutes is 1, etc.) The plotted points are then joined by a *smooth* curve (since the x-values can be assumed to increase smoothly and without discontinuities).

Cumulative frequency curves can be used to determine x-values lying any fraction of the way through the distribution. In this example the median is obtained by reading from the curve the value of the 50th typing

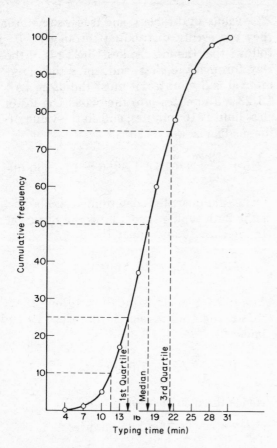

Figure 8.4 Cumulative frequency curve of typing times

the x-value lying 95% of the way through: this equals 26.5 minutes in the typing times example.

Quartiles, deciles, percentiles, and other values lying various fractions of the way through a distribution are known as 'fractiles'. They are calculated when it is required to segment the distribution in some way. For example, it might be required to segment the population into tenths according to height in order to devise a sizing system for clothes; or it might be required to fail a certain percentage of candidates sitting an exam, in which case the pass mark must be made equal to the appropriate percentile.

RELATIVE FREQUENCY AND PROBABILITY

Table 8.6 is the relative frequency table for the distribution of typing times. The relative frequency of a class is the class frequency divided by the total frequency, and it shows what proportion of the values lies in that class.

Table 8.6   Relative frequencies of the typing times

Class (minutes)	Frequency	Relative frequency (= probability, p)
4 and under 7	1	0.01
7 and under 10	4	0.04
10 and under 13	12	0.12
13 and under 16	20	0.20
16 and under 19	23	0.23
19 and under 22	18	0.18
22 and under 25	13	0.13
25 and under 28	7	0.07
28 and under 31	2	0.02
Totals	100	1.00

time: the horizontal line through 50 on the vertical scale intersects the curve at the point corresponding to 17.7 minutes on the horizontal scale. The quartiles are determined similarly, as indicated in the figure.

x-values lying various tenths of the way through a distribution are called 'deciles'. The first decile, for example, is the x-value lying one-tenth of the way through, that is the tenth typing time in our example. As indicated in Figure 8.4, this equals 11.5 minutes. The fourth decile, for example, is the x-value lying four-tenths of the way through the distribution; the reader should confirm that for the typing times example this equals 16.5 minutes.

'Percentiles' are x-values lying various hundredths of the way through the distribution. The 95th percentile, for example, is

It is a measure which is independent of the total number of values, and it thus enables frequency distributions with differing total numbers to be compared. We shall use relative frequencies rather than ordinary frequencies in subsequent chapters.

There is an obvious association between relative frequency and probability. The first definition of probability given in Chapter 3 was:

$$P(\text{success}) = \frac{\text{number of successes}}{\text{number of trials}}$$

In the typing times example we have 100 'trials' (i.e. observed typing times). If 'success' is, for example, taking between 10 and under 13 minutes to type, then there are 12 successes and

$$P(\text{success}) = \frac{12}{100} = 0.12$$

The probability calculation is identical to the relative frequency calculation. The relative frequency distribution given in Table 8.6 can therefore be regarded as a probability distribution.

It should, however, be emphasized that relative frequency and probability are not identical concepts. If we have a playing die which we believe to be accurately machined and therefore unbiased, then we will not equate the probability of throwing a four with the relative frequency with which a four is thrown over a number of trials. We will assign probabilities on the basis of the second definition given in Chapter 3: the probability of throwing a four is, we believe, $\frac{1}{6}$. The relative frequency should, of course, tend to this value as the number of trials increases.

The various summary measures can be calculated from a relative frequency distribution in just the same way as they are calculated from an ordinary frequency distribution. If relative frequency is equated with probability (as has been done in Table 8.6), then some of these summary measures take on a special meaning. The mode of a probability distribution is the value with the highest probability, in other words the value which is 'most likely' to occur. If a letter were selected at random and we were required to guess its typing time, we should choose the mode, 17.0 minutes.

For most purposes the most useful average of a probability distribution is the mean, usually referred to as the 'expected value' or 'expectation'. To calculate it the formula for the mean is used, with f replaced by p, the symbol for probability:

$$\text{Expected value} = \frac{\Sigma px}{\Sigma p}$$

Since Σp, the sum of the probabilities, must equal 1, it follows that this formula can be written:

$$\text{Expected value} = \Sigma px$$

As we shall see in Chapter 17, expected values have important applications. For example, businessmen can make the 'best' choice between alternative courses of action by selecting the one with the highest expected value.

LORENZ CURVES

Although Lorenz curves are not directly related to the main subject matter of this chapter, they involve the construction of frequency tables, and it is therefore convenient to deal with them at this point in the text.

Lorenz curves are used to show inequalities in the distribution of, for example, wealth among the population, productivity among firms in an industry, turnover among companies, etc. The example used in this section shows the inequality in the distribution of pre-tax personal income in the U.K. in 1975/76. The curve is shown in Figure 8.5, and it is constructed by plotting cumulative percentage number of incomes against cumulative percentage total income. These cumulative percentages are calculated by summing successive percentages in the usual way, and the results are shown in Table 8.7.

From the cumulative percentage columns of this table it can be seen that the 3.1% lowest income earners received only 0.8% of the total income, the 10.0% lowest income earners received only 3.1% of the total income, and so on. The top 0.2% income earners, on the other hand, received 2.0% of the total income. If the total income were equally divided among income earners, then the 3.1% of income earners referred to above would receive 3.1% of the total income, the 10.0% of income earners would receive 10.0% of the total income and so on.

The Lorenz curve shows this in graphical form. The line of equal distribution (Figure 8.5) shows the situation if incomes were equally distributed: each fraction of income earners receives a corresponding fraction of

Figure 8.5 Lorenz curve showing the inequality in the distribution of personal income in the UK

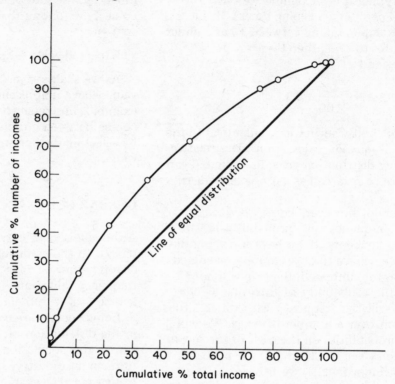

Table 8.7   The distribution of pre-tax personal incomes in the UK (from the 1975/76 Annual Survey)

Annual income (£)	Number of incomes (Thousands)	(%)	(cum. %)	Total income (£m)	(%)	(cum. %)
Under 750	644	3.1	3.1	441	0.8	0.8
750 and under 1000	1411	6.9	10.0	1239	2.3	3.1
1000 and under 1500	3256	15.8	25.8	4076	7.6	10.7
1500 and under 2000	3372	16.4	42.2	5913	11.0	21.7
2000 and under 2500	3299	16.0	58.2	7397	13.8	35.5
2500 and under 3000	2840	13.8	72.0	7783	14.5	50.0
3000 and under 4000	3780	18.4	90.4	12961	24.2	74.2
4000 and under 5000	617	3.0	93.4	3340	6.2	80.4
5000 and under 10000	1160	5.6	99.0	7329	13.7	94.1
10000 and under 20000	158	0.8	99.8	2070	3.9	98.0
20000 and over	33	0.2	100.0	1056	2.0	100.0
	20570			53605		

Source: *Annual Abstract of Statistics*

the total income. The curve shows the actual situation, and the extent to which this curve diverges from the line of equal distribution indicates the degree of inequality. By drawing on the same graph Lorenz curves for income distribution in other countries, it is possible to compare the inequality in income distribution in one country with the inequality in another: those countries with the greatest inequality have curves lying furthest from the line of equal distribution. Any changes in the inequality of income distribution from one year to another can be similarly monitored (see question 6 below).

EXERCISES

1. Forty families live in a certain street. The numbers of families with no children, one child, two children, etc., are shown in the histogram in Figure 8.6. You are required to write down the frequency distribution and from it compute the mean and the standard deviation.

2. A biased die is thrown 600 times with the following results: a one was thrown 130 times; a two, 60 times; a three, 70 times; a four, 110 times; a five, 120 times; and a six, 110 times.
    (a) Write down the frequency distribution of the dice throws and from it deduce the probability distribution (leave the probabilities as fractions).
    (b) Compute the expected value of a dice throw. What is the most likely value?
    (c) What is the expected value of a throw of an unbiased die? Is the above die biased towards the low or the high scores?

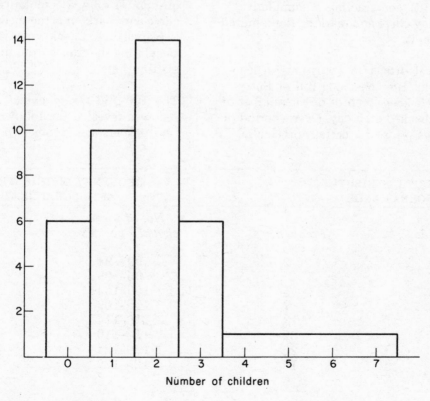

Figure 8.6 Histogram for question 1

3. The marks of 50 students sitting an exam were as follows:

$$
\begin{array}{cccccccccc}
70 & 42 & 55 & 48 & 64 & 56 & 59 & 65 & 51 & 52 \\
76 & 51 & 62 & 54 & 49 & 68 & 45 & 43 & 33 & 40 \\
57 & 62 & 53 & 58 & 40 & 38 & 56 & 48 & 65 & 54 \\
65 & 62 & 37 & 68 & 56 & 58 & 57 & 63 & 73 & 55 \\
59 & 53 & 61 & 52 & 42 & 54 & 56 & 51 & 56 & 56 \\
\end{array}
$$

Construct a frequency distribution table using between 8 and 12 classes, and from it determine:

(a) The mean and the standard deviation
(b) The median, the quartile deviation, and the 4th decile
(c) The pass mark if it is desired to fail 20% of the students
(d) The distinction mark if it is desired to award distinctions to the top 10% of students.

Check the results of your calculations in (b) to (d) constructing a cumulative frequency curve and marking the required values on it.

4. A clerical officer in a customs office spends his time checking Bill of Entry forms. He keeps records of the number of forms checked each day. Over a period of 100 days prior to a certain procedural change, the daily numbers of forms checked were as shown on the left below. Over a period of 80 days following the change, the daily numbers checked were as shown on the right.

(a) Compare the two frequency distributions by calculating for each:
  (i) The relative frequencies and from them drawing histograms — each with the same vertical scale
  (ii) The mean, the standard deviation, and the coefficient of skewness.
  Comment on the results of your calculations.

(b) What is the probability that on the 81st day following the change the number of forms checked is: (i) 120 or more; (ii) 100 or less; (iii) exactly 110.

5. For each frequency distribution given in question 4 draw a cumulative frequency curve and mark on it the median and the two quartiles. Check your results by calculating the values from the frequency distributions.

6. The 1964/65 *Quinquennial Survey of Incomes* revealed the following information on personal incomes (before tax):

FREQUENCY DISTRIBUTION BEFORE CHANGE		FREQUENCY DISTRIBUTION AFTER CHANGE	
No. of forms checked per day	Frequency	No. of forms checked per day	Frequency
55– 64	2	90– 94	2
65– 74	3	95– 99	6
75– 84	5	100–104	12
85– 89	7	105–109	17
90– 94	13	110–114	20
95– 99	22	115–119	13
100–104	25	120–124	7
105–109	18	125–129	3
110–114	5		80
	100		

Annual income (£)	No. of incomes (000s)	Total income (£m)
Under 500	4100	1594
500 and under 1000	9037	6760
1000 and under 1500	5517	6649
1500 and under 2000	1411	2386
2000 and under 3000	592	1408
3000 and under 4000	180	615
4000 and under 5000	84	372
5000 and under 10000	120	804
10000 and under 15000	21	252
15000 and over	12	309
	21074	21149

(a) Construct a Lorenz curve for the above data.

(b) Draw on the same graph the Lorenz curve for the 1975/76 Annual Survey (see Table 8.7). What change has there been in the distribution of incomes over the 10-year period between the surveys?

Nine

Frequency Curves

In a frequency distribution (such as that of the typing times considered in the last chapter) the observed values are most widely dispersed at the extremities of the distribution, and are most densely grouped together at the mode. The number of values per unit interval is called the 'frequency density', and for most distributions involving continuous data this measure increases smoothly as the observed values depart from the extremities and approach the mode.

The average frequency density of a class is obtained by dividing the class frequency by the class interval. It was this fraction that was used to determine the heights of the histrogram bars in Figures 8.1, 8.2 and 8.3, and it follows that 'height' in those figures represents frequency density.

The histogram is not an entirely satisfactory method of representing frequency distributions, for it portrays the frequency density as increasing in a series of steps. To show the reality of a smoothly increasing frequency density, a frequency curve is necessary. The way in which this is derived from the histogram is explained below.

FREQUENCY CURVES

Figure 9.1 shows, superimposed on the histogram of typing times, a 'frequency polygon' which, although not a true curve, at least does not exhibit a step-like appear-ance. It is constructed by marking the midpoints of the tops of the histogram bars and joining up these points by straight lines. (Note that the polygon must start and finish on the horizontal axis at the midpoints of the empty classes adjoining the extremities of the distribution.)

As indicated in the figure, the areas of the triangles subtracted from the histogram equal the triangles added to it, and so the total area under the frequency polygon equals the total histogram area. This is an important point, for it means that the essential characteristic of the histogram (that area = frequency) is retained by the frequency polygon.

Histograms and frequency polygons can be drawn to represent relative frequencies instead of ordinary frequencies (a relative frequency polygon differs from a frequency polygon only in the scale used on the vertical axis). The total area under a relative frequency polygon equals the total relative frequency, which is 1, the advantage of this being that the area is then independent of the total number of observed values. It is from relative frequency polygons that frequency curves are derived.

To replace the angular appearance of the polygon by the smooth appearance of the curve, we suppose that the number of observed values is increased, and that the size of each class interval is decreased. The total area will be unaltered (since total

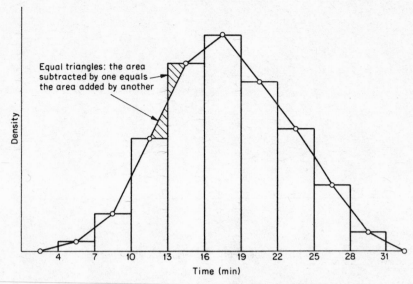

Figure 9.1   Frequency polygon of typing times

relative frequency always equals 1), but as this process approaches the limit (of an infinitely large number of observed values and infinitesimal class intervals), the polygon becomes a smooth frequency curve.

If this process were carried out for the distribution of typing times (by recording the times of many thousands of letters and constructing a frequency distribution with a class interval of just a few seconds), the frequency curve might be as shown in Figure 9.2. It is almost symmetrical (though a slight positive skew can be detected), and it is bell-shaped. As indicated in the figure, the area under any part of the curve represents the relative frequency of the corresponding interval of the distribution.

Figure 9.3 shows the frequency curve of

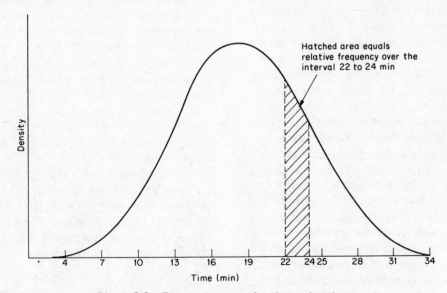

Figure 9.2   Frequency curve for the typing times

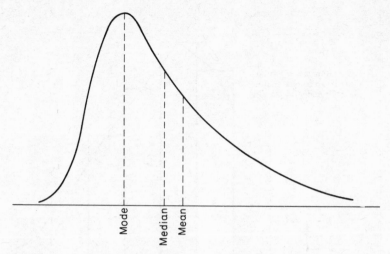

Figure 9.3   Positively skewed frequency curve

a distribution with a large positive skew, and the relative positions of the mean, median, and mode should be noted. Negatively skewed frequency curves (which are rarely encountered in practice) have the median and mode to the right of the mean.

NORMAL FREQUENCY CURVES

A large number of frequency distributions give rise to symmetrical bell-shaped frequency curves. Examples include distributions of heights of adults, intelligence quotients, lifetimes of electric light bulbs, and lengths of components produced by an automatic machine. Such distributions are called 'normal'.

Since normal frequency curves are symmetrical, it follows that the mean, median, and mode coincide, and the coefficient of skewness is therefore zero. In fact, normal distributions differ from one another only in their central tendency and dispersion. It follows from this that one normal distribution can be transformed to any other normal distribution by altering its mean and standard deviation by the method of assumed means — in particular any normal distribution can be transformed to what is known as the

'standard normal distribution', which has $\overline{x} = 0$ and S.D. = 1. The great value of this particular transformation is that the areas under every part of the standard normal frequency curve have been determined (see Appendix I, page 193), and since area = relative frequency, it follows that the relative frequency of any interval of any normal distribution can be calculated.

We illustrate the method by applying the transformation to the distribution of the very large number of typing times referred to in the previous section. We assume for the purposes of this calculation that the mean has been found to be 18.5 minutes and the standard deviation 5.0 minutes. As sometimes occurs in practice, the distribution is slightly skewed (see Figure 9.2), and so the standard normal curve areas only approximately apply to it. It is, however, so nearly normal that the resulting error will be very small.

To transform to the standard normal distribution, the procedure is: (a) subtract the mean from each x-value; (b) divide the remainders by the standard deviation. For example, the transformed value of the typing time $x = 23.5$ minutes is:

$$\frac{23.5 - 18.5}{5.0} = 1.$$

Values obtained using this transformation are called 'standard normal units' and are denoted by the letter z. Thus the typing time $x = 23.5$ corresponds to $z = 1$. The transformation procedure can be written down as a formula involving z and x:

$$z = \frac{x - \overline{x}}{\text{S.D.}}$$

z-values corresponding to some other x-values of the typing times distribution are as follows:

1. For the mean typing time ($x = 18.5$)

$$z = \frac{18.5 - 18.5}{5.0}$$

$$= 0$$

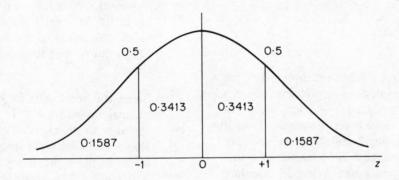

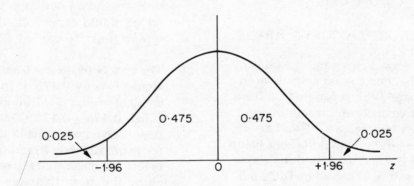

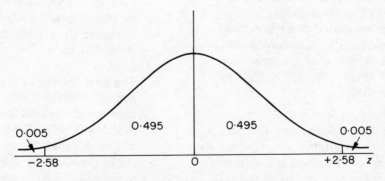

Figure 9.4 Selected normal curve areas

2. For the typing time $x = 13.5$ minutes (which lies one standard deviation below the mean)

$$z = \frac{13.5 - 18.5}{5.0}$$

$$= -1$$

3. For the typing time $x = 28.5$ (which lies two standard deviations above the mean

$$z = \frac{28.5 - 18.5}{5.0}$$

$$= 2$$

It is clear from these examples that we can think of z-values as expressing x-values in terms of the number of standard deviations they lie away from the mean. Thus the typing time lying 2 standard deviations below the mean ($x = 8.5$) transforms to $z = -2$, the typing time lying $1\frac{1}{2}$ standard deviations below the mean ($x = 11$) transforms to $z = -1.5$, and so on.

STANDARD NORMAL CURVE AREAS

The standard normal curve and the table of standard normal curve areas are shown in Appendix I (page 193). It can be seen from the table that virtually the whole of the distribution lies between $z = -3$ and $z = +3$, that is, between 3 standard deviations below the mean and 3 standard deviations above the mean. (It will be observed in Table 8.3 that none of the 100 typing times discussed in the last chapter lie more than 3 S.D.s from the mean.) The areas given in Appendix I are measured from the mean (the hatched part of the standard normal curve illustrated). Some of the most commonly used of these areas are as follows (refer to Figure 9.4):

1. The area between $z = 0$ and $z = 1$ is 0.3413. It follows that the relative frequency of the interval $z = 0$ (which is the mean) to $z = 1$ (which is 1 standard deviation above the mean) is 0.3413.

Hence 34.13% (roughly one-third) of the observed values lie in this interval. About one-third of the typing times, for example, will lie in the interval 18.5 to 23.5 minutes.

2. Since the standard normal curve is symmetrical about $z = 0$, it follows that the area between $z = -1$ and $z = 0$ is also 0.3413, and hence that 34.13% of the observed values from a normal distribution lie in the interval 1 standard deviation below the mean to the mean (13.5 to 18.5 minutes in the case of the typing times).

3. Since the total area under the standard normal curve equals 1, it follows that the area to the right of $z = 0$ equals 0.5. Hence the area lying under the 'tail' of the curve to the right of $z = 1$ is $0.5 - 0.3413 = 0.1587$. This means that 15.87% of values from a normal distribution lie more than 1 standard deviation above the mean. So we would expect about 16% of the typing times to exceed 23.5 minutes.

4. The area between $z = 0$ and $z = 1.96$ is almost exactly 0.475. It follows that the area between $z = -1.96$ and $z = +1.96$ equals $0.475 + 0.475 = 0.950$. So 95% of the observed values lie in the interval 1.96 (or approximately 2) standard deviations below the mean to 2 standard deviations above the mean (between 8.5 and 28.5 minutes in the case of the typing times). 2.5% of the values are further than 1.96 standard deviations below the mean, 2.5% are more than 1.96 standard deviations above the mean.

5. The area between $z = 0$ and $z = 2.58$ is almost exactly 0.495. Hence the area between $z = -2.58$ and $z = +2.58$ equals $0.495 + 0.495 = 0.99$, and so 99% of observed values lie in the interval 2.58 (or approximately 2.6) S.D.s below the mean to 2.58 S.D.s above.

6. It can also be seen from Appendix I that 99.75% of the distribution lies within $z = 3$ and $z = +3$, and that therefore only 0.25% lies more than 3 S.D.s from the mean.

The relative frequency of any interval of a normal distribution can be determined from the table of normal curve areas. For example, to determine the relative frequency of the interval 22 to 24 minutes illustrated in Figure 9.2, we first calculate the z-values of the interval limits: for a typing time of 22 minutes,

$$z = \frac{22 - 18.5}{5.0}$$

$$= 0.7$$

and for 24 minutes,

$$z = \frac{24 - 18.5}{5.0}$$

$$= 1.1$$

From Appendix I, the standard normal curve area between $z = 0$ and $z = 0.7$ is 0.2580, and the area between $z = 0$ and $z = 1.1$ is 0.3643. It follows that the area between $z = 0.7$ and $z = 1.1$ is $0.3643 - 0.2580 = 0.1063 \simeq 0.1$, and this is the required relative frequency. One-tenth of the typing times lie in the interval 22 to 24 minutes.

EXAMPLE

The lengths of bolts produced by a certain machine are normally distributed with a mean of 20.0 cm and a standard deviation of 0.1 cm. If 1000 bolts were selected on a random basis, how many would you estimate have lengths of: (a) between 20.0 and 20.2 cm; (b) more than 20.2 cm; (c) between 20.1 and 20.2 cm; (d) between 19.74 and 20.26 cm?

ANSWER

(a) 20.0 cm is the mean, and so corresponds to $z = 0$ in standard normal units. 20.2 cm is 2 S.D.s above the mean, and so corresponds to $z = +2$. The area between $z = 0$ and $z = 2$ is 0.4772, and this is therefore the relative frequency of the class 20.0 to 20.2 cm. The total number of bolts is 1000, and so the required frequency is

$$0.4772 \times 1000 = 477$$

(Note that the number of bolts from such a sample with lengths between 20.0 and 20.2 cm is unlikely to be exactly 477, due to the effect of sampling errors. The effect of sampling errors on estimates such as this is dealt with in the next chapter.)

(b) The area under the tail of the curve above $z = 2$ is $0.5 - 0.4772 = 0.0228$. Hence the estimated number of bolts with lengths in excess of 20.2 cm is

$$0.0228 \times 1000 = 23$$

(c) 20.1 cm is 1 S.D. above the mean, and so corresponds to $z = +1$. The area between $z = 0$ and $z = 2$ is 0.4772, the area between $z = 0$ and $z = 1$ is 0.3413, and hence the area between $z = 1$ and $z = 2$ is $0.4772 - 0.3413 = 0.1359$. Hence the number of bolts with lengths between 20.1 and 20.2 is

$$0.1359 \times 1000 = 136$$

(d) 19.74 is 2.6 S.D.s below the mean, and so corresponds to $z = -2.6$. 20.26 cm corresponds to $z = +2.6$. The area between $z = -2.6$ and $z = +2.6$ is $0.4953 + 0.4953 = 0.9906$, and so the required number of bolts is

$$0.9906 \times 1000 = 991$$

FREQUENCY CURVES AND PROBABILITY

Since relative frequencies can be used as probability estimates (see page 86), it follows that the table of normal curve areas can be used to determine the probability that an observed value from a normal distribution will lie between given limits. For example, the probability that a bolt selected at random in the above problem has a length between 19.8 and 20.2 cm is 0.4772 + 0.4772 = 0.95 approximately.

This probability estimate can be expressed in the following way: we are 95% confident that a bolt selected at random will have a length between these two limits. There is only 1 chance in 20 that this prediction will be wrong, and that the bolt selected will have a length outside these limits. If we wish to make a prediction in which we have 99% confidence (that is which has only 1 chance in 100 of being wrong), we have to select an interval under the frequency curve enclosing an area of 0.99. Such an interval is 19.74 to 20.26 cm (part (d) of the above example). This concept of 'confidence' has important implications for sampling theory, the subject of the next two chapters.

EXERCISES

1. The lifetimes of electric light bulbs produced by a certain company are found to be normally distributed with a mean of 1600 hours and a standard deviation of 100 hours.
   (a) 500 bulbs are selected at random. How many would you expect to have lifetimes:
      (i) Of between 1600 and 1650 hours
      (ii) Of between 1500 and 1700 hours
      (iii) In excess of 1800 hours
      (iv) Of between 1700 and 1800 hours.
   (b) What percentage of the bulbs produced by the company have lifetimes which are:
      (i) Less than 1300 hours
      (ii) Between 1400 and 1500 hours.
   (c) One bulb is selected at random. What is the probability that it will have a lifetime which is:
      (i) More than 1500 hours
      (ii) Less than 1750 hours
      (iii) Either less than 1340 hours or more than 1860 hours?

2. A survey of men's heights showed that the mean was 175 cm and the standard deviation was 5 cm.

   (a) Write down the relative frequency distribution using class intervals of 2.5 cm over the range 160 to 190 cm.
   (b) Construct the histogram of this relative frequency distribution and insert the frequency polygon.

3. The marks of students sitting a certain exam are found to be normally distributed with a mean of 51.5 and a standard deviation of 8.0. You are required to calculate:
   (a) The percentage of students who have failed the exam (the pass mark is 40)
   (b) The mark above which the top 5% lie
   (c) The median and the two quartiles.

Ten

Estimation

Sampling theory, the subject of this chapter and the next, is concerned with the method by which conclusions about populations can be drawn from sample data. In pursuing this subject it is necessary to distinguish between population summary measures and sample summary measures. When referring to populations, the mean, standard deviation, etc., are called the population 'parameters' and are denoted by Greek letters (μ, σ, etc.). When referring to samples, these measures are called sample 'statistics' and are denoted by English letters ($\overline{x}$, s, etc.). In this chapter we examine the estimation of population parameters from sample statistics. It should be noted that the underlying assumption throughout is that the samples are *random*.

ESTIMATORS OF μ AND σ.

In the sample of 100 letter-typing times considered in Chapter 8, the sample mean was found to be 17.9 minutes and the standard deviation was found to be 5.0 minutes. Due to the effect of sampling errors, this sample is unlikely to be absolutely representative of the population of typing times, and the population mean and standard deviation are therefore unlikely to equal exactly the sample mean and standard deviation. What conclusions, then, can we draw about these population parameters?

Our first task is to decide which of the possible sample statistics our conclusions should be based on. Should we base our estimate of the population mean upon the sample mean, or upon the sample median, for instance? Is the sample standard deviation the best measure to use as an estimator of the population standard deviation?

It is possible to show mathematically that the sample mean ($\overline{x}$) is, in fact, the best estimator of μ. Provided the sample is random, it is unbiased (that is, it is as likely to give a high estimate as a low estimate), and it is consistent (that is, it approximates more closely to μ as the sample size increases). The sample standard deviation is not, however, the best estimator of σ. To estimate σ from a sample we should sum the squared deviations of the sample values from μ and compute

$$\sqrt{\frac{\Sigma(x - \mu)^2}{n}}$$

The sample standard deviation is calculated by summing the squared deviations of the sample values from $\overline{x}$, and this sum will be less than the sum of the squared deviations from any other value, including μ. As an estimator of σ, therefore, the sample standard deviation is biased on the low side.

It can be shown that an unbiased estimate of σ is obtained by multiplying the sample standard deviation by the fraction

$$\sqrt{\frac{n}{n-1}}$$

where n is the sample size. The sample standard deviation, when adjusted by this fraction, has the formula:

$$s = \sqrt{\frac{\Sigma(x - \overline{x})^2}{n - 1}}$$

For computational purposes the following formula (derived from the above by expanding the squared bracketed term and manipulating the summations) is more convenient:

$$s = \sqrt{\frac{\Sigma x^2}{n-1} - \frac{(\Sigma x)^2}{n(n-1)}}$$

Provided n is sufficiently large (30 or more), the fraction $\sqrt{\dfrac{n}{n-1}}$ is very nearly equal to 1, and the difference between s and the ordinary standard deviation is negligible. For small samples, however, s should be used as the estimator of σ.

THE STANDARD ERROR OF THE MEAN

Having determined that the sample statistics $\overline{x}$ and s are the best estimators of μ and σ, we can now proceed to a consideration of the estimation procedure. $\overline{x}$ and s are, of course, subject to sampling errors, and so it is impossible to derive exact values for μ and σ from them. With regard to σ these errors are usually of little significance, but any error in the estimate of μ can be important. For example, an error of 5% in the mean weight of a product sold in 450 g jars could seriously affect the manufacturer's profits — he might be supplying on average 472 g instead of 452 g. But an error of 5% in the standard deviation is of no consequence — it does not matter if the standard deviation in this case is 0.63 g instead of 0.60 g.

It is usually not necessary, therefore, to indicate the effect of sampling errors on the estimate for σ. It is sufficient simply to quote as the estimate the sample statistic s. A simple estimate of this sort, lacking any indication of the errors inherent in it, is called a 'point estimate'. With regard to μ, however, a point

estimate is usually insufficient, and it is necessary to indicate the size of the errors by specifying a range of values within which μ lies with a given probability. Such an estimate is called an 'interval estimate'.

To construct an interval estimate for μ the first step is to determine the effect of sampling errors on the estimator $\overline{x}$, and this is done by calculating the 'standard error of the mean'. To explain the meaning of this term, let us return to the typing times example and suppose that the population parameters μ and σ are 18.5 and 5.0 minutes respectively (that is to say, if every letter typed during the period of the survey were timed, the population mean would be 18.5 and the population standard deviation would be 5.0 minutes).

The sample of 100 times given in Chapter 8 had a mean of 17.9 minutes. If a different sample of size 100 had been taken, this might have had a mean of 19.0 minutes, and a third sample of size 100 might have had a mean of 18.4. If we carried on taking samples of size 100, we would find that the sample means would all lie within about 1.5 minutes of the population mean. We could then construct a frequency distribution of these sample means — this is called a 'sampling distribution of means' — and we would find that this was a normal distribution with mean equal to μ (18.5 minutes) and standard deviation equal to the population standard deviation divided by the square root of the sample size

$$\text{i.e.} \frac{\sigma}{\sqrt{n}} = \frac{5.0}{\sqrt{100}}$$
$$= 0.5$$

If a frequency curve of this sampling distribution were constructed, it would be as shown in Figure 10.1. (The way in which a sampling distribution of this sort could be constructed in the class room is indicated in Appendix IV, assignment C2 (page 199).)

The standard deviation of this sampling distribution is called the 'standard error (of the mean)'. The formula for it given above involves the population standard deviation,

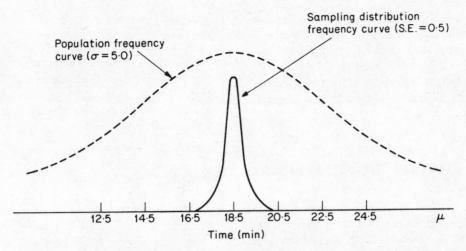

Population frequency
curve ($\sigma = 5.0$)

Sampling distribution
frequency curve (S.E. = 0.5)

| 12.5 | 14.5 | 16.5 | 18.5 | 20.5 | 22.5 | 24.5 | μ |

Time (min)

Figure 10.1 Sampling distribution of means — samples of size 100 of letter-typing times

but since this is usually unknown it is necessary to replace it by its estimator, the sample statistic s. The formula is then:

$$\text{S.E.} = \frac{s}{\sqrt{n}}$$

(The error resulting from the use of s instead of σ in this formula is negligible.)

These facts about sampling distributions are embodied in one of the most important theorems of mathematics, the central limit theorem. A further important result of this theorem is that these facts (including the fact that the sampling distribution is normal) hold even if the population frequency distribution is not normal, provided that the sample size n is sufficiently large (that is, greater than 30). This means that we can take a sample (of size greater than 30) from *any* population and apply the estimation methods described in this and the following section. (The proof of the central limit theorem lies outside the scope of this text.)

INTERVAL ESTIMATES FOR μ

Having determined that the sample mean $\overline{x}$ is the best estimator of μ, and having seen how the effect of sampling errors on $\overline{x}$ can be quantified by calculating the standard error,

the final step is to derive an interval estimate for μ.

The sampling distribution of means is normal, and so the table of normal curve areas (Appendix I) can be applied to it. From this table it can be seen that 95% of the area under a normal curve lies within the interval 1.96 standard deviations below the mean to 1.96 standard deviations above the mean. It follows that in a sampling distribution 95% of sample means lie within 1.96 standard errors of the population mean — or, equivalently, that the population mean has a probability of 0.95 of lying within 1.96 standard errors of the sample mean. In other words, we are 95% confident that μ lies in the interval 1.96 standard errors below $\overline{x}$ to 1.96 standard errors above $\overline{x}$.

This is called the '95% confidence interval', and its limits ($\overline{x} - 1.96$ S.E. and $\overline{x} + 1.96$ S.E.) are called the '95% confidence limits'. For our sample of 100 typing times, $\overline{x} = 17.9$, S.E. = 0.5, and so the 95% confidence interval for μ is $17.9 - 1.96 \times 0.5$ to $17.9 + 1.96 \times 0.5$, that is, 16.92 to 18.88 minutes.

Interval estimates for any specified level of confidence can be determined from the table of normal curve areas. For example, to obtain the 99% confidence limits, we must take 2.58 standard errors (since the standard normal interval $z = -2.58$ to

$z = +2.58$ encloses 99% of the normal curve area). In the case of the typing times sample, these limits are $17.9 - 2.58 \times 0.5$ and $17.9 + 2.58 \times 0.5$, that is, 16.61 and 19.19 minutes. We are therefore 99% confident that μ lies somewhere in the interval 16.61 to 19.19 minutes.

SMALL SAMPLES: THE t-DISTRIBUTION

The distribution of sample means is normal only if the sample size is greater than 30. The distribution of means of samples of size less than 30 is flatter than the normal distribution, the flatness becoming more pronounced as the sample size decreases, and it has higher tails. It is known as the t-distribution. As a result of its shape, the 95% confidence limits are more than 1.96 standard errors removed from the mean, the 99% confidence limits are more than 2.58 standard errors from the mean, and so on for other confidence limits. It is therefore necessary, when estimating the 95% or 99% confidence limits for μ, to multiply the standard error not by 1.96 or 2.58 but by larger numbers. These numbers, or t-values, are given in Appendix II (page 194). Like Appendix I, the areas quoted lie between the mean and the given value above the mean. In order to use the table the number of 'degrees of freedom' has to be determined. As the following reasoning shows, this number is simply the sample size minus 1.

In selecting a sample of size n from a population there are n degrees of freedom — there are no restraints on the values that the n observations can take. However, in order to calculate the standard error, we need to introduce the restraint that the sample statistic s is equal to the population standard deviation. This reduces the number of degrees of freedom by 1, since, once the first $n-1$ items in the sample are chosen, there is only one value that the nth item can take for s to equal σ. Hence the number of degrees of freedom is $n-1$.

EXAMPLE

A random sample of 16 light bulbs produced by a certain process is selected, and $\overline{x}$ and s are found to be 1450 hours and 80 hours respectively. Estimate the population mean at: (a) the 95% confidence level; and (b) the 99% confidence level.

ANSWER

$$\text{Standard error} = \frac{s}{\sqrt{n}} = \frac{80}{\sqrt{16}}$$

$$= 20 \text{ hours}$$

$$\text{Number of degrees of freedom} = 16 - 1$$

$$= 15$$

(a) Area between the mean ($t = 0$) and $t = 2.131$ is 0.475, and so the 95% confidence limits are $2.131 \times 20 \simeq 43$ hours below and above $\overline{x}$. Hence we are 95% confident that μ lies in the interval 1407 to 1493 hours.

(b) Area between $t = 0$ and $t = 2.947$ is 0.495, and so the 99% confidence limits are $2.947 \times 20 \simeq 59$ hours below and above $\overline{x}$. Hence the 99% confidence interval for μ is 1391 to 1509 hours.

ESTIMATION OF POPULATION PROPORTIONS

Samples are frequently taken with the object of determining the proportions that certain groups form of a total population. Examples are the proportion of people who intend to vote for a certain party, or the proportion of total production which is defective. The sample proportion (denoted by p) is the best estimator of the population proportion (denoted by the Greek letter π). The procedure for estimating confidence limits for π is similar to the procedure outlined above for μ.

Suppose that 20% of the population

watched a certain television programme. Then

$$\pi = \frac{20}{100}$$

$$= 0.2$$

This proportion will not, of course, be known, and it will have to be estimated by selecting a sample from the population. Due to the effect of sampling errors, it is unlikely that the sample proportion p will exactly equal π — it might, for example, equal 0.215. A second sample of the same size might give $p = 0.192$, and a third sample of the same size might give $p = 0.199$. The values of p from successive samples form what is known as a binomial distribution. The properties of the binomial distribution are examined in Chapter 18; it is sufficient to note here that if p is not too small or too large, and if the sample size n is sufficiently large,* then this distribution approximates to the normal distribution with mean equal to π and standard error equal to

$$\sqrt{\frac{\pi(1-\pi)}{n}}$$

π will usually be unknown, and so an estimate of the standard error must be obtained by using p instead of π:

$$\text{S.E.} = \sqrt{\frac{p(1-p)}{n}}$$

It is conventional to denote the term $(1-p)$ by q, and so

$$\text{S.E.} = \sqrt{\frac{pq}{n}}$$

This fact means that we can use the table of normal curve areas to estimate population proportions from sample data.

EXAMPLE

Programmes A, B, and C were broadcast at a certain time. Out of a random sample of

*The distribution of p is approximately normal if $np \geqslant 5$, provided that $p \leqslant q$. If $p > q$, then nq must be greater than or equal to 5.

400 people, 80 watched A, 40 watched B, and 4 watched C. Estimate the population proportions at the 95% confidence level.

ANSWER

For programme A, $p = \frac{80}{400} = 0.2$, $q = 1 - p = 0.8$, hence

$$\text{S.E.} = \sqrt{\frac{pq}{n}}$$

$$= \sqrt{\frac{0.2 \times 0.8}{400}}$$

$$= \frac{0.4}{20}$$

$$= 0.02$$

From the table of normal curve areas, the 95% confidence limits lie 1.96 standard errors ($\simeq 0.04$) below and above p. Hence the 95% confidence interval for π is $0.2 - 0.04$ to $0.2 + 0.04$, that is, 0.16 to 0.24. So we are 95% confident that between 16% and 24% of the population watched programme A.

For programme B, $p = \frac{40}{400} = 0.1$, $q = 1 - p = 0.9$, hence

$$\text{S.E.} = \sqrt{\frac{0.1 \times 0.9}{400}}$$

$$= \frac{0.3}{20}$$

$$= 0.015$$

The 95% confidence limits for π lie $1.96 \times 0.015 \simeq 0.03$ below and above p, that is, they are 0.07 and 0.13. So at 95% confidence, between 7% and 13% watched programme B.

For programme C, $np < 5$, so the normal approximation to the binomial distribution cannot be used. The Poisson distribution, dealt with in Chapter 18, can be applied in this case.

Although the sample size in the above example is reasonably large, the calculated confidence interval is very wide. This is because sampling errors have a greater effect on proportions than on means. Large samples are therefore usually taken when it is required to estimate proportions, and the use of small sample theory is rarely needed when dealing with proportions.

EXERCISES

1. (a) The lengths of 100 randomly selected components produced by a certain process are measured, and $\bar{x}$ and s found to be 4.108 and 0.020 cm respectively. Estimate the population mean at (i) the 95% and (ii) the 99% level of confidence.
    (b) The process is adjusted, and a further random sample of 10 components is selected. The lengths, in cm, are found to be as follows: 4.14, 4.12, 4.09, 4.10, 4.14, 4.13, 4.08, 4.13, 4.12, 4.13.
    Compute $\bar{x}$ and s using the method of assumed means, and estimate the population mean at (i) the 95% and (ii) the 99% level of confidence.

2. For each of the following examples, estimate the population mean at the 95% level of confidence:
    (a) Sample of 400 bolt lengths, $\bar{x} = 24.97$ cm, $s = 0.10$ cm
    (b) Sample of 64 weights of tins, $\bar{x} = 16.02$ oz, $s = 0.16$ oz
    (c) Sample of 16 I.Q.s of students $\bar{x} =$

114, $s = 4$
    (d) Sample of 9 lettuce prices, $\bar{x} = 9$p, $s = 1.5$ p.

3. For each of the following examples, estimate the population proportion at the 99% level of confidence:
    (a) Sample of 500 voters, 46% intend to vote Labour
    (b) Sample of 700 workers, 180 come home to a mid-day meal
    (c) Sample of 40 bottles of home-made wine, 14 are undrinkable.

4. One hundred invoices are selected at random from a file and analysed. It is found that (i) the mean value of an invoice is £36.80 with a standard deviation of £8.50; and (ii) 10 of the invoices contain an error.
    (a) Estimate the population mean from (i) and the population proportion from (ii) at the 99.75% level of confidence.
    (b) The accountant is satisfied with a confidence level of 99.75%, but he considers the confidence intervals quoted in the answer to (a) to be too wide. What size sample must be taken if it is required to reduce the width of the confidence interval for the population mean to £1.00? What size sample must be taken if it is required to reduce the width of the confidence interval for the population proportion to 0.06?

Eleven

Significance Tests

In this second chapter on sampling theory we turn from the problem of estimating unknown population parameters from sample statistics to the related problem of determining whether or not data found by sampling from an unknown population allows us to hold a given belief (or 'hypothesis') about that population.

TESTING A HYPOTHESIS ABOUT A POPULATION MEAN

The example used in this section is of an automatic machine which has been set up to produce steel bolts of mean length 20.00 cm and standard deviation 0.10 cm. To check the machine's performance a sample of 100 bolts is taken each day and the lengths measured. If the mean length of one such sample happens to be 19.00 cm then it will be apparent that our belief that the machine is producing bolts of mean length 20.00 cm can no longer be held: clearly a fault has developed, and the machine must be stopped and the fault rectified.

But suppose that the mean length of the sample is 19.978 cm. Are we in this case justified in abandoning the above belief? The sample mean is, after all, only 0.022 cm from the believed population mean, and sampling errors could be the cause of this.

To answer this question we adopt the method used in science for testing hypotheses.

We assert the 'null hypothesis', that is we assume that the population mean has not altered, but is in fact the value we believe it to be. We then deduce what the experimental results (that is, the sample mean) should be. If the observed results are consistent with these expected results, then our case for accepting the null hypothesis is strengthened (but not proved), and we have no grounds for rejecting it. If, however, there is an appreciable discrepancy between the observed results and the expected results, then the null hypothesis is unlikely to be correct, and we are justified in rejecting it.

The null hypothesis in this example is that the mean length of bolts produced by the machine has not altered but is still 20.00 cm. We must now determine by how much the observed results (that is, the actual sample mean) can differ from this value before we reject the explanation that sampling errors are the sole cause and instead reject the null hypothesis. In determining this, the risk of accepting the null hypothesis when it is false has to be balanced against the risk of rejecting it when it is true, and in balancing these risks each case must be judged on its merits. If, in this example, the act of stopping and adjusting the machine causes expensive delays elsewhere in the plant, then we need to be very confident that sampling errors are not the cause of the difference between the observed sample mean and the believed population mean. We might then decide that we shall reject the null hypothesis only if the probability that sampling errors are the sole cause is as low as 0.01. If the discrepancy is so large that this probability is, in fact, only 0.01, then the difference is said to be 'significant at the 0.01 (or 1%) level'.

If, however, subsequent stages of the production process make it imperative that the mean bolt length is very close to 20.00 cm, then we are less willing to take the risk of accepting the null hypothesis when it is false. We shall then be prepared to reject the null hypothesis if the above probability is more than 0.01, and the figure we might decide upon is 0.05. In this case we shall be testing the null hypothesis at the 0.05 (or 5%) significance level.

To carry out the test we use the table of normal curve areas (see Appendix I, page 193). (For small samples the *t*-distribution must be used — see page 102.) On the assumption that the null hypothesis is true, it can be seen from the table that the probability that a sample mean differs by more than 2.58 standard errors from the population mean is 0.01 (since 1% of the area lies under the two tails of the normal curve below $z = -2.58$ and above $z = +2.58$). Hence, if we are testing at the 1% significance level, the critical number of standard errors is 2.58. If the difference between the observed sample mean and the believed population mean exceeds this, then we reject the null hypothesis.

The probability that a sample mean differs by more than 1.96 S.E.s from the population mean is 0.05 (since 5% of the area lies under the tails of the curve below $z = -1.96$ and above $z = +1.96$). Hence, if we are testing at the 5% significance level, the critical number of standard errors is 1.96. If the difference between the observed sample mean and the believed population mean exceeds this, then we reject the null hypothesis. The 5% and 1% significance levels are commonly used in hypothesis testing, and are equivalent to the 95% and 99% confidence levels used in estimating.

In the bolt length example the null hypothesis is that the population mean has not altered from 20.00 cm, and for samples of size 100 the standard error is $\frac{\sigma}{\sqrt{n}} = \frac{0.1}{\sqrt{100}} =$ 0.01 cm. The difference between the sample mean and the believed population mean is 0.022 cm, that is, 2.2 S.E.s. If we are testing at the 5% significance level, then this *exceeds* the critical number of standard errors (1.96). The probability that this difference is caused solely by sampling errors is therefore unacceptably low, and we *reject* the null hypothesis. The conclusion is that the population mean is not 20.00 cm, and the machine must therefore be shut down and the fault recified.

If we are testing at the 1% level, however, then the difference between the observed sample mean and the believed mean is *less than* the critical number of standard errors (2.58). We are not therefore prepared to rule out sampling errors as the sole cause, and we therefore *accept* the null hypothesis.

ONE-TAILED TESTS

The above test is called a two-tailed test, because in determining the critical number of standard errors the probabilities are apportioned to both tails of the normal curve. A two-tailed test is used when the null hypothesis ignores the direction of the difference between the sample mean and the believed population mean, so that it will be rejected if $\overline{x}$ is significantly less than *or* significantly greater than μ. If, however, the null hypothesis is such that it will be rejected only if $\overline{x}$ is significantly less than μ (as in the following example), or if it is such that it will be rejected only if $\overline{x}$ is significantly greater than μ (as in question 3, page 114), then a one-tailed test must be applied. In this the critical number of standard errors is determined by setting the probability equal to the area under just one tail of the normal curve.

To illustrate one-tailed tests we return to

the letter-typing times example used in previous chapters, for which μ = 18.5 minutes and σ = 5.0 minutes. Suppose that new procedures are proposed, such as modifications in the letter layout and the use of continuous stationery, which it is claimed will reduce the typing times. The procedures are adopted, and a random sample of 100 typing times is subsequently taken. If the sample mean is found to be 17.7 minutes, can the claim that the new procedures reduce the typing times be accepted?

The null hypothesis in this example is that the new procedures have not reduced the typing times, that is, the population mean has not decreased from its original value of 18.5. We are concerned only with values of $\overline{x}$ which are smaller than μ, for if $\overline{x}$ were larger than μ we should automatically accept the null hypothesis. (In question 3b, the null hypothesis is that the mean has not increased; in this case we are concerned only with values of $\overline{x}$ which are larger than μ.)

Having stated the null hypothesis we must now determine how far $\overline{x}$ must lie below μ for us to rule out the explanation that sampling errors are the sole cause and instead reject the null hypothesis. From Appendix I (page 193) the area under the tail of the normal curve below $z = -1.64$ is seen to equal $0.5 - 0.45 = 0.05$. Hence the critical number of standard errors for the one-tailed test at the 5% significance level is 1.64. (It can be similarly seen that the critical number of standard errors for this test at the 1% level is 2.33, and the critical number at the 0.1% level is 3.09.)

The standard error for a sample of 100 typing times is $5.0 / \sqrt{100} = 0.5$ minutes. The difference between the observed sample mean (17.7 minutes) and the believed population mean (18.5 minutes) is 0.8 minutes, that is $0.8/0.5 = 1.6$ standard errors. Since this does not exceed 1.64 standard errors, it follows that we cannot reject the null hypothesis at the 5% significance level. The evidence has not convinced us that the new procedures reduce typing times.

TESTING A DIFFERENCE BETWEEN TWO SAMPLE MEANS

In this section we are concerned with testing whether there is a significant difference between two sample means. The test used is based upon the fact that if the observed values of one normally distributed variable are subtracted from the observed values of another, then the resulting differences are themselves normally distributed with mean equal to the difference between the original means, and variance (standard deviation squared) equal to the sum of the two original variances. The test is similar to those already described. It involves determining whether the difference between the two sample means $\overline{x}_1$ and $\overline{x}_2$ exceeds the critical number of standard errors, the standard error in this case being the standard error of the difference between the sample means. These differences are normally distributed, and the formula for the standard error is

$$\text{S.E.}_{\text{diff}} = \sqrt{(\text{S.E.}_1)^2 + (\text{S.E.}_2)^2}$$

where S.E._1 denotes the standard error of the first sample mean and S.E._2 denotes the standard error of the second sample mean.

Consider the following example. In a certain college the 36 female students sitting an exam achieve a mean mark of 56.1 with a standard deviation of 9.0, and the 49 male students sitting the exam achieve a mean mark of 52.5 with a standard deviation of 9.1. Can we conclude that male and female students perform differently at this exam?

The null hypothesis is that males and females perform equally well at this exam. It does not specify the direction of the difference between the two sample means, and so we apply a two-tailed test.

$$\text{S.E.}_1 = \frac{9.0}{\sqrt{36}}$$

$$= 1.5$$

$$\text{S.E.}_2 = \frac{9.1}{\sqrt{49}}$$

$$= 1.3$$

and so

$$\text{S.E.}_{\text{diff}} = \sqrt{(1.5^2 + 1.3^2)}$$

$$\simeq 2.0$$

The observed difference is $\overline{x}_1 - \overline{x}_2 = 56.1 - 52.5 = 3.6$, i.e. $3.6/2.0 = 1.8$ standard errors. This is not significant at the 5% level (for which the critical number of standard errors is 1.96), nor indeed at the 1% level, so if we are testing at these levels we should accept the null hypothesis. We must attribute the difference between the mean performance of this sample of females and this sample of males to sampling errors. We cannot conclude, on the evidence available, that males and females perform differently at this exam.

If we are required to test whether female students do *better* at this exam than male students, then the null hypothesis is that female students do not do better than male students. We are then concerned with the direction of the difference between the two sample means (for if the mean mark for the male students exceeded the mean for the female students, we should automatically accept the null hypothesis) and we therefore apply a one-tailed test. If we are testing at the 5% level, the critical number of standard errors is 1.64. The observed difference exceeds this, and so we reject the null hypothesis and conclude that female students do in fact do better than male students at this exam.

TESTS ON SMALL SAMPLES AND TESTS ON PROPORTIONS

Tests involving the means of samples of size less than 30 are identical to the above tests, except that the *t*-distribution given in Appendix II (page 194) must be used instead of the standard normal distribution. The use of this distribution is described in Chapter 10.

Tests involving sample proportions are also identical to the above, with the proviso that the table of normal curve areas can only be applied if $np > 5$ when $p \leqslant 0.5$ (or $nq > 5$ when $q < 0.5$). If this condition is not fulfilled, then the binomial or Poisson distributions described in Chapter 18 must be used.

EXAMPLE

Prior to an advertising campaign, 35% of a sample of 400 housewives used a certain product. After the campaign, 40% of a second sample of 400 housewives used the product. Did the campaign increase sales? Test at the 1% significance level.

ANSWER

The null hypothesis is that sales have not increased, and so we are concerned with the direction of the difference. A one-tailed test must therefore be applied, and for this the critical number of standard errors at the 1% level is 2.33. The standard errors of the two sample proportions are

$$\sqrt{\frac{0.35 \times 0.65}{400}} \text{ and } \sqrt{\frac{0.4 \times 0.6}{400}}$$

and so

$$\text{S.E.}_{\text{diff}} = \sqrt{\frac{0.35 \times 0.65}{400} + \frac{0.4 \times 0.6}{400}}$$

$$= 0.034.$$

The difference between the second sample proportion and the first sample proportion is $0.40 - 0.35 = 0.05$, i.e. $0.05/0.034 = 1.47$ standard errors. This is less than the critical number, and so we must accept the null hypothesis — we cannot conclude that the campaign has increased sales.

STATISTICAL QUALITY CONTROL

Statistical quality control involves sampling the output of a process and applying the technique described above to ensure that the quality conforms to specified standards. In the bolt-length example described earlier, variations can occur in both the mean length of bolts coming off the machine and in the standard deviation, and in both cases the result can be an increase in the number of bolts lying outside the specified quality limits. It is therefore necessary to check both the mean and the standard deviation of the output by sampling at regular intervals.

To simplify quality control work and to provide a visual indication of quality variations, the sample statistics are plotted on quality control charts. The quality of output from a production process often deteriorates progressively, and one important advantage of using control charts is that this progressive deterioration is made quickly apparent by the consistent trend of the plotted points.

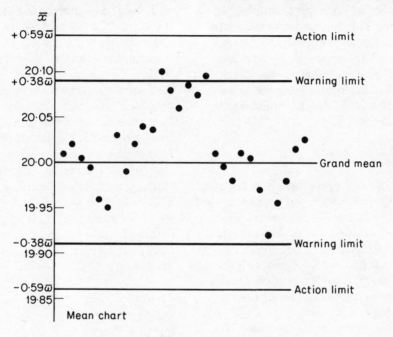

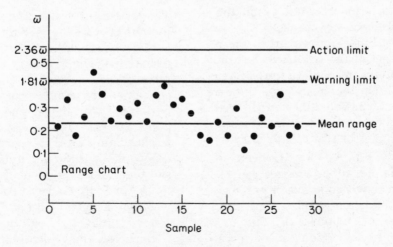

Figure 11.1   Mean and range charts

The calculations are simplified by using the range instead of the standard deviation to measure the dispersion of the sample values. There is a close connexion between the range and the standard deviation — almost all the values of a normal distribution lie within the range $\bar{x} - 3$ S.D. to $\bar{x} + 3$ S.D. The range suffers from the disadvantage that it fluctuates widely from one sample to the next, and to reduce the effect of these fluctuations it is necessary to take, not one large sample, but 10 or more small samples, and calculate from these the mean range. When divided by a conversion factor the mean range provides an estimate of the population standard deviation. It is often found convenient to take samples of size 5, and for these the conversion factor is 2.33:

$$\sigma = \frac{\text{mean range}}{2.33}$$

The quality control procedure is as follows. At regular intervals a number of small samples (we shall assume of size 5) are taken. The mean $(\bar{x})$ and the range (w) of each sample are calculated and plotted on the mean control chart and the range control chart (Figure 11.1), and the grand mean $(\bar{\bar{x}})$ and the mean range $(\bar{w})$ are determined. If a point lies outside the 'warning limits' then a look-out is kept for possible faults in the process. If a point lies outside the 'action limits' then there is a strong indication of trouble and the process must be carefully checked.

The warning limits correspond to the 5% significance level of the two-tailed test, and the action limits correspond to the 0.2% significance level. On the mean chart they are therefore set at 1.96 and 3.09 standard errors respectively above and below the process mean. For samples of size 5, 1.96 S.E. = $0.38\bar{w}$, and 3.09 S.E. = $0.59\bar{w}$. (Conversion factors for samples of other sizes can be obtained from conversion tables.) In the case of the range chart, the warning limit is at $1.81\bar{w}$, and the action limit is at $2.36\bar{w}$. Since the warning and action limits are based upon sample data, they will not be known

accurately until a number of samples have been taken.

Figure 11.1 shows hypothetical control charts for the bolt-length example. It is assumed that the process mean is 20.00 cm and the standard deviation is 0.10 cm. For samples of size 5 the expected value of $\bar{w}$ is 2.33 σ = 2.33 × 0.1 = 0.233. The warning limits on the mean chart are therefore at 20.00 ± 0.38 × 0.233, i.e. 19.91 and 20.09, and the action limits are at 20.00 ± 0.59 × 0.233, i.e. 19.86 and 20.14. For the range chart the warning limit is at 1.81 × 0.233 = 0.42, and the action limit is at 2.36 × 0.233 = 0.55.

If quality control of a process involves checking that the proportion of defective items lies within given limits, then a 'number defective control chart' must be constructed. In this case the standard error of the proportion of defectives is determined, and the warning and action limits set at 1.96 and 3.09 S.Es from the process proportions. For this test, single large samples must be taken (otherwise the standard errors are uselessly large) and the sample proportions plotted on the chart.

THE CHI SQUARED TEST (1): GOODNESS OF FIT TESTS

The tests dealt with so far are called 'parametric', because they test hypotheses involving parameters (means, proportions, and standard deviations). The χ^2 test (χ is the Greek letter pronounced 'ky') is non-parametric. It is concerned not with the parameters of a distribution but with the frequencies of the component classes. The procedure in this test is to calculate what the expected frequencies (E) would be if the null hypothesis were true, and then to use the table of the χ^2 distribution (Appendix II, page 194) to determine whether or not the observed frequencies (O) differ significantly from these expected frequencies. The value of chi squared is calculated using the formula

$$\chi^2 = \Sigma \frac{(O-E)^2}{E}$$

It should be noted that the χ^2 test can only be applied to frequencies. It is not valid for percentages, relative frequencies, proportions, or other derived numbers. In addition, no more than one in five expected frequencies should have a value less than 5. (Ideally, none of the expected frequencies should be this low. If necessary, classes should be combined so that expected frequencies of

Table 11.1 Calculations for the goodness of fit test

(1)	(2)	(3)	(4)	(5)	(6)
Class (x-values)	Class (z-values)	Relative frequency (=area)	Expected frequency (E)	Observed frequency (O)	$\frac{(O-E)^2}{E}$
4 and under 7	→ − 2.18	0.5000 −0.4854 / 0.0146	5.71	5	0.0883
7 and under 10	−2.18 to −1.58	0.4854 −0.4429 / 0.0425			
10 and under 13	−1.58 to −0.98	0.4429 −0.3365 / 0.1064	10.64	12	0.1738
13 and under 16	−0.98 to −0.38	0.3365 −0.1480 / 0.1885	18.85	20	0.0702
16 and under 19	−0.38 to +0.22	0.1480 +0.0871 / 0.2351	23.51	23	0.0111
19 and under 22	+0.22 to +0.82	0.2939 −0.0871 / 0.2068	20.68	18	0.3473
22 and under 25	+0.82 to +1.42	0.4222 −0.2939 / 0.1283	12.83	13	0.0023
25 and under 28	+1.42 to +2.02	0.4783 −0.4222 / 0.0561	7.78	9	0.1913
28 and under 31	+2.02 →	0.5000 −0.4783 / 0.0217			
					0.8843

5 or more are obtained, as has been done in Table 11.1.)

In this section we deal with 'goodness of fit' tests, that is tests which determine whether an observed frequency distribution can be adequately described by a theoretical distribution such as the normal distribution. By way of example we test the assumption made in previous chapters that the frequency distribution of 100 typing times given in Table 8.3 came from a population of typing times which was normally distributed. The calculations required for this test are set out in Table 11.1, the explanation of which is given below.

The expected frequency distribution for the sample of 100 typing times is calculated on the assumption that the null hypothesis is true (that the times are normally distributed with the same mean and standard deviation as was calculated in Table 8.3: $\mu = 17.9$ and $\sigma = 5.0$). The class limits (column 1) are first transformed to standard normal z-values (column 2 — note that the lowest and highest z-values extend to the extremities of the distributions), and then the relative frequencies of the classes are determined by reference to the table of normal curve areas (column 3). The expected frequencies (column 4) are calculated by multiplying the relative frequencies by the total frequency (100).

The observed frequencies are now inserted alongside the expected frequencies (column 5), and the fraction

$$\frac{(O-E)^2}{E}$$

is calculated for each class (column 6). For the combined class '4 and under 10', for example

$$\frac{(O-E)^2}{E}$$

$$= \frac{(5-5.71)^2}{5.44}$$

$$= 0.0883$$

Finally,

$$\chi^2 = \Sigma \frac{(O-E)^2}{E}$$

is determined by summing all the figures in column 6, the answer in this case being 0.8843.

Clearly the larger the value of χ^2, the greater the difference between the expected and the observed frequencies, and the greater the justification for rejecting the null hypothesis. The question is, what is the critical value of χ^2 below which we decide to accept the null hypothesis and above which we decide to reject that hypothesis?

Appendix II (page 194) gives the critical values at the 5% and 1% significance levels. In order to use this table it is necessary to determine the number of degrees of freedom (df), and this is done by subtracting the number of restraints from the number of classes. In the above example there are 3 restraints: (i) the mean of the expected distribution must equal 17.9; (ii) the standard deviation must equal 5.0; and (iii) the total frequency must equal 100. There are 7 classes, and there are therefore $7 - 3 = 4$ degrees of freedom.

As can be seen from Appendix II, to be significant at the 5% level, the value of χ^2 with 4 degrees of freedom must exceed 9.49. The value of χ^2 calculated in Table 11.1 is less than this, and hence the observed frequency distribution does not differ significantly at the 5% level from the expected frequency distribution. Hence we can accept the null hypothesis that the distribution of typing times is normal.

THE CHI SQUARED TEST (2): CONTINGENCY TESTS

The χ^2 test can be used to determine whether the possession of one attribute (or characteristic) is related to, or 'contingent upon', another. The procedure is to list the observed frequencies in a contingency table, compare these with the frequencies which would be expected if the null hypothesis (that no relationship exists) were true, and compute χ^2 as for the goodness of fit test.

This type of test can be used to determine, for instance, whether age or sex affects consumer preferences for certain goods, whether absenteeism is related to size of firm or type of occupation, and so on. In the following example the χ^2 test is used to determine whether or not the number of accidents in a large factory is related to the age of the worker.

Suppose that there are 1000 men in the factory, and that over a certain year 880 have no accidents, 80 have 1 accident, and 40 have 2 or more accidents. Of the workers with no accidents, 240 are under 25 years of age, 250

are 25 to under 35, and so on — the classification of the three groups of workers by age is given in Table 11.2. To calculate χ^2 for this data a contingency table is drawn up, as shown in Table 11.2, the explanation of which is as follows.

The proportion of the workforce which has no accidents is 880/1000 = 0.88, and if we accept the null hypothesis that no relationship exists between age of worker and number of accidents, then we would expect 0.88 of each age-group to have 0 accidents. There are in total 315 workers in the class 'under 25', and we would expect 315 × 0.88 = 277.2 of these to have 0 accidents. Similarly, the expected number with 0 accidents in the class '25 to under 35' is 276 × 0.88 = 242.9, the expected frequency in the class '35 to under 50' is 211 × 0.88 = 185.7, and the expected frequency in the class '50 to under 65' is 198 × 0.88 = 174.2.

The proportion of the workforce which has 1 accident is 80/1000 = 0.08, and hence the expected frequency in the class 'under 25' with 1 accident is 315 × 0.08 = 25.2. The expected frequencies in the other classes are calculated similarly and inserted in the appropriate spaces, or 'cells' in the table. $\frac{(O-E)^2}{E}$ is now calculated for each cell, and

Table 11.2   Number of accidents in a factory

AGE OF WORKER	NUMBER OF ACCIDENTS		
	0	1	2 *or more*
Under 25	240	50	25
25 to under 35	250	19	7
35 to under 50	200	6	5
50 to under 65	190	5	3
Total	880	80	40

Table 11.3   Contingency table

AGE OF WORKER	NUMBER OF ACCIDENTS						TOTAL
	0		1		2 *or more*		
	O	*E*	*O*	*E*	*O*	*E*	
Under 25	240	277.2 (4.99)	50	25.2 (24.41)	25	12.6 (12.20)	315
25 to under 35	250	242.9 (0.21)	19	22.1 (0.43)	7	11.0 (1.48)	276
35 to under 50	200	185.7 (1.10)	6	16.9 (7.03)	5	8.4 (1.40)	211
50 to under 65	190	174.2 (1.43)	5	15.8 (7.44)	3	7.9 (3.06)	198
Total	880		80		40		1000

χ^2 = 4.99 + 0.21 + 1.10 + . . . + 3.06 = 65.18

the results inserted in brackets as shown. To obtain $\chi^2 = \Sigma\dfrac{(O - E)^2}{E}$ these bracketed numbers are added, the result being 65.18.

The number of degrees of freedom in a contingency table is the number of rows minus 1 multiplied by the number of columns minus 1 (the bottom 'total' row and the right-hand 'total' column are ignored in this calculation). In the above example the number of degrees of freedom is $(4 - 1)(3 - 1) = 6$.

The reason why this gives the number of degrees of freedom is that each column has one restraint (namely that the E-values must add up to the given total at the bottom), and therefore in Table 11.3 the number of degrees of freedom for each column is $4 - 1$, and each row has one restraint (the E-values must add up to the given total on the right), and therefore the number of degrees of freedom for each row is $3 - 1$. Hence the total number of degrees of freedom for the table is $(4 - 1)(3 - 1)$.

Referring to Appendix II (page 194) it can be seen that with 6 degrees of freedom $\chi^2 = 65.18$ is highly significant. We can therefore reject the null hypothesis, and conclude that the number of accidents is related to the age of the worker.

EXERCISES

1. In each of the examples below, test at the 5% significance level the null hypothesis that the population mean has not altered.

2. For the examples in question 1, test at the 1% significance level the null hypothesis that the population mean has not decreased.

3. In each of the examples opposite, test the null hypothesis that the population proportion has: (a) not altered; (b) not increased. Test at both the 5% and the 1% significance levels.

4. In each of the examples opposite, determine whether there is a significant difference between the sample proportions. Test at the 5% and the 1% significance levels.

5. Refer to the 'before change' frequency distribution of question 4 page 90. The claim is made that this sample of size 100 came from a population which was normally distributed. Test at the 1% level.

6. Over the period October 1967 to September 1973, 459 long-range regional temperature forecasts were made, 124 of which predicted below average temperatures, 173 predicted average temperatures, and 162 predicted above average temperatures. The observed temperatures were compared with the predicted temperatures, and the results are tabulated opposite. Test at the 5% significance level the null hypothesis that there is no relationship between the predicted and the observed temperatures.

Population	Believed population mean	Sample size	Sample mean	Sample S.D.(s)
(a) Lengths of bolts produced by a certain machine	10.00 cm	64	9.99	0.04
(b) Weights of tins of a brand	16.04 oz	49	16.02	0.05
(c) I.Q.s of students	115	16	111	8
(d) Prices of a certain commodity	£3.90	9	£3.80	£0.15

Examples for question 3

Population	Believed population proportion	Sample size	Sample proportion
(i) Voters' intentions	0.43 Labour	800	0.47
(ii) I.Q.s of students	0.30 greater than 120	80	0.40
(iii) Components produced by a machine	0.10 faulty	100	0.16

Examples for question 4

POPULATION	Size	FIRST SAMPLE Proportion	Size	SECOND SAMPLE Proportion
(a) Workers in a certain area	150	0.28 from area *A* come home for midday meal	300	0.38 from area *A* come home
(b) Invoices from a certain firm	100	0.10 from firm *A* have an error	100	0.20 from firm *A*
(c) Home-made wines	50	0.25 undrinkable	80	0.50 undrinkable

Temperatures for question 6

	OBSERVED TEMPERATURES			
Forecast	*Below average*	*Average*	*Above average*	*Totals*
Below Average	54	25	45	124
Average	56	61	56	173
Above Average	64	46	52	162
Totals	174	132	153	459

7. Refer to the advertising campaign example on page 108. Convert the sample percentages to numbers of housewives, construct a contingency table, and apply the χ^2 test to determine whether the sample results differ significantly at the 1% level.

Twelve

Correlation and Regression

INTRODUCTION

Our attention so far has been almost exclusively confined to the analysis of problems involving one variable — typing-times of letters produced by a typing pool, lengths of bolts produced by a machine, and so on. We must now turn to problems involving two related variables. If two variables are related, then changes in the value of one are associated with changes in the value of the other, and in this chapter we discuss the techniques used to measure this association.

Two-variable problems were introduced in Chapter 2, and it was seen there that relationships between variables can be modelled by graphs and by equations. Figure 2.1 illustrates a relationship which is very straightforward, that between the variable 'Billy's height' and the variable 'Billy's age'. Changes in one variable follow changes in the other in a very exact manner, and there is no difficulty in determining from the graph the value of Billy's height at any given age.

The situation depicted in the scattergraph in Figure 2.3 is, however, much less straightforward. There appears to be some sort of relationship between the variable 'sales' and the variable 'advertising expenditure', for increases in one tend to be accompanied by increases in the other, but it is far from being a close relationship. The plotted points are scattered about the line of best fit, and although that line indicates that a company

which spends, for example, £20,000 on advertising can anticipate sales of about £175,000, this is a prediction which is subject to some uncertainty. We should not be very surprised if a company which actually did spend this amount on advertising in fact achieved sales as low as £150,000 or as high as £200,000.

The analysis of situations of this sort is based upon the statistical theory discussed in preceding chapters. We have in this example a sample of seven companies from an industry, each with a certain annual sales and a certain annual advertising expenditure. The line of best fit can be regarded as the sample 'mean' around which the plotted points are scattered. If the points lie close to the line, the 'dispersion', or degree of scatter, is low, and it is reasonable to conclude that a close association exists between the two variables. If the points are widely dispersed about the line, then the association is weak or perhaps non-existent, and any predictions which are made will be subject to a large error.

The analysis utilizes two techniques:

1. *Correlation* — the determination of the degree of dispersion of the plotted points about the line. The technique is analogous to that used for calculating ordinary standard deviations, and the answer obtained (called the 'correlation coefficient') indicates the closeness of the association between the two variables. If no associa-

tion is indicated, then there is little point in applying the second technique — regression.

2. *Regression* — the determination of the equation of the mean line which best indicates the trend of the points. This is called the 'regression line', and it shows what the relationship between the two variables is.

These two techniques are closely connected, and the results of the correlation calculations can be used in the regression-line determination. The proof of the regression formulae is based upon the techniques of calculus discussed in Chapter 16, and the correlation formulae can be quite easily derived from the regression formulae. Owing to lack of space, proofs are not supplied in this text.

Example: selling price and takings of freehold grocery shops

The example used in this chapter is of a firm of business transfer agents (similar to estate agents) which specializes in the sale of grocery shops, and which wishes to determine what the relationship is between the selling price of freehold shops and their weekly takings. The firm has first to establish that a relationship does in fact exist between the variable 'selling price' and the variable 'weekly takings' (this is a correlation problem). If a relationship does exist (and this seems likely, for we should expect that shops with high takings sell for more than shops with low takings), then the firm has to determine what that relationship is (this is a regression problem).

The firm must first take a sample of freehold grocery shops which have recently been sold. To obtain valid results this sample must be representative of the population of recently-sold, freehold grocery shops, and so we shall suppose that a simple random sample is taken. The sample should normally be reasonably large (at least of size 30) but, in order to reduce the calculations, we shall suppose that in this case it consists of just

7 shops. The weekly takings and the selling price of each of the 7 shops is shown in Table 12.1.

Table 12.1 Weekly takings and selling prices of freehold grocery shops

Grocery shop	Weekly takings (£s) (x)	Selling price (£s) (y)
A	1000	25 400
B	550	14 900
C	500	16 000
D	800	21 800
E	1650	38 400
F	750	18 000
G	1500	28 000

'Weekly takings' is the independent variable, and it is therefore denoted by x. 'Selling price' is the dependent variable (it depends upon the takings), and so it is denoted by y. The scattergraph of y against x is shown in Figure 12.1, with the line of best fit inserted (see Chapter 2 for the method of construction).

LINEAR AND CURVILINEAR CORRELATION AND REGRESSION

The location of the scattergraph points indicates that the line of best fit should be straight rather than curved, and it follows that the relationship between the variables can be modelled by a linear regression equation (i.e. an equation of the form $y = a + bx$). If a scattergraph, when drawn, indicates that a curved line best fits a set of points, then the relationship should be modelled by a non-linear regression equation. An exponential equation may fit the data, and to determine whether this is the case the points should be plotted on semi-logarithmic graph paper. If now the points are best fitted by a straight line, the regression equation will take the form $y = ab^x$ (see Chapter 2). The procedure in this case for determining the correlation coefficient and the regression equation is

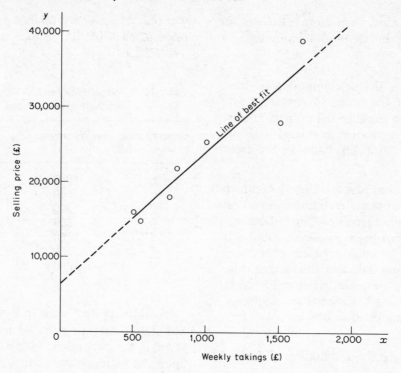

Figure 12.1   Scattergraph of selling price of grocery shops against weekly takings

identical to that described below for linear correlation and regression, except that logarithms must first be taken of the *y*-values. The method is illustrated in the answer to question 5 (page 205).

If scattergraphs plotted on natural scale and on semi-logarithmic graph paper both indicate a pronounced curvilinear (curved line) relationship between the variables, then the techniques of curvilinear correlation and regression must be applied. The mathematics is then very complex, and lies outside the scope of this course.

THE COEFFICIENT OF CORRELATION

The points of the scattergraph shown in Figure 12.1 lie fairly close to the line of best fit, and this indicates that selling price and takings are closely associated, or 'strongly correlated'. The line of best fit has a positive slope (that is

it slopes upwards from left to right, showing that an increase in the value of one variable is normally accompanied by an increase in the other), and the correlation is therefore said to be 'positive'.

Figure 12.2, in contrast, illustrates 'weak negative correlation'. The points are quite widely scattered about the line, which has a negative slope (downwards from left to right, showing that an increase in the value of one variable tends to be accompanied by a decrease in the other).

Figure 12.3 shows the scattergraph of two variables which are 'uncorrelated', that is, not associated. In this case the points exhibit no discernible trend.

To measure the strength of the association between two variables we determine the dispersion of the scattergraph points by means of the 'Pearsonian' (or 'product-moment') coefficient of correlation. This is denoted by the symbol *r*, and its formula incorporates the

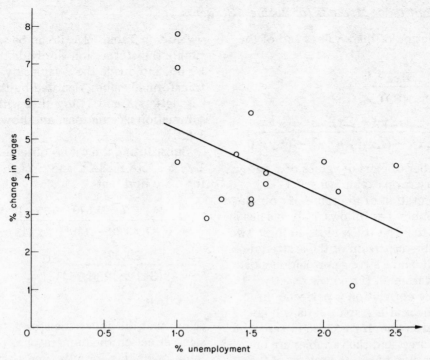

Figure 12.2 Scattergraph of percentage change in wages against percentage unemployment for the period 1952–66, illustrating weak negative correlation (r = –0.5)

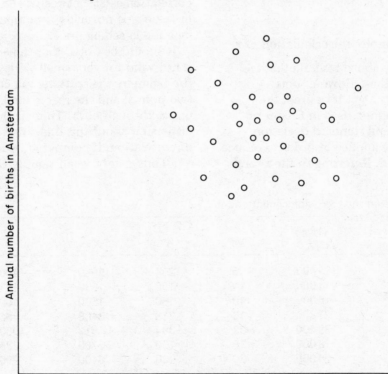

Annual number of storks flying over Amsterdam

Figure 12.3 Scattergraph illustrating zero correlation

standard deviation of the x-values and of the y-values:

$$r = \frac{n\Sigma xy - \Sigma x \Sigma y}{n^2(\text{S.D.}_x)(\text{S.D.}_y)}$$

$$= \frac{n\Sigma xy - \Sigma x \Sigma y}{\sqrt{\{(n\Sigma x^2 - (\Sigma x)^2)(n\Sigma y^2 - (\Sigma y)^2)\}}}$$

(n is the number of pairs of values of x and y; for the grocery shop example $n = 7$.)

The interpretation of the value of r obtained from this formula is as follows. r always lies in the range -1 to $+1$; if it lies close to these two values, then the dispersion of the scattergraph points is small, and a strong correlation exists **between** the variables. If r equals exactly -1 or $+1$, then the correlation is perfect — in this case all the scattergraph points will lie on the regression line. If r is close to zero, the dispersion is large, and the variables are un-correlated. A value of r in the region of 0.5 generally indicates weak correlation. The minus or plus sign indicates negative or positive correlation.

Grocery shop example: the calculation of r

It is clear from the above formula that we need to compute the following sums: Σx, Σy, Σxy, Σx^2, Σy^2. If desired, the transformation method used in Chapter 6 to simplify mean and standard deviation calculations can be applied in order to reduce the labour involved. Referring to the x- and y-values in Table 12.1, it can be seen that a simple transformation is: divide the x-values by 50, and divide the y-values by 100. The transformed values, denoted by the upper case letters X and Y, together with the summation calculations, are shown in Table 12.2.

Substituting the values obtained for ΣX, ΣY, ΣXY, ΣX^2, and ΣY^2 in the formula for r, we find that

$$r = \frac{7 \times 35{,}579 - 135 \times 1625}{\sqrt{\{(7 \times 3091 - 135^2)(7 \times 418{,}097 - 1625^2)\}}}$$

$$= \frac{29{,}678}{\sqrt{(3412 \times 286{,}054)}}$$

$$= 0.95$$

(Note that the above transformations have the same effect on the numerator as on the denominator of this formula, and they therefore have no effect on the value obtained for r.)

$r = 0.95$ indicates that a strong positive correlation exists between x and y: an increase in takings is normally accompanied by an increase in selling price.

It should be noted that the correlation test is not valid for very small values of n. If $n = 2$, for example, the scattergraph consists of just two points, and the regression line necessarily passes through both. There is therefore zero dispersion about this line, and the coefficient of correlation, if computed, would be -1 or $+1$. Thus a very small sample taken from

Table 12.2 Correlation and regression computations

Shop	Takings (x)	Price (y)	X	Y	XY	X^2	Y^2
A	1000	25 400	20	254	5080	400	64 516
B	550	14 900	11	149	1639	121	22 201
C	500	16 000	10	160	1600	100	25 600
D	800	21 800	16	218	3488	256	47 524
E	1650	38 400	33	384	12 672	1089	147 456
F	750	18 000	15	180	2700	225	32 400
G	1500	28 000	30	280	8400	900	78 400
Totals			135	1625	35579	3091	418097

uncorrelated variables will yield a high value of r. As indicated earlier, the minimum sample size should be around 30 for the test to be valid.

It should also be noted that, owing to the effect of sampling errors, the sample chosen for the correlation test may not be representative of the population. Our sample of grocery shops, for example, may exhibit a relationship between selling price and takings which does not exist in the population of recently-sold grocery shops. r is an estimator of the population coefficient of correlation, and, like other estimators of population parameters, it is subject to sampling errors. To determine whether a given value of r differs significantly from zero it is necessary to apply the t-test. The statistic

$$t = \sqrt{\frac{r^2(n-2)}{1-r^2}}$$

is calculated, and this follows the t-distribution with $n - 2$ degrees of freedom.

In the above example, $t = \sqrt{\dfrac{0.95^2(7-2)}{1-0.95^2}} =$ 6.80. Applying the two-tailed test at the 0.01 significance level, the critical value of t for 5 df is 4.03 (see Appendix II), and since the calculated value of t exceeds this it can be concluded that correlation exists in the population of recently-sold grocery shops.

It should be noted that the above significance test is valid only if the two variables x and y are normally or approximately normally distributed.

Spurious Correlation

The above correlation test does not, in itself, prove that two variables are associated. It may be a coincidence that movements in one variable tend to match movements in another, and unless there are grounds for supposing that there is some direct causal connextion between the two it is foolhardy to claim that a genuine correlation exists. For example, many attempts have been made to correlate sunspot activity with events on the earth, and a correlation has been found between sunspot activity and each of the following: car production; skirt lengths; Beatlemania; anti-war protest in America; the rabbit population; the Dow-Jones Stock Index. There is no evidence for supposing that a causal connexion exists between sunspot activity and fluctuations in any of the above, and it must therefore be concluded that the correlation is 'spurious'. In the grocery shop example, however, there is a causal connexion between takings and selling price, and so it can be concluded that the correlation is genuine.

THE REGRESSION EQUATIONS

The equation of the regression line is obtained by what is known as 'the method of least squares', so-called because the procedure involves minimizing the sum of the squared deviations (i.e. the standard deviation) of the scattergraph points from the line. These deviations can be measured in the vertical direction, in which case the standard deviation of the y-values from the line is minimized, the line obtained being 'the regression line of y on x'. Alternatively the deviations can be measured horizontally, in which case the standard deviation of the x-values from the line is minimized, a different line being obtained which is referred to as 'the regression line of x on y'.

If it is required to predict y when x is given (in our example this means predicting the selling price of a freehold grocery shop from a knowledge of its takings), then it is necessary to obtain the regression line of y on x. If, however, it is required to predict x when y is given (in our example this means predicting what takings can be expected from a grocery shop selling at a given price), then it is necessary to obtain the regression line of x on y. It is the former type of prediction which is normally required, the regression line of x on y being only rarely needed.

The formulae for obtaining the regression equations are as follows:

1. *The regression line of y on x*
   The equation of the line is $y = a + bx$, where

   $$b = \frac{n\Sigma xy - \Sigma x \Sigma y}{n\Sigma x^2 - (\Sigma x)^2}$$

   and

   $$a = \frac{\Sigma y - b\Sigma x}{n}$$

2. *The regression line of x on y*
   The xs and ys are reversed in the above formula, so that the equation of the line is $x = a + by$, where

   $$b = \frac{n\Sigma xy - \Sigma x \Sigma y}{n\Sigma y^2 - (\Sigma y)^2}$$

   and

   $$a = \frac{\Sigma x - b\Sigma y}{n}$$

Grocery shop example: the regression line of y on x

To determine the equation of the regression line of y on x (i.e. selling price on takings), it is necessary to substitute the values of ΣX, ΣY, etc. (calculated in Table 12.2) in the first regression formula given above. The numerator and denominator of b have in fact already been computed for the correlation test, and using the results of those computations we obtain

$$b = \frac{29{,}678}{3412}$$

$$= 8.698$$

$$\simeq 8.7$$

Substituting this value of b in the formula for a, we obtain

$$a = \frac{1625 - 8.698 \times 135}{7}$$

$$= 64.393 \simeq 64.4$$

The equation of the regression line is therefore

$$Y = 64.4 + 8.7X$$

To obtain the regression equation in the original units (i.e. in x and y), it is necessary to reverse the transformation by substituting $X = x/50$ and $Y = y/100$:

$$\frac{1}{100}y = 64.4 + 8.7\left(\frac{1}{50}x\right)$$

$$\therefore y \quad = 6440 + 17.4x$$

This equation can be used to predict selling price from takings. For example, if the proprietor of a freehold grocery shop with weekly takings of £900 wished to sell his business, the price he could expect to get is $y = 6440 + 17.4(900) = 6440 + 15{,}660 = $ £22,100.

Regression line of x on y

Suppose that a prospective purchaser can raise £30,000 to buy a freehold grocery shop. What weekly takings can he expect from a shop costing this amount? To predict takings from selling price (i.e. x from y) the regression line of x on y is required, and this is obtained by substituting the values of ΣX, ΣY, etc., in the second regression formula. The numerator and denominator have already been worked out (see the correlation computations), and

$$b = \frac{29{,}678}{286{,}054}$$

$$= 0.10375$$

$$\simeq 0.1$$

Substituting this in the formula for a, we obtain

$$a = \frac{135 - 0.10375 \times 1625}{7}$$

$$= -4.799$$

$$\simeq -4.8.$$

The regression equation of takings on selling price is therefore $X = -4.8 + 0.1Y$. To transform this back to the original units, substitute $X = 1/50x$ and $Y = 1/100y$:

$$\frac{1}{50}x = -4.8 + 0.1 \frac{1}{100}y$$

$$\therefore x = -240 + 0.05y$$

To estimate the weekly takings that a purchaser buying a shop for £30,000 can expect, substitute $y = 30,000$ in this equation:

$$x = -240 + 0.05(30,000)$$

$$= -240 + 1500$$

$$= £1260$$

The two regression lines are shown in Figure 12.4. They intersect at the point $(\overline{x}, \overline{y})$, that is at the mean of the x-values and the mean of the y-values. Because x and y are strongly correlated in this example, the angle between the lines is small. Were the correlation weaker, the angle would be larger. In the case of zero correlation, the angle is $90°$. In the case of perfect correlation, the angle reduces to zero (i.e. the two regression lines coincide), and all the scattergraph points lie on the one line.

UNCERTAINTY IN REGRESSION

Unless two variables are perfectly correlated, predictions obtained from regression equations are always subject to uncertainty, and if the correlation is weak the degree of uncertainty may be large. For example, in the previous section we made the prediction that by spending £30,000 a purchaser would obtain a shop with weekly takings of £1260. However, he may choose to buy a shop of this price, with takings below this figure, but which is pleasantly situated with superior living accommodation over and a large garden at the rear. Or he may buy a shop with takings higher than this figure, but which is

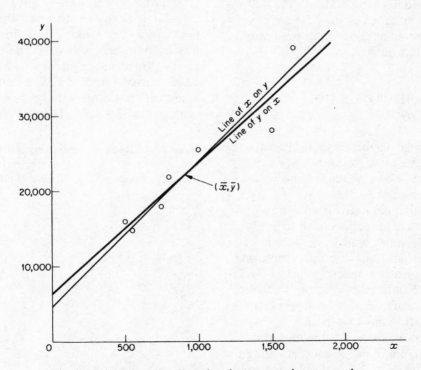

Figure 12.4   Regression lines for the grocery shop example

open for long hours, or has poor accommodation over. In this example the correlation is straong, and the uncertainty is therefore not too great.

Predictions should normally only be made within the range of the available data. In the grocery shop example the range is $500 \leqslant x \leqslant 1650$, and the scattergraph indicates that the line of best fit is straight and therefore that a linear regression equation is approximately valid over this range. We cannot be sure how the variables behave outside this range, and the regression equation then ceases to be valid. For example, we may attempt to use the regression equation of y on x to predict the selling price of a vacant shop. This has no takings, so its x-value is $x = 0$. Substituting this value in the equation $y = 6440 + 17.4\,x$, we obtain the predicted selling price of £6440 — an estimate which is much too low.

The process of making predictions within the range of the available data is called 'interpolation'. The making of predictions outside this range is called 'extrapolation'. Predictions made outside the range of the data are clearly subject to more uncertainty than predictions made within that range.

THE COEFFICIENT OF RANK CORRELATION

The discussion so far has been limited to variables which can be measured against an objective scale. Some variables, however, cannot be measured in this way — for example, pictures entered for an art competition. In this case the judges have to apply a subjective assessment, and by a process of comparing one with another must rank one picture 'first', another 'second', and so on. If it is required to determine whether variables of this sort are correlated, then the coefficient of rank correlation must be used.

Suppose that a survey is being undertaken by a hi-fi magazine of music-centres selling for under £200. The magazine wishes to determine

Table 12.3   Prices and quality rankings of eight music-centres

Music-centre	Retail price (£s)	Quality ranking by hi-fi expert
A	199	1
B	184	4
C	175	3
D	164	2
E	164	5
F	149	8
G	126	6
H	110	7

whether the quality of reproduction is related to price, and it accordingly selects eight music-centres and employs a hi-fi expert to rank them in order of sound quality. The results are given in Table 12.3, and they show that the expert considered that the music-centre costing £199 had the highest quality, and was ranked 1, the one costing £164 was second, and so on.

In order to compare quality ranking with price, it is necessary to place the prices in rank order. The ranking direction for quality was from highest to lowest, and so this must be the direction for prices: the highest price, £199, must be ranked 1, £184 must be ranked 2, and £175 is ranked 3. There are two music-centres costing £164; rather than arbitrarily

Table 12.4   Rank correlation computations

Price (£)	Price ranking	Quality ranking	d	d^2
199	1	1	0	0
184	2	4	2	4
175	3	3	0	0
164	$4\frac{1}{2}$	2	2.5	6.25
164	$4\frac{1}{2}$	5	0.5	0.25
149	6	8	2	4
126	7	6	1	1
110	8	7	1	1
			Σd^2	= 16.5

ranking one of them 4 and the other 5, it is preferable to split the difference by ranking them both $4\frac{1}{2}$. These rankings should be set out as shown in Table 12.4.

The symbol r' is used to denote the coefficient of rank correlation, and the formula for calculating its value is

$$r' = 1 - \frac{6\Sigma d^2}{n(n^2 - 1)}$$

where d is the difference between the rankings, and n is the number of pairs of rankings. (Although this formula looks quite different from the formula for r used earlier, it is in fact derived from it.)

In this example d denotes the difference between each price ranking and the corresponding quality ranking, and Σd^2 (calculated in Table 12.4) is found to be 16.5. $n = 8$, and so

$$r' = 1 - \frac{6 \times 16.5}{8 \times 63}$$

$$= 1 - 0.196$$

$$\simeq 0.8$$

The rules given previously for interpreting r also apply to r', and so we can conclude that the two variables are positively correlated — generally speaking, the buyer who pays more gets the higher quality.

Note that the ranking process results in a loss of information — for example, the actual prices given in Table 12.4 are more informative than the price rankings. Because of this the coefficient of rank correlation is a less reliable indicator of correlation than the Pearsonian coefficient considered earlier, and should only be used when it is impossible or impractical to use the Pearsonian coefficient.

EXERCISES

1. At the start of the autumn term a group of business studies students at Hangover College set up a plant to brew beer for (illicit) sale to other students. Each month they vary the price charged, the results being as shown below:

Month	Price per pint (pence)	Number of pints sold
October	8	400
November	9	320
December	11	280
January	12	240
February	8	360

(a) Draw a scattergraph and insert by eye the line of best fit (this line must pass through the point $(\overline{x}, \overline{y})$)

(b) Compute the following sums: Σx, Σy, Σxy, Σx^2, Σy^2 (to simplify the calculations make a suitable transformation of the variable 'Number of pints sold')

(c) Compute the correlation coefficient r and state what it shows

(d) Determine the equation of the regression line of 'Number of pints sold' on 'Price'

(e) If the students set the price at 10p per pint, how many pints can they expect to sell per month?

(f) Determine the equation of the regression of 'Price' on 'Number of pints sold'

(g) What price should the students charge if they wish to sell 400 pints per month?

(h) What are the main causes of uncertainty in the predictions made in (e) and (g) above?

(i) Insert the two regression lines on the scattergraph

(j) Compute the coefficient of rank correlation and comment on the result.

2. A large state enterprise runs five factories in various parts of the country. Rates of pay for a certain grade of operatives vary from factory to factory, and are shown in the table below. In order to determine

how rate of pay affects rate of work, the Work Study Section measures the rates of work of these operatives in each of the five factories. The average work-study ratings are shown in the table.

Factory	Hourly rate of pay (£)	Work-study rating
A	1.80	80
B	2.00	110
C	1.85	100
D	1.95	120
E	1.90	90

(Note: the higher the work-study rating, the faster the speed of work.)

(a) Denote 'hourly rate of pay' by x and 'work-study rating' by y, and make the transformation $X = 20(x - 1.80)$, and $Y = y/10$

(b) Calculate the correlation coefficient and state what it shows

(c) The management wishes to increase the rate of work of the operatives in factory A to 100. By computing the appropriate regression equation estimate what the rate of pay should be increased to.

3. The national income of a small country during the period 1970–75 was as follows:

Year:	1970	1971	1972	1973	1974	1975
N.I. (£millions):	136	140	164	180	188	188

(a) Plot the above data on a scattergraph.

(b) Using x to denote 'year' and y to denote 'national income', make the transformation $X = x - 1970$, and an appropriate transformation of y. By computing the appropriate regression line, estimate what the national income will be in 1978.

(c) Comment on the reliability of your result.

4. Figure 12.2 shows the scattergraph of percentage rise in wages (y) on percentage unemployment (x) for each of the 15 years 1952–66. The following sums have been computed: $\Sigma x = 23.4$, $\Sigma y = 63.7$, $\Sigma xy = 94.21$, $\Sigma x^2 = 39.46$, $\Sigma y^2 = 307.15$, $n = 15$.

(a) Compute the correlation coefficient r and test the significance of this value.

(b) By the use of regression analysis, compute what percentage rise in wages might be expected in a year when percentage unemployment fell to zero. How much reliance can be placed on the result?

5. Refer to the data in question 4 in the exercises for Chapter 2 (page 27). Let x represent the passage of time in years since 1970, and let y represent the sales in £000s.

(a) Construct a table to calculate Σx, $\Sigma \log y$, $\Sigma x \log y$, Σx^2, and $\Sigma(\log y)^2$

(b) Calculate the correlation coefficient r (y must be replaced by $\log y$ in the formula)

(c) Calculate the regression equation of $\log y$ on x.

Thirteen

The Analysis of Time Series

INTRODUCTION

A time series consists of the successive values of a variable which changes over time. It is a special case of the two-variable situation encountered in the last chapter, 'time' being the independent variable (x).

A typical example of a time series is afforded by the monthly takings of the launderette business discussed in Chapter 5 (see Table 5.3 columns 2 and 3). The takings of this business fluctuate from month to month, and the causes of these fluctuations can be attributed to the following three factors:

1. *The trend* in takings (in this case upwards over the first part of the series, but downwards at the end)

2. *Seasonal variations* (in this case a peak in the winter and a trough in the summer)

3. *Residual fluctuations*, that is, random irregularities in the takings caused by events such as machine breakdowns, the amount of rainfall, and so on.

Most time series encountered in business are subject to these three influences. Some are also subject to *cyclical fluctuations* — these fluctuations are similar to seasonal variations, and are analysed in the same way, but the interval between successive peaks in the cycle is some period other than one year. One example is the 24-hour cycle in electricity

demand; another is the four-yearly peaks and troughs of the business cycle.

The analysis of a time series involves the isolation and measurement of these influences so that the direction in which events are heading can be determined, and future values of the series predicted. This facilitates the planning and control of enterprises — investment plans, for example, are based upon predictions of future demand for products.

In this chapter we shall carry out an analysis of the launderette takings, but in order to reduce the figure-work we shall use quarterly rather than monthly figures. Table 13.1 shows the quarterly figures for the business for the three-year period 1977-79. These figures are graphed in Figure 13.1, and two possible trend lines are shown. The winter peaks and summer troughs can be clearly seen.

There are two main methods of determining the trend line, and there are two methods of determining the seasonal variations and residual fluctuations.

Table 13.1 Quarterly takings of the launderette business

| Year | Quarters | | | |
	1	2	3	4
1977	4750	4130	3520	4580
1978	4690	4220	3530	5790
1979	6030	4670	3790	5280

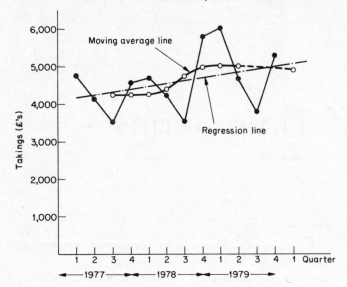

Figure 13.1   Time series graph

1. *The trend-line methods*

The two trend-line methods are (a) to plot moving annual averages on a graph and join the points by hand, or (b) to use regression analysis to calculate the equation of the trend line. The advantage of (a) is that the calculations are fairly easy, and in extrapolating future figures it is possible to take account of any changes in the trend line indicated by the final moving average figures. For example, the final moving average figures plotted in Figure 13.1 indicate that the trend has begun to decline, and this decline can be projected forwards on the graph to give future trend figures. This freehand method of projection must be used with caution, however, as the exact location of the projected trend line depends upon subjective judgement rather than mathematical calculation. For this reason it is infrequently used in practice, the regression method being generally preferred.

The advantage of (b) — the regression method — is that short-term 'wobbles' in the trend figures do not unduly influence the trend line, and the projected line is calculated in a mathematically exact manner. If the levelling out of the moving average trend line in Figure 13.1, for example, is thought to be a short-term phenomenon, and the trend figures are expected to rise again, predictions made by the regression method will be more reliable than predictions made by the moving average method.

2. *The seasonal variations and residual fluctuations*

Seasonal variations and residual fluctuations can be determined (a) on the assumption that their magnitude is not affected by the magnitude of the trend figures, or (b) on the assumption that their magnitude is proportional to the magnitude of the trend. Assumption (a) regards the actual figure for a period as being made up as follows:

$$A = T + S + R$$

where A is the actual figure, T is the trend, S is the seasonal variation, and R is the residual fluctuation. This is called the 'additive model'. Assumption (b) regards the composition of the actual figure as being

$$A = T \times S \times R$$

This is called the 'multiplicative model'.

The advantage of (a) is that the calculations are somewhat easier, and the assumption will be approximately true if the trend figures are altering only slightly over the period of the analysis. Assumption (b), however, is likely to lead to more reliable results. One would, for example, expect the seasonal variations of a business with takings of £100,000 per annum to be considerably larger than those of a similar business with takings of only £20,000 per annum.

In the next section we shall consider the simplest method of analysing a time series, involving the determination of the trend by the method of moving averages and the determination of the seasonal and residual fluctuations on the assumption that they are not related to the magnitude of the trend (i.e. the additive model). Then we shall consider the more complicated (but more reliable) method involving the determination of the trend using the regression approach and the determination of the seasonal and residual fluctuations on the assumption that they are proportional to the magnitude of the trend (i.e. the multiplicative model).

THE ANALYSIS (1): T BY THE MOVING AVERAGES METHOD, S AND R BY THE ADDITIVE MODEL

The analysis of the time series in Table 13.1 by this first method is set out in Tables 13.2 and 13.3. The explanation of these tables is given below (the paragraph numbers refer to the numbered columns of Table 13.2).

1. The method of calculating the moving annual totals is similar to that used in the Z-chart calculations in Chapter 5. In this

Table 13.2 Time series calculations

Quarter		Quarterly figures (A)	(1) M.A.T.	(2) Moving averages	(3) Trend (T)	(4) Variation from trend (A−T = S+R)	(5) Seasonal variations (S)	(6) Residual fluctuations (R=A−T−S)
1977	1	4750						
	2	4130						
				4245				
	3	3520			4237.5	−717.5	−982	+264
				4230				
	4	4580	16 980		4241.25	+338.75	+570	−231
				4252.5				
1978	1	4690	16 920		4252.5	+437.5	+694	−256
				4252.5				
	2	4220	17 010		4403.75	−183.75	−282	+ 98
				4555				
	3	3520	17 010		4722.5	−1202.5	−982	−220
				4890				
	4	5790	18 220		4946.25	+ 843.75	+570	+274
				5002.5				
1979	1	6030	19 560		5036.25	+ 993.75	+694	+300
				5070				
	2	4670	20 010		5006.25	− 336.25	−282	− 54
				4942.5				
	3	3790	20 280					
	4	5280	19 770					

Table 13.3 Seasonal variations

Year	Quarter 1	Quarter 2	Quarter 3	Quarter 4
1977			− 717.5	+ 338.75
1978	+ 437.5	−183.75	−1202.5	+ 843.75
1979	+ 994.75	−336.25		
Totals	+1431.25	−520	−1920	+1182.5
Averages	+ 715.625	−260	− 960	+ 591.25
				(Sum = +86.875)
Correcting factor	− 21.72	− 21.72	− 21.72	− 21.72
Seasonal variations	+ 694	−282	− 982	+ 570

case the quarterly figures are added in 4s — for example, the M.A.T. for the period quarter 1 to quarter 4 of 1977 is 4750 + 4130 + 3520 + 4580 = 16,980. The next M.A.T. can be obtained by subtracting from this the 1977 quarter 1 figure and adding the 1978 quarter 1 figure: 16,980 − 4750 + 4690 = 16,920.

2. The moving averages are obtained by dividing the M.A.T.s by 4. They show the average quarterly takings over the four quarterly periods to which they refer. Because they are averages, they must be located at the *mid-points* of those periods. For example, the moving average for the period referred to in (1) above is 16,980/4 = 4245 and it is located midway between quarter 2 and quarter 3 of 1977.

3. The moving averages of column (2) cannot be used to show the quarterly trend because they are located between quarters. To obtain trend figures which refer to specific quarters, it is necessary to take the moving averages in pairs and find a further average. For example, the average of the first two figures in column (2) is $(4245 + 4230) \div 2 = 4237.5$. This is located midway between those two figures, i.e. on the third quarter of 1977. These further averages can therefore be used to show the trend (T) and it is these which are plotted in Figure 13.1.

4. The variation from trend figures show how much the actual quarterly figures (A) depart from the trend (T), and they are obtained by calculating $A − T$. Since $A = T + S + R$, it follows that these figures are equal to $S + R$.

5. To obtain the seasonal variations (S) it is necessary to calculate for each quarter the average variation from trend (this is done in Table 13.3), and then to adjust these averages by a correcting factor. This adjustment has to be made because the averages do not add up to zero — in this case they add up to 86.875. Now $86.875 \div 4 \simeq 21.72$, and this therefore is the correcting factor to be subtracted from each average. The resulting figures are the seasonal variations — which, over the course of a year, cancel each other out: $694 − 282 − 982 + 570 = 0$.

6. T and S have now been isolated, and the final task is to determine the residual fluctuations (R). Since $A = T + S + R$, it follows that $R = A − T − S$, and it can therefore be seen that R is obtained by subtracting the column (5) figures from the column (4) figures. Inspection of column (6) shows that the residual fluctuations can cause the takings to increase or decrease by up to £300 in a quarter.

FORECASTING BY THE MOVING AVERAGES METHOD

To forecast figures for future quarters from the above analysis, it is necessary to extend the moving average trend line on the graph. The further into the future that this line is extended, the more unreliable the results become. In figure 13.1 this line is extended just to the first quarter of 1980 — but even over this short distance there is a difference of about £150 between the forecast made by this method and the forecast made by the regression method. (Forecasts made by the regression method will also, of course, become progressively more unreliable the further they are extended into the future.)

The graph indicates that the value of the moving average trend at the first quarter of 1980 will be about £4900. This figure is then adjusted by the first quarter seasonal variation of + £694 to give predicted quarterly takings of £4900 + £694 ≃ £5600. Owing to the effect of residual fluctuations, this forecast is subject to an error of ± £300. As has been emphasized above, this forecast must be treated with some caution.

THE ANALYSIS (2): *T* BY THE REGRESSION METHOD, *S* AND *R* BY THE MULTIPLICATIVE MODEL

In this section we analyse the data in Table 13.1 by (a) computing the trend line by the regression method, and (b) computing the seasonal variations and residual variations and residual fluctuations on the assumption that they are proportional to the magnitude of the trend, that is by assuming that $A = T \times S \times R$.

In this text we deal with linear regression only, and so we must assume that the trend line is straight. This is often approximately true, but it is unlikely to be exactly true, and this inexactness will introduce an error into any forecasts that are made. The time series should normally be plotted on a graph before the analysis is undertaken, in order to determine whether the assumption of a linear trend line is realistic. If a markedly non-linear trend is indicated, and it appears that exponential growth (or decay) is occurring, then the series should be plotted on semi-logarithmic graph paper. If the trend then appears to be linear, logarithms of the y-values should be taken, and the regression line of log y on x calculated (see the section on curvilinear correlation and regression in Chapter 12). The remainder of the analysis

Table 13.4 Time series calculations

Year and Quarter	(1) Quarter number x	(2) $X = 2(x-6\frac{1}{2})$	(3) Quarterly figures (A) y	(4) Xy	(5) X^2	(6) Trend (T)	(7) Actual Trend $(\frac{A}{T} = S \times R)$	(8) Seasonal variations (S)	(9) Residual fluctuations $(\frac{A}{T \times S} = R)$
1977 1	1	−11	4750	−52 250	121	4183	1.136	1.150	0.988
2	2	−9	4130	−37 170	81	4256	0.970	0.955	1.016
3	3	−7	3520	−24 640	49	4328	0.813	0.783	1.038
4	4	−5	4580	−22 900	25	4400	1.041	1.112	0.936
1978 1	5	−3	4690	−14 070	9	4472	1.049	1.150	0.912
2	6	−1	4220	− 4220	1	4545	0.928	0.955	0.972
3	7	1	3520	3520	1	4617	0.762	0.783	0.973
4	8	3	5790	17 370	9	4689	1.235	1.112	1.111
1979 1	9	5	6030	30 150	25	4761	1.267	1.150	1.102
2	10	7	4670	32 690	49	4834	0.966	0.955	1.012
3	11	9	3790	34 110	81	4906	0.773	0.783	0.987
4	12	11	5280	58 080	121	4978	1.061	1.112	0.954
Totals		0	54 970	20 670	572				

Table 13.5 Seasonal variations

Year	Quarter 1	2	3	4
1977	1.136	0.970	0.813	1.041
1978	1.049	0.928	0.762	1.235
1979	1.267	0.966	0.773	1.061
Total	3.452	2.864	2.348	3.337
Average	1.151	0.955	0.783	1.112
				(Sum = 4.001)
S = average × $\frac{4}{4.001}$	1.150	0.955	0.783	1.112

proceeds exactly as for the linear regression method outlined below.

The analysis is set out in Tables 13.4 and 13.5. The numbered paragraphs in the explanation below refer to the numbered columns of Table 13.4.

1. The independent variable (x) in the regression calculation is 'time', and the first step is to obtain the x-values by numbering the twelve quarters in the series consecutively.

2. There is a constant interval (of 1) between successive x-values, and a useful transformation to make in this situation is to take the middle value of the series as the assumed mean (the effect of this is to make $\Sigma X = 0$, thus simplifying the regression calculations). In this example the middle value is $6\frac{1}{2}$, and so this is subtracted from each x-value. To eliminate $\frac{1}{2}$s from the transformed values, we multiply the answers by 2: our transformed variable X is therefore equal to $2(x - 6\frac{1}{2})$. (Note that if there were an odd number of quarters in the series, there would be no $\frac{1}{2}$s, and it would not then be necessary to multiply by 2.)

3. The quarterly figures are the independent variable (y). The trend is determined by

calculating the regression line of y on X, the equation of the line being $y = a + bX$. Since $\Sigma X = 0$, the formulae for a and b given in Chapter 12 reduce to the following:

$$a = \frac{\Sigma y}{n}$$

$$b = \frac{\Sigma Xy}{\Sigma X^2}$$

Σy (the sum of the quarterly figures) is 54,970, n is 12, and so $a = 54{,}970 \div 12 = 4580.8$.

4.
5. ΣXy and ΣX^2 are calculated in the usual way, and in this case are equal to 20,670 and 572 respectively. Hence $b = 20{,}670 \div 572 = 36.13636$.

6. The equation of the trend line is therefore

$$y = 4580.8 + 36.13636X$$

In order to reverse the transformation made in column (2), substitute $X = 2(x - 6\frac{1}{2})$ in this equation

$$y = 4580.8 + 36.13636 \times 2(x - 6\tfrac{1}{2})$$

$$= 4580.8 + 72.27x - 469.8$$

$$= 4111 + 72.27x$$

The quarterly trend figures are obtained by substituting the quarter numbers (x) in this equation. For the first quarter of 1977, $x = 1$, and so $y = 4111 + 72.27 = 4183$. For the second quarter of 1977, $x = 2$, and so $y = 4111 + 72.27 \times 2 = 4256$. The remaining trend figures are calculated in the same way, and are shown in column (6).

7. We are using the multiplicative model for the seasonal variations and residual fluctuations, i.e. $A = T \times S \times R$, and so to determine $S \times R$ it is necessary to divide A (the quarterly figures in column (3)) by T (the trend figures in column (6)).

8. The column (7) figures for each quarter are now averaged to obtain the seasonal variations (see Table 13.5). The sum of these averages should be exactly 4 (since there are four quarters); it is in fact 4.001, and so it is necessary to correct the averages by multiplying them by 4/4.001. To avoid errors introduced by rounding it is best to base the calculations on the totals rather than the averages:

$$S = \text{total} \times \frac{4}{3 \times 4.001}$$

The corrected figures now sum to 4, as required, and these are the seasonal variations (S).

9. Since $A = T \times S \times R$, it follows that

$$R = \frac{A}{T \times S}$$

To obtain R (the residual fluctuations), it is therefore necessary to divide the column (7) figures by the column (8) figures. The results (shown in column (9)) show that R lies between about 0.9 and 1.1, indicating that the residual fluctuations can affect the takings by as much as 10% (since the $T \times S$ figures have to be multiplied by a factor as low as 0.9 or as high as 1.1 to obtain the actual figures).

The calculation of R concludes the analysis of the time series by this second method.

FORECASTING BY THE REGRESSION METHOD

To forecast the takings for a future quarter, it is necessary merely to insert the quarter number into the regression equation to obtain the value of the trend, and then to adjust this value by the seasonal variation. For the first quarter of 1980, for example, (i.e. quarter 13), substitute $x = 13$ in the equation to obtain the trend value:

$$y = 4111 + 72.27 \times 13$$
$$= 5051$$

Multiplying this by the first quarter seasonal variation, we obtain the predicted takings:

$$5051 \times 1.150 = 5809$$
$$\simeq £5800$$

Owing to the effect of residual fluctuations, this is subject to an error of ± 10%.

As stated previously, this forecast is not entirely reliable, due to the fact that a linear regression line is an approximate model only of the trend. The forecasts become progressively more unreliable the further they are extended into the future.

CYCLICAL FLUCTUATIONS

Although many time series met with in business are subject to annually recurring seasonal variations, some are subject to cyclical fluctuations the peaks and troughs of which recur with some other frequency — for example, every six years. Such fluctuations can be analysed in the same way as seasonal variations, except that the number of 'seasons' is not four but (in the case of a six-year cycle) six. The fluctuations in this case will have to be averaged in sixes instead of in fours, and, in the case of the moving average method, six-yearly moving averages must be calculated. For an example, see question 2, page 134.

DESEASONALIZING A TIME SERIES

In order to remove the effects of seasonal variations from a time series it is necessary merely to calculate $A - S$ in the case of the additive model, or A/S in the case of the multiplicative model.

Referring to the additive model in Table 13.2, the deseasonalized figure for the second quarter of 1979 is $4670 - (-282) = 4952$, and for the fourth quarter of 1979 the figure is $5280 - 570 = 4710$. The corresponding figures for the multiplicative model in Table 13.4 are $\frac{4670}{0.955} = 4890$ (second quarter) and

$\frac{5280}{1.112} = 4748$ (fourth quarter).

Unemployment, trading and financial statistics are frequently adjusted in this way to enable the underlying trends to be discerned.

EXERCISES

(Answers not given to questions 3 and 4.)

1. The new registrations of cars for the period third quarter 1974 to second quarter 1977 are shown below (in thousands):

| | | Quarters | | |
Year	1	2	3	4
1974			110.5	81.7
1975	116.0	96.4	107.6	68.5
1976	115.3	109.7	106.6	87.1
1977	116.5	106.1		

(a) Plot the figures on a graph.
(b) Using the method of moving averages and the additive model, compute the trend, the seasonal variations, and the residual fluctuations.
    Insert the trend line on the graph.
(c) Deseasonalize the data.

(d) Forecast the number of new car registrations for the third quarter of 1977.

2. The index of industrial production for the period 1961–73 was as follows:

| Year: | 1961 | 1962 | 1963 | 1964 | 1965 | 1966 | 1967 |
| Index number: | 76.7 | 77.4 | 79.7 | 86.5 | 89.1 | 90.6 | 91.7 |

| Year: | 1968 | 1969 | 1970 | 1971 | 1972 | 1973 |
| Index number: | 97.2 | 99.9 | 100.0 | 100.3 | 102.5 | 110.0 |

(a) Plot the figures on a graph, and confirm that they are subject to five-yearly cyclical fluctuations
(b) Determine the trend by the regression method, and the cyclical fluctuations and residual fluctuations using the multiplicative model
(c) Estimate the index for 1960, and compare your answer with the actual index for that year (75.8).

3. Answer question 1 using the regression method to find the trend and the multiplicative model to find the seasonal variations and residual fluctuations.

4. Answer question 2 using the method of moving averages to find the trend and the additive model to find the cyclical and residual fluctuations.

Part Three

Algebraic Methods

Fourteen

Growth and Decay

An important business application of mathematics is to situations involving growth and decay, examples being growth in the value of investments, and decay (or depreciation) in the value of assets. The only mathematical difference between a growth situation and a depreciation situation is that the growth rate (or interest rate) in the former is positive, whereas in the latter it is negative. The same mathematical theory can be applied to both.

This subject was introduced in Chapter 2 to illustrate the application of exponential equations to business. A much more comprehensive treatment is given in this chapter, beginning with a consideration of progressions, from which the exponential equations describing growth can be derived.

ARITHMETIC AND GEOMETRIC PROGRESSIONS

The fundamental concept in this branch of mathematics is that of a 'sequence' of numbers. A sequence is a set of numbers arranged in order (there being a first number, a second number, and so on) exhibiting some regular pattern of growth or decay, so that the value of any number in the sequence can be determined from its position in that sequence. The following are examples of sequences:

1.   10,   13,   16,   19,   22, . . .

2. $1\frac{1}{2}$,   1, $\frac{1}{2}$,   0, $-\frac{1}{2}$, . . .
3.   1,   3,   9, 27,   81, . . .
4.   100,   50,   25, $12\frac{1}{2}$, $6\frac{1}{4}$, . . .

In example (1), each number (or term) is 3 more than its predecessor. The sixth term in this sequence will obviously be 25. In example (2) each term is $\frac{1}{2}$ less than its predecessor; the sixth term in this case will be -1. In example (3) each term is three times as large as its predecessor, and in example (4) each term is half as large as its predecessor.

(1) and (2) are examples of 'arithmetic progressions' (A.P.s), these being sequences in which each term is obtained by adding a fixed number to its predecessor. This fixed number is called the common difference, and is denoted by d. In example (1) $d = 3$, and in example (2) $d = -\frac{1}{2}$. If we denote the first term of an arithmetic progression by a, then the second term is $a + d$, the third term is $(a + d) + d = a + 2d$, the fourth term is $(a + 2d) + d = a + 3d$, and so on. It follows that:

The nth term of an A.P. $= a + (n-1)d$

(This is a linear equation, with n as the independent variable.)

(3) and (4) above are examples of 'geometric progressions' (G.P.s), these being sequences in which each term is obtained by multiplying its predecessor by a fixed number. This fixed number is called the common ratio,

and is denoted by r. In example (3) $r = 3$, and in example (4) $r = \frac{1}{2}$. If the first term of a geometric progression is a, then the second term is ar, the third term is $(ar)r = ar^2$, the fourth term is $(ar^2)r = ar^3$, and so on. It follows that:

The nth term of a G.P. $= ar^{n-1}$

(This is an exponential equation, with n as the independent variable.)

Other sequences besides A.P.s and G.P.s exist, but they are of no concern to us here.

EXAMPLE

Determine the 16th term in sequence (1) and in sequence (4) above.

For sequence (1), $a = 10$, $d = 3$, $n = 16$, and so the required term is

$$a + (n - 1)d = 10 + 15 \times 3$$

$$= 55$$

For sequence (4), $a = 100$, $r = \frac{1}{2}$, $n = 16$, and so the required term is

$$ar^{n-1} = 100(\tfrac{1}{2})^{15}$$

$$= 0.00305$$

APPLICATION TO INTEREST AND DEPRECIATION

Rates of interest and depreciation are normally expressed as percentages. For the purposes of calculation, however, it is more convenient to express them as decimals: an interest rate of 5%, for example, is $5/100 = 0.05$. In the formulae given below the symbol i is used to denote rate of interest (as a decimal). These formulae can be applied to depreciation as well as to interest problems, provided it is remembered that depreciation is to be treated as negative interest: if, for instance, a machine is depreciated at the rate of 20% per annum, then $i = -0.2$. The other symbol used is P,

which denotes the 'principal', that is, the initial value of an investment. (In the case of a depreciation problem P will denote the initial value of the asset to be depreciated.)

We begin by assuming that the interest is calculated and paid once a year at the end of each year. Some investments (for example, Savings Bonds) earn simple interest, that is interest which is not added to the principal but is paid into a separate account. The amount of money earning interest in this case therefore remains unchanged, and the amount of interest earned is also unchanged from year to year — it is the principal multiplied by the interest rate $= Pi$. The way in which the value of the investment increases is therefore as follows:

At start	After 1 year	After 2 years	After 3 year.
Value: P	$P + Pi$	$(P + Pi) + Pi$ $= P + 2Pi$	$(P + 2Pi) + P$ $= P + 3Pi$

This sequence is an arithmetic progression, with common difference $= Pi$. The amount after n years (i.e. at the start of the $(n + 1)$th year) is

$$A = P + nPi$$

$$= P(1 + in)$$

For example, if £500 earns simple interest at $8\frac{1}{2}\%$ per annum, the amount after 5 years is

$$A = 500(1 + 0.085 \times 5)$$

$$= 500 \,(1.425)$$

$$= £712.50$$

Most investments earn compound interest, that is interest which is added to the principal and earns further interest in subsequent years. In this situation the principal P increases to $P + Pi$ at the end of the first year, and at the end of the second year the interest earned is $(P + Pi)i$ which is added to the increased principal of $P + Pi$. The amount at the end of the second year is therefore

$$A = (P + Pi) + (P + Pi)i$$
$$= (P + Pi)(1 + i)$$
$$= P(1 + i)(1 + i)$$
$$= P(1 + i)^2$$

Similarly, the amount at the end of the third year is $P(1 + i)^3$, and after the fourth year it is $P(1 + i)^4$.

This sequence is a geometric progression, with common ratio $= (1 + i)$. The amount at the end of n years (i.e. at the start of the $(n + 1)^{th}$ year) is

$$A = P(1 + i)^n$$

In Chapter 2 the effect of increasing the rate at which interest is accrued was briefly discussed. If interest at the rate of i per annum is compounded every 6 months, then the amount at the end of n years is

$$A = P(1 + \frac{i}{2})^{2n}$$

This can be proved by writing out the successive terms of the geometric progression. At the start the amount is P, after 6 months it is

$$P + P(\frac{i}{2}) = P(1 + \frac{i}{2})$$

after 1 year it is

$$P(1 + \frac{i}{2})^2$$

and so on. If interest is accrued every quarter, then the amount after n years can be similarly shown to be

$$P(1 + \frac{i}{4})^{4n}$$

Generally, if interest at the rate of i per annum is accrued m times per year, then the amount after n years is

$$A = P(1 + \frac{i}{m})^{mn}$$

In the above examples the growth in the value of the investment takes place in a series of discontinuous steps. The value remains fixed at £P until the end of the first period of time, when it jumps to

$$P(1 + \frac{i}{m})$$

It remains fixed at this new level until the end of the second period of time, when it jumps to

$$P(1 + \frac{i}{m})^2$$

and so on. In many growth situations, however, the increase takes place continuously. For example, the general level of prices in an inflationary situation is increasing continuously; populations are increasing continuously; technological change is increasing continuously. The above formula can be applied to such a situation if m, the frequency with which the interest is accrued, is allowed to become infinitely large.

The effect of increasing the value of m can be seen by considering the simple example of an investment of £1 earning interest at 100% per annum (i.e. $P = 1$ and $i = 1$). The amount at the end of 1 year (i.e. when $n = 1$) for various values of m is shown below:

Rate of compounding (m)	Amount at end of year ($A = (1 + \frac{1}{m})^m$)
Once a year	$(1 + 1)^1 = 2$
Twice a year	$(1 + \frac{1}{2})^2 = 2.25$
4 times a year	$(1 + \frac{1}{4})^4 = 2.44$
12 times a year	$(1 + \frac{1}{12})^{12} = 2.613$
100 times a year	$(1 + \frac{1}{100})^{100} = 2.704$
1000 times a year	$(1 + \frac{1}{1000})^{1000} = 2.717$

As m gets larger and larger, the amount approaches a limiting number known as the exponential constant (e), whose value is, approximately

$e = 2.71828$

The compound interest formula

$A = P(1 + \dfrac{i}{m})^{mn}$

becomes, when m is infinitely large

$A = Pe^{in}$

This gives the amount after n years when £P earns continuously compounded interest at the rate of i per annum.

EXAMPLE

An investment of £100 earns interest at 10% p.a. What will be the amount after 10 years if interest is: (a) simple interest; (b) interest compounded (i) annually (ii) quarterly (iii) continuously?

ANSWER

$P = 100, i = 0.1, n = 10$
(a) $A = P(1 + in)$

$\quad = 100(1 + 0.1 \times 10)$

$\quad = 100 \times 2 \ = £200$

(b) (i) $A = P(1 + i)^n$

$\qquad = 100(1.1)^{10}$

$\qquad = £259.37$

(ii) $A = P(1 + \dfrac{i}{4})^{4n}$

$\qquad = 100(1.025)^{40}$

$\qquad = £268.41 \text{ (by logs)}$

(iii) $A = Pe^{in}$

$\qquad = 100 \times 2.71828^{0.1 \times 10}$

$\qquad = 100 \times 2.71828$

$\qquad = £271.83$

EXAMPLE

A machine is purchased for £1000 and is depreciated at 15% p.a. What is its value after 5 years: (a) if the annual depreciation remains constant at 15% of the original value (straight line depreciation); (b) if the annual depreciation is at 15% of the value at the beginning of each year (reducing balance depreciation)?

ANSWER

$P = 1000, i = -0.15, n = 5$
(a) Straight line depreciation is analogous to simple interest:

$\quad A = P(1 + in)$

$\qquad = 1000(1 - 0.15 \times 5)$

$\qquad = 1000 \times 0.25$

$\qquad = £250$

(b) Reducing balance depreciation is analogous to compound interest:

$\quad A = P(1 + i)^n$

$\qquad = 1000(1 - 0.15)^5$

$\qquad = 1000 \times 0.85^5$

$\qquad = £443.71$

EFFECTIVE INTEREST RATES

An interest rate of 10% p.a. compounded quarterly is obviously more valuable to the investor than a rate of 10% p.a. compounded semi-annually. But how does it compare with, say, an interest rate of 10.1% compounded semi-annually? In order to compare interest rates compounded at different intervals we determine for each the equivalent rate if interest is compounded annually — called the effective rate. The most straightforward method of doing this is to calculate the amount that £1 will be increased by after 1 year.

In the above example, 10% compounded quarterly over a period of 1 year increases £1 to

$$1(1 + \frac{0.1}{4})^4 = 1.025^4$$

$$= £1.1038$$

It is therefore equivalent to an interest rate of 0.1038 compounded annually. Hence the effective rate is 10.38%.

10.1% compounded semi-annually over a period of 1 year increases £1 to

$$1(1 + \frac{0.101}{2})^2 = £1.1036.$$

This is therefore equivalent to an interest rate of 0.1036 compounded annually. The effective rate in this case is 10.36%.

10% compounded quarterly gives the highest effective rate, and is therefore the most valuable.

SUM OF A PROGRESSION

The sum (S) of the first n terms of an arithmetic progression is:

$$S = a + (a + d) + (a + 2d) + \ldots +$$

$$(a + (n-2)d) + (a + (n-1)d)$$

By reversing the order of the terms, this can be rewritten:

$$S = (a + (n-1)d) + (a + (n-2)d) + \ldots +$$

$$(a + 2d) + (a + d) + a$$

Adding the corresponding terms in these two expressions for S, we obtain:

$$2S = (2a + (n-1)d) + (2a + (n-1)d) + \ldots +$$

$$(2a + (n-1)d) + (2a + (n-1)d)$$

There are n of these equal bracketed terms, and so it follows that:

$$2S = n(2a + (n-1)d)$$

Hence, for an A.P., the formula for the sum to n terms is:

$$S = \frac{n}{2}(2a + (n-1)d)$$

The sum of the first n terms of a geometric progression is:

$$S = a + ar + ar^2 + \ldots + ar^{n-1}$$

Multiplying by r, we obtain:

$$rS = ar + ar^2 + ar^3 + \ldots + ar^{n-1} + ar^n$$

Subtracting rS from S, we get:

$$S - rS = a + (ar - ar) + (ar^2 - ar^2) + \ldots +$$

$$(ar^{n-1} - ar^{n-1}) - ar^n$$

$$= a - ar^n$$

i.e.

$$(1 - r)S = a(1 - r^n)$$

Hence, for a G.P., the formula for the sum to n terms is:

$$S = \frac{a(1 - r^n)}{1 - r}$$

EXAMPLE

A man opens two shops, both of which have sales of £1000 in the first month. If shop A's sales increase each month at the rate of £10 per month, and shop B's sales increase at the rate of 1% per month on the previous month's sales, what will be their combined sales: (a) in the twelfth month of trading; (b) in the first year of trading?

ANSWER

Shop A's sales form an A.P. with $a = 1000$ and $d = 10$. Shop B's sales form a G.P. with $a = 1000$ and $r = 1 + i = 1.01$

(a) To find the sales in the twelfth month, determine the twelfth term of each progression:

For shop A, the required term is
$a + (n-1)d = 1000 + 11 \times 10 = £1110$

For shop B, the required term is
$ar^{n-1} = 1000 \times 1.01^{11} = £1115.67$

Hence the combined sales for the two shops is £2225.67.

(b) To find the sales in the first year, determine the sum of the first 12 terms of each progression:

For shop A, $S = \dfrac{n}{2}(2a + (n-1)d)$

$$= \dfrac{12}{2}(2000 + 11 \times 10)$$

$$= £12,660$$

For shop B, $S = \dfrac{a(1 - r^n)}{1 - r}$

$$= \dfrac{1000(1 - 1.01^{12})}{1 - 1.01}$$

$$= \dfrac{1000(1 - 1.126825)}{-0.01}$$

$$= £12,682.50$$

Hence the combined sales for the two shops is £25,342.50.

PRESENT VALUES

What sum of money, if invested at an interest rate of 10% p.a. compounded annually, will give £100 in 5 years' time? To find the answer the formula

$$A = P(1 + i)^n$$

must be applied, where P is the sum we are trying to find, $A = £100$, $i = 0.1$, and $n = 5$:

$$100 = P(1 + 0.1)^5$$

$$\therefore \quad P = \dfrac{100}{1.1^5} \simeq £62$$

£62 is said to be the present value (or discounted value) of £100 due at the end of 5 years. The 10% is said to be the discount rate. What this means is that £62 now is equivalent to £100 in 5 years' time. This has nothing to do with inflation; £1 now is always worth more than £1 in the future, simply because that £1 can be used to earn more money. When a business borrows money, it is in effect exchanging a larger sum of future money for a smaller sum of present money, which can be utilised now to increase its earning power.

The formula for calculating the present value of a future amount A at a discount rate of i can be seen, from the above, to be

$$P = \dfrac{A}{(1 + i)^n}$$

where n is the number of years in the future in which the amount is due. When calculating present values, the discount rate used is normally either the prevailing rate of interest on money borrowed by the business, or the best rate of return that the business can obtain by investing the money.

Present values have a number of financial applications. One example is discounted cash flow (D.C.F.), which involves the calculation of the present value of a series of future cash flows. (A cash flow is the difference between the money flowing into a business (from receipts) over a certain period and the money flowing out (from payments).)

Suppose that the current year's cash flow is A_0, next year's cash flow is expected to be A_1, the following year's is expected to be A_2, and so on. The present value of A_n, the expected cash flow in the nth year from now, is:

$$\dfrac{A_n}{(1 + i)^n}$$

If the expected cash flow of each year is discounted in this way, then the sum of these discounted cash flows (called the net present value (N.P.V.)) is:

$$\text{N.P.V.} = A_0 + \dfrac{A_1}{(1 + i)} + \dfrac{A_2}{(1 + i)^2} + \ldots +$$

$$\dfrac{A_n}{(1 + i)^n}$$

By calculating the net present value of a proposed investment project a business can ascertain its present worth. Businesses are often faced with a choice between alternative investments, and the calculation of their N.P.V.s provides a valid means of comparison.

EXAMPLE

A firm must choose between two plants, one of which costs £70,000, the other £55,000. They each have a useful life of four years. The expected annual cash flows in £000s from the plants are shown below (a negative sign represents a net cash outflow, a positive sign represents a net cash inflow). Which plant should the firm purchase if the discount rate is 10%?

	$A_0 = cost$	A_1	A_2	A_3	A_4
Plant A:	−70	+8	+20	+40	+30
Plant B:	−55	+10	+30	+20	+ 5

ANSWER

Plant A's N.P.V. (in £000s) =

$$-70 + \frac{8}{1.1} + \frac{20}{1.1^2} + \frac{40}{1.1^3} + \frac{30}{1.1^4}$$

$$= 4.34465 \text{ (i.e. £4345)}$$

Plant B's N.P.V. =

$$-55 + \frac{10}{1.1} + \frac{30}{1.1^2} + \frac{20}{1.1^3} + \frac{5}{1.1^4}$$

$$= -2.67433 \text{ (i.e. −£2674)}$$

Plant A has the highest N.P.V., so this should be chosen.

In this example the negative N.P.V. of plant B shows that this plant will yield a return on investment which is less than the current discount rate. A project with a negative N.P.V. is not viable, since either the firm will not be able to cover the cost of its borrowing, or, if it has spare cash, it can invest it more profitably elsewhere.

A frequently used method of appraising investment projects is to determine the discounted rate of return on the investment—the discount rate which will give an N.P.V. of zero. Suppose, in the above example, that plant A is no longer available and the firm is forced to buy plant B if it wishes to go ahead with the project. What discount rate will give a zero N.P.V. and thus make the project viable?

The 10% discount rate applied above gives a negative N.P.V. For a zero N.P.V. the discount rate must therefore be less than this, and to determine what it is we proceed by a process of trial and error. Let us begin by trying a discount rate of 8%:

$$\text{N.P.V.} = -55 + \frac{10}{1.08} + \frac{30}{1.08^2} + \frac{20}{1.08^3} + \frac{5}{1.08^4}$$

$$= -0.46878$$

This is still rather less than 0, so try 7%:

$$\text{N.P.V.} = -55 + \frac{10}{1.07} + \frac{30}{1.07^2} + \frac{20}{1.07^3} + \frac{5}{1.07^4}$$

$$= 0.68939$$

This is positive, so the discount rate must lie between 7% and 8%. Inspection of the above N.P.V.s indicates that it lies rather closer to 8% than to 7%, so try 7.6%:

$$\text{N.P.V.} = -55 + \frac{10}{1.076} + \frac{30}{1.076^2} + \frac{20}{1.076^3} + \frac{5}{1.076^4}$$

$$= -0.01$$

This is very close to zero, and so the discounted rate of return is 7.6%.

The expected returns from this project will therefore repay the original investment of £55,000 and give a return on that investment of 7.6% p.a. Provided, therefore, that the firm can borrow money at an interest rate of less than 7.6%, the project is viable.

ANNUITIES

An annuity is a series of cash flows at constant intervals and of constant amount. If the amount of each cash flow is £A, and if the cash flows are to be made at annual intervals starting next year and continuing for n years, then the present value is:

$$P = \frac{A}{1+i} + \frac{A}{(1+i)^2} + \frac{A}{(1+i)^3} + \ldots + \frac{A}{(1+i)^n}$$

where i is the discount rate.

This is a geometric progression with first term

$$a = \frac{A}{1+i}$$

and common ratio

$$r = \frac{1}{1+i}$$

Applying the formula for the sum of a geometric progression, we obtain:

$$P = \frac{a(1-r^n)}{1-r}$$

$$= \frac{A}{1+i} \times \frac{1-\left(\frac{1}{1+i}\right)^n}{1-\frac{1}{1+i}}$$

$$= \frac{A(1-(1+i)^{-n})}{1+i-1}$$

$$= \frac{A}{i}(1-(1+i)^{-n})$$

An example of the use of this formula is given in question 10 below.

EXERCISES

1. Write down the first five terms of the following progressions:
    (a) A.P. with $a = 5$ and $d = 4$
    (b) A.P. with $a = 20$ and $d = -10$
    (c) G.P. with $a = 10$ and $r = 2$
    (d) G.P. with $a = 2$ and $r = -3$.

2. Write down the 20th term and the sum to 20 terms of the following progressions:
    (a) 10, 14, 18, 22, ...
    (b) 20, 17, 14, 11, ...
    (c) 1, 2, 4, 8, 16, ...
    (d) 2700, 900, 300, 100, $33\frac{1}{3}$, ...

3. A firm anticipates that its profits will increase geometrically over the next 8 years, so that each year's profit will be 15% more than the previous year's profit. If the profit in the first year is £25,000, what will it be in the eighth year, and what will be the total profit over the 8 years?

4. A man agrees to repay a loan of £10,000 over a 10-year period by paying £250 each quarter plus interest at 10% p.a. on each quarter's opening balance. Compute the total amount of interest paid.

5. (a) What will an investment of £500 be worth after 4 years if interest at 8% p.a. is compounded:
    (i) semi-annually;
    (ii) quarterly;
    (iii) continuously?
    (b) Calculate the effective interest rate for each of the above cases.

6. (a) A machine costing £5000 is depreciated in a firm's books at 20% per annum. What is its book value after 5 years if:
    (i) the straight line method of depreciation is used;
    (ii) the reducing balance method is used?
    (b) At the end of the five years the machine is sold for scrap for £389. What was the actual rate of depreciation (reducing balance method)?

7. (a) What is the present value of £500 in 5 years' time discounted at 5% p.a.?
    (b) Mr Smith buys a new house with a bridging loan on which he is paying interest at 12% p.a. The buyer of his old house has agreed to complete the purchase in six months' time, when he will buy it for £30,000. What is the present value of this amount to Mr Smith?

8. A man is retired at the age of 60 and plans to buy a launderette business which he will sell when he reaches 65. There is a

launderette for sale in the town in which he lives and he has to decide between purchasing this and starting up a new launderette on a prime site in the main shopping area. The expected annual cash flows (in £s) from these two alternatives are as follows:

	Existing launderette	*New launderette*
Immediately (purchase of business)	−8000	−12000
After 1 year's trading	+4500	+ 4000
After 2 years' trading	+4700	+ 5500
After 3 years' trading	+4000	+ 6500
After 4 years' trading	+4000	+ 6500
After 5 years' trading (including sale of business)	+8000	+12500

Which alternative should he choose if the discount rate is 11%?

9. A company plans to undertake a project which will result in annual cash flows as shown below (i.e. cash outflows of £20,000 immediately, and £25,000 in a year's time, and cash inflows over the remaining 4 years of its life). What is the discounted rate of return on the investment?

Year:	0	1	2
Cash flow:	−20,000	−25,000	+10,000

Year:	3	4	5
Cash flow:	+30,000	+30,000	+15,000

10. Under the terms of a certain policy a man can receive either a lump sum payment of £4000 immediately, or an annuity consisting of five annual payments of £1000, the first payment being made in one year's time. If the current discount rate is 8%, which should be choose?

Fifteen

Linear Programming

Included in the subject area of quantitative methods is a family of techniques known as 'mathematical programming'. These have been developed to determine how best to allocate personnel, equipment, materials, finance, land, transport, etc., so that profits are maximized, or costs are minimized, or some other optimization criterion is achieved. Linear programming, so-called because all the equations involved are linear, is the most commonly used of these techniques.

To illustrate linear programming we shall consider the example of a baker who makes two products, large loaves and small round loaves. We shall suppose that he can sell up to 280 of the large loaves per day in his shop, and up to 400 small loaves. Each large loaf occupies 0.01 m³ of shelf space, each small loaf occupies 0.008 m³ of space, and there is 4 m³ of shelf space available. There are 8 hours available each night for baking, and he can produce large loaves at the rate of 40 per hour, and small loaves at the rate of 80 per hour. If he makes 5p profit on each large loaf, and 3p profit on each small loaf, what number of large and small loaves should he produce to maximize his profits?

This is typical of the type of problem which is amenable to solution by linear-programming methods. Different products are being made, and there are various 'constraints' on the amounts that can be produced—storage space, availability of labour and equipment, and so on. We are required to determine the optimum product mix.

THE MATHEMATICAL MODEL

The first step is to construct a mathematical model of the problem, and to do this it is necessary to denote the variables in it by the symbols x, y, z, etc. In this example there are just two variables, namely, the number of large loaves produced and the number of small loaves produced, and we shall denote these by x and y respectively. The constraints on the values that x and y can take are the amounts that can be sold, the storage space, and the hours available for baking, and these constraints can be written in mathematical form as a set of inequalities:

1. The maximum number of large loaves that can be sold is 280, and so the first constraint is:

    $x \leqslant 280$ (i.e. x must be less than or equal to 280).

    (A mathematical relationship involving, as this does, a $<$ or $>$ sign is called an 'inequality'.)

2. The maximum number of small loaves that can be sold is 400, and so the second constraint is:

    $y \leqslant 400$.

3. The third constraint is the 4 m³ of shelf space. Each large loaf occupies 0.01 m³ of space, and so x large loaves occupy $0.01x$ m³. Each small loaf occupies 0.008 m³, so

y small loaves occupy $0.008y$ m^3. The total space occupied by the loaves is therefore $0.01x + 0.008y$ m^3 and, since this cannot exceed 4 m^3 the third constraint can be written:

$$0.01x + 0.008y \leqslant 4$$

The rules for manipulating equations also apply to inequalities: each side of the inequality can be multiplied or divided by the same number, or the same number can be added to or subtracted from each side. We can therefore simplify the above inequality by carrying out a suitable operation on both sides. The best operation in this case is to multiply through by 500:

$$5x + 4y \leqslant 2000.$$

4. The fourth constraint is the 8 hours of production time available. Large loaves are produced at the rate of 40 per hour, and each loaf therefore requires 1/40 hours of production time. x large loaves therefore require $x/40$ hours. Small loaves are produced at the rate of 80 per hour, and each loaf therefore requires 1/80 hours. y small loaves therefore require $y/80$ hours. The total number of production hours required is therefore $x/40 + y/80$, and since this cannot exceed 8 hours the fourth constraint can be written:

$$\frac{x}{40} + \frac{y}{80} \leqslant 8$$

Multiplying through by 80, we obtain

$$2x + y \leqslant 640$$

5. A further condition is that negative numbers of loaves cannot be produced, i.e. $x \geqslant 0$ and $y \geqslant 0$. This is a condition which applies to all linear programming problems, and it is not necessary to state it formally.

The final part of the model is the 'objective function', that is the equation which expresses the profit, or cost, or other optimization parameter in terms of the variables. In this example we are required to maximize the profit. Each large loaf contributes 5p to the profit, and so the profit (in pence) from x large loaves is $5x$. Each small loaf contributes 3p to the profit, and so the profit from y small loaves is $3y$. The total profit is therefore $5x + 3y$, and so the objective function (F) is:

$$F = 5x + 3y.$$

GRAPHICAL SOLUTION

There are only two variables in this example, and so the above model can be represented by a graph with an x- and y-axis. If more variables than two appear in a problem, then a solution by graph is not possible, and the method outlined in the next section must be applied. For the graphical solution, the x and y axes are drawn in the usual way (Figure 15.1), and the inequalities representing the constraints inserted.

The first inequality is $x \leqslant 280$. To represent this on the graph, the line $x = 280$ is drawn (this is the vertical line through $x = 280$ on the horizontal axis). x cannot exceed 280, and so the right-hand side of this line is hatched; the non-hatched area to the left of the line (and including the line itself) is called the 'feasible region'—x can take any value in this region.

The second inequality is $y \leqslant 400$. The horizontal line $y = 400$ is drawn, and its upper side hatched, indicating that y can take any value below or on the line. The feasible region for x and y is now the area in the 'box' bounded by the axes, the line $x = 280$, and the line $y = 400$. (Note that, since $x \geqslant 0$ and $y \geqslant 0$ in any linear programming problem, the axes invariably bound the feasible region.)

To represent the third constraint, the line $5x + 4y = 2000$ is drawn. (Two points on this line are (0, 500) and (400, 0). The line is therefore obtained by joining the point 500 on the y-axis to the point 400 on the x-axis.) The area above this line is hatched, indicating that x and y are restricted to values below the line or on it. The feasible region is now

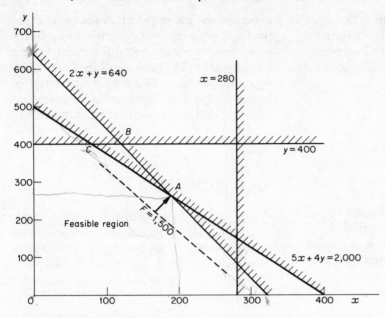

Figure 15.1 *Linear programming graph for maximization problem*

restricted to the area within the 'box' bounded by this line.

The fourth constraint ($2x + y \leqslant 640$) is drawn and hatched in the same way. The feasible region is the area bounded by all the hatched lines (Figure 15.1)—x and y can take any values within this region, but they cannot lie outside it.

We now have to determine the point within the feasible region at which the profits are maximized. To do this we plot a line representing the objective function $F = 5x + 3y$. There are an infinite number of possible values of F (the profits), and these give rise to an infinite number of parallel lines. We are limited to lines which actually pass through the feasible region, and we are looking for the one which has the highest value of F. The procedure to find this line is to draw any one of the possible lines, and then to determine by eye the line parallel to this which maximizes F.

Let us choose $F = 1500$ (representing profits of 1500p). The objective function is then

$$1500 = 5x + 3y$$

Two points on this line are:

$$x = 0, \quad y = \frac{1500}{3} = 500$$

and $$y = 0, \quad x = \frac{1500}{5} = 300$$

Thus the line is obtained by joining 500 on the y-axis to 300 on the x-axis (Figure 15.1). A value of F smaller than 1500 will give a line parallel to this but closer to the origin; a value of F larger than 1500 will give a parallel line which is further from the origin. To achieve maximum profits we therefore need the parallel line which is at the greatest distance from the origin, but which still passes through the feasible region. The required line passes through the point A, i.e. the intersection of the lines $5x + 4y = 2000$ and $2x + y = 640$. It can be seen from the graph that the co-ordinates (i.e. the x- and y-values) of this point are approximately (185, 265), showing that to maximize his profits the baker should produce 185 large loaves and 265 small loaves each day. The daily profit at this output is $5 \times 185 + 3 \times 265 = 1720$p.

The graph also shows the effect of altering the constraints. For example, if the baker decides to install additional shelving, so that the shelf space constraint line ($5x + 4y = 2000$) is shifted outwards beyond the point B in Figure 15.1, then the optimum objective function line (i.e. the line which lies furthest from the origin) will pass through *B*. This point has co-ordinates (120, 400), and maximum profits will therefore be achieved when 120 large loaves and 400 small loaves are produced. The daily profit in this case will be $5 \times 120 + 3 \times 400 = 1800$p. The baker will therefore increase his maximum daily profits by 80p through increasing his shelf space.

SOLUTION BY THE SIMPLEX METHOD

The graphical method outlined above can only be applied to problems containing two variables. A graph can have only two axes, and if our baker produced buns in addition to large and small loaves, there is no way of representing the third variable, 'number of buns', on the graph. When three or more variables are involved it is therefore necessary to abandon the graphical method and turn to more powerful algebraic methods. These methods can be reduced to a sequence of simple repetitive steps, and they thus lend themselves to computer processing (most linear-programming problems are solved by computer). To illustrate these methods we will solve algebraically the problem discussed in the last section.

In any linear programming problem the optimum point (where profits are maximized, or costs are minimized, etc.) lies at one of the corners of the feasible region. The co-ordinates of these corners can be determined by solving successive pairs of simultaneous equations. In Figure 15.1 the corner *A* can be determined by solving $5x + 4y = 2000$ and $2x + y = 640$; the corner *C* can be determined by solving $y = 400$ and $5x + 4y = 2000$; and so on.

By substituting the co-ordinates of each corner in the objective function, the one which gives the maximum value for *F* (that is, the maximum profits) can be determined.

Outlined below is the most commonly used way of carrying out these steps, called the simplex method. Although quite straightforward, this method is based upon an area of mathematics not dealt with in this text

(matrix algebra) and we cannot therefore go into the reasoning behind it.

In order to shorten the explanation we shall simplify the problem by assuming that there is no limitation on the number of loaves that the baker can sell. We therefore eliminate from consideration the inequalities $x \leqslant 280$ and $y \leqslant 400$. Our problem is then reduced to maximizing the objective function

$$F = 5x + 3y$$

subject to the constraints

$$5x + 4y \leqslant 2000$$

and

$$2x + y \leqslant 640$$

To make the problem amenable to solution by algebra we must, as a preliminary step, convert these inequalities to equalities. This is done by inserting into them what are known as 'slack variables' These variables indicate the amount of 'slack', or surplus capacity, and they cannot take negative values.

The first constraint is $5x + 4y \leqslant 2000$. If we write $2000 - (5x + 4y) = s_1$, it is clear that s_1 must be greater than or equal to zero. This is our first slack variable, and inserting it into the constraint we obtain:

$$5x + 4y + s_1 = 2000$$

In just the same way the second constraint can be rewritten

$$2x + y + s_2 = 640$$

where s_2 is the second (non-negative) slack variable.

The simplex method involves setting out the information contained in these equations in tabular form, and carrying out appropriate operations on the rows and columns of this table until the optimum solution (the solution which maximizes profits) is achieved. The steps involved in the method are as follows:

1. The columns of the table are headed with the variables that appear in the equations (x, y, s_1, s_2). Above these headings are

$5x + 4y$

written the coefficients that these variables take in the objective function. (The co-efficient of a variable is the number by which it is multiplied.) Referring to the objective function, it will be observed that the coefficient of x is 5 and the coefficient of y is 3. The slack variables, which do not appear in this function, can be regarded as each having a coefficient of zero—in other words, we can rewrite the objective function thus:

$$F = 5x + 3y + 0s_1 + 0s_2$$

This row of coefficients is labelled C (see the table below).

C		5	3	0	0	*First*
		x	y	s_1	s_2	*solution*
0	s_1	5	4	1	0	2000
0	s_2	2	1	0	1	640

2. The first solution is now inserted into the table. The optimum solution lies at one of the corners of the feasible region and, since we do not know which, we can try the solution attained at any corner. The origin is invariably one corner of a feasible region, and so this is always used as the first solution. It will never be the optimum solution, but computers—for which this method is ideally suited—need to proceed in a series of steps which can be rigidly applied to any problem.

At the origin $x = 0$ and $y = 0$, and substituting these values into the two constraint equations, we obtain $s_1 = 2000$ and $s_2 = 640$. We incorporate this first solution into the table by using the variables that appear in the solution (s_1 and s_2) as row headings, and inserting 2000 and 640 in the s_1 and s_2 rows under the heading 'First solution'.

3. The coefficients of the variables in the constraint equation containing s_1 (i.e. $5x + 4y + s_1 = 2000$) are now inserted in the s_1 row in the appropriate columns (the coefficient of x is 5, so 5 is written in

the x column, the coefficient of y is 4, of s_1 is 1, and of s_2 is 0). The coefficients of the variables in the constraint equation containing s_2 are written in the s_2 row in a similar way.

4. The coefficients that the solution variables (s_1 and s_2) take in the objective function are written to the left of the solution variables, outside the body of the table. This column of coefficients is headed C.

5. All the information contained in the constraint equations and the objective function is now in the table. The next task is to determine whether the first solution is optimal. The procedure is to insert into the table a further row headed Z. The numbers in this row represent the total profits of the solution variables when they take the values shown in the body of the table. These Z-values are obtained by multiplying each value in the C column by the corresponding values in the other columns, and summing the results. The Z-value in the x column is therefore

$$\Sigma Cx = 0 \times 5 + 0 \times 2 = 0$$

For the y column

$$Z = \Sigma Cy = 0 \times 4 + 0 \times 1 = 0$$

and the Z-values in the s_1 and s_2 columns (ΣCs_1 and ΣCs_2) are also 0. The Z-value in the solution column is calculated similarly. (For convenience the first solution table is reproduced below, with the Z row inserted.)

C		5	3	0	0	*First*	*Solution*
		x	y	s_1	s_2	*solution*	$\div x$
0	s_1	5	4	1	0	2000	400
0	s_2	②	1	0	1	640	320 ←
	Z	0	0	0	0	0	
	$C–Z$	5	3	0	0		
Incoming		↑					
row: x		1	$\frac{1}{2}$	0	$\frac{1}{2}$	320	

6. A final row, headed '$C - Z$', is now inserted. This is obtained by subtracting the numbers in the Z row from the numbers in the C row at the top of the table. For the x column, $C - Z = 5 - 0 = 5$; for the y column, $C - Z = 3 - 0 = 3$; and so on.

If all the numbers in the $C - Z$ row are negative or zero, then the optimum solution has been reached. Since this is not the case in this instance, it follows that the solution $s_1 = 2000$, $s_2 = 640$ does not maximize the profits, and an alternative solution must therefore be tried. We proceed systematically, replacing one of the existing solution variables s_1, s_2 by one of the other variables (x or y).

7. The largest positive number in the $C - Z$ row (marked with an arrow) indicates which of the variables should next appear in the solution. In this case the largest number lies in the x column (which is referred to as the 'pivot' column), and so x is to be the new solution variable. To determine which of the existing solution variables should be discarded, the numbers in the solution column are divided by the corresponding values in the pivot column. The row with the smallest positive value (marked with an arrow) is called the pivot row, and indicates which of the variables is to be discarded. In this case 320 is the smallest positive value, and s_2 is therefore the outgoing solution variable. The pivot column and the pivot row have an element in common, which in this example is the number 2. This is referred to as the 'pivot', and is circled.

8. A second solution table must now be drawn up with x replacing s_2 as a row heading. The numbers that are to be inserted in the new x row are determined by dividing the numbers in the existing s_2 row by the value of the pivot (2). The incoming x row therefore has the values $1, \frac{1}{2}, 0, \frac{1}{2}, 320$, and for convenience these numbers are shown at the foot of the first

solution table. The reason for dividing by the value of the pivot, and the reason for the further operations that are to be carried out in stage (9) below, is as follows.

In the first solution table the number at the intersection of a row with the correspondingly labelled column is always 1: the number at the intersection of the s_1 row with the s_1 column is 1, and the number at the intersection of the s_2 row with the s_2 column is also 1. The number lying at the intersection of a row with a column headed by a different row-labelling variable is always 0: the number at the intersection of the s_1 row with the s_2 column is 0, as is the number at the intersection of the s_2 row with the s_1 column. This is always the case at a corner of the feasible region, and in order to achieve this (and thus ensure that the solution found applies to a corner) the following steps are necessary:

(a) The incoming x row must have the number 1 in the x column
(b) The x column must have 0 in the s_1 row.

(There will normally be more than two rows in a linear-programming problem. These rules must then be extended, and it must be ensured that the column headed by the incoming variable has zeros in every position except the incoming row position, where it must have the number 1.)

To achieve (a) (i.e. the number 1 in the x column) every number in the pivot row must be divided by the value of the pivot (2). To achieve (b) (i.e. 0 at every other position in the x column) it is necessary to carry out what are known as 'row operations': the incoming x row is multiplied or divided by suitable numbers and subtracted from other rows. (By carrying out these steps we are, in effect, solving a pair of simultaneous equations and finding the x- and y-values of their intersection.)

9. In this example we have to apply operation (b) to one row only, namely the s_1 row. To obtain 0 at the intersection of this row with the x-column it is necessary to multiply the incoming x row values by 5 and subtract the answers from the s_1 row values. The resulting numbers are 0, $4 - 2\frac{1}{2} = 1\frac{1}{2}$, 1, $-2\frac{1}{2}$, $2000 - 1600 = 400$. These numbers are inserted in the new s_1 row of the second solution table.

10. The coefficient of x in the objective function is 5, and so this number is inserted in the C column to the left of the x row. The C row at the top of the first table is transferred unchanged to the second table. The information in the problem, together with the second solution, is now in the table (see below).

C		5	3	0	0	*Second*	*Solution*
		x	y	s_1	s_2	*solution*	$\div y$
0	s_1	0	$1\frac{1}{2}$	1	$-2\frac{1}{2}$	400	266.7 ←
5	x	1	$\frac{1}{2}$	0	$\frac{1}{2}$	320	640
	Z	5	$2\frac{1}{2}$	0	$2\frac{1}{2}$	1600	
	$C-Z$	0	$\frac{1}{2}$	0	$-2\frac{1}{2}$		
Incoming			↑				
row:	y	0	1	2	$-\frac{5}{3}$	266.7	

11. The numbers in the Z row are computed as before ($\Sigma Cx = 5$, $\Sigma Cy = 2\frac{1}{2}$, etc.) and inserted in the table, and the $C - Z$ row determined. The largest positive number in this row is $\frac{1}{2}$, and since this is in the y row, we must try y as the next solution variable. Dividing the solution column by the y column, we obtain the solution $\div y$ column. The smallest positive value in this column lies in the s_1 row, and so the solution variable s_1 must be replaced by y. $1\frac{1}{2}$ is the pivot, and so the incoming y row is obtained by dividing the existing s_1 row by $1\frac{1}{2}$.

12. The third solution table is drawn up in a similar manner to the second. The incoming y row replaces the s_1 row, and

this y row is divided by 2 and subtracted from the existing x row to give the new x row (with 0 in the y column):

C		5	3	0	0	*Third*
		x	y	s_1	s_2	*solution*
3	y	0	1	$\frac{2}{3}$	$-\frac{5}{3}$	266.7
5	x	1	0	$-\frac{1}{3}$	$\frac{4}{3}$	186.7
	Z	5	3	$\frac{1}{3}$	$1\frac{2}{3}$	1733.3
	$C-Z$	0	0	$-\frac{1}{3}$	$-1\frac{2}{3}$	

The Z row is determined by calculating ΣCx, ΣCy, etc., and the $C - Z$ row is obtained. All the numbers in this last row are zero or negative, and this shows that the optimum solution has been reached. The values of x and y which maximize profits are therefore

$x = 186.7$, i.e. 186 large loaves

$y = 266.7$, i.e. 266 small loaves

and the profits (shown at the foot of the solution column) are 1733p.

Linear-programming problems generally involve many more variables than are present in this simple example. A large number of possible solutions have normally to be tried before the optimum one is reached, the steps outlined above being repeated until all the $C - Z$ values are negative or zero. This repetitive process is ideal for the computer, but monotonous and time-consuming when carried out manually.

A MINIMIZATION PROBLEM: GRAPHICAL SOLUTION

Although most linear programming problems are concerned with maximizing the value of the objective function, some, like the example below, are concerned with minimizing that function. In this case the constraints will take the form of minimum requirements.

We shall suppose that in a time of acute food rationing a man tries to meet his normal daily requirements for protein, calcium, and iron from corned beef and sardines. The amounts of these substances in each ounce of corned beef and sardines are shown in the table below, together with the man's normal daily requirements. We wish to determine what amounts of these two foods he should eat each day in order to minimize the number of ration coupons spent. We shall assume first that 1 oz of corned beef costs one coupon, and 1 oz of sardines also costs one coupon; we shall then assume that the price of corned beef is altered, so that 1 oz costs two coupons, the price of sardines remaining unchanged at 1 oz for one coupon.

		Protein	*Calcium*	*Iron*
(x)	Corned beef (amount per oz)	10 g	3 mg	3 mg
(y)	Sardines (amount per oz)	8 g	125 mg	1 mg
	Normal daily requirements	80 g	800 mg	12 mg

The two variables in this example are the number of ounces of corned beef consumed per day, and the number of ounces of sardines consumed per day. We shall denote these by x and y respectively.

The first constraint is that at least 80 g of protein must be consumed daily, and from the table it can be seen that each ounce of corned beef contributes 10 g to this, and each ounce of sardines contributes 8 g. x oz of corned beef therefore contributes $10x$ g, and y oz of sardines contributes $8y$ g, and it follows that the total contribution is $10x + 8y$, which must equal or exceed 80. The first constraint can therefore be written

$$10x + 8y \geqslant 80$$

(Note that the direction of the inequality is reversed in this minimization problem compared to the direction in the previous maximization problem.)

As in the maximization example, this inequality is represented on the graph by drawing the line $10x + 8y = 80$ (see Figure 15.2), but in this case the area *below* the line is hatched. The feasible region lies above the line or on it, for it is only there that total protein consumption exceeds or equals 80 g.

The second constraint (that at least 800 mg of calcium should be consumed daily) gives the inequality

$$3x + 125y \geqslant 800$$

and the third constraint (that at least 12 mg of iron should be consumed daily) gives the inequality

$$3x + y \geqslant 12$$

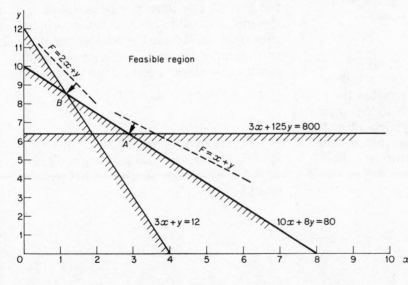

Figure 15.2 Linear programming graph for minimization problem

These inequalities are represented on the graph in the usual way, the feasible region being the non-hatched area above the lines.

The first part of the problem states that 1 oz of corned beef costs 1 ration coupon, and 1 oz of sardines costs 1 coupon. If x oz of corned beef is consumed and y oz of sardines is consumed, then the expenditure is $x + y$ coupons. Hence the objective function is

$$F = x + y$$

where F is the total number of coupons spent.

As in the maximization example, the objective function gives rise to an infinite number of parallel lines. To draw one of these lines, choose a value of F, say $F = 10$. Then $10 = x + y$, and the line representing this equation is shown in Figure 15.2. To minimize F, we need the line parallel to this which lies as close to the origin as possible but which passes through the feasible region. Inspection of the graph shows that the required line passes through the point A. The co-ordinates of this point are $(2.9, 6.2)$, and these give the quantities of the two foods that the man should buy in order to meet his daily requirements at minimum cost: 2.9 oz of corned beef, 6.2 oz of sardines.

The second part of the problem states that 1 oz of corned beef costs two coupons, and 1 oz of sardines costs one coupon. The objective function, representing the total expenditure of coupons, is therefore

$$F = 2x + y$$

Again we choose a value for F, say $F = 12$, and the line representing $12 = 2x + y$ is drawn on the graph. The parallel line within the feasible region which lies closest to the origin passes through the point B, whose co-ordinates are $(1.15, 8.5)$. The amounts the man should consume to minimize expenditure are therefore 1.15 oz of corned beef and 8.5 oz of sardines.

THE MINIMIZATION PROBLEM: SIMPLEX SOLUTION

We shall now apply the simplex method of solution to the above problem. In order to reduce the amount of work we shall ignore the calcium restraint ($3x + 125y \geqslant 800$), and we shall solve the second part only of the problem. We are therefore left with the task of minimizing

$$F = 2x + y$$

subject to the constraints

$$10x + 8y \geqslant 80$$
$$3x + y \geqslant 12$$

We begin by converting these inequalities to equalities by inserting into them non-negative slack variables. In the first constraint, $10x + 8y$ must be at least as large as 80, and so to convert this to an equality it is necessary to *subtract* the first slack variable s_1:

$$10x + 8y - s_1 = 80$$

The second slack variable s_2 must similarly be subtracted from the second inequality, giving:

$$3x + y - s_2 = 12$$

This, however, leaves us with the difficulty that the first solution (at $x = 0$, $y = 0$) is $s_1 = -80$, $s_2 = -12$. Negative solutions are not feasible (we have a negative solution in this case because in a minimization problem the origin lies outside the feasible region), and to overcome this it is necessary to insert artificial variables a_1 and a_2 into the equations:

$$10x + 8y - s_1 + a_1 = 80$$
$$3x + y - s_2 + a_2 = 12$$

The first solution is now at $x = 0$, $y = 0$, $s_1 = 0$, $s_2 = 0$, and this gives $a_1 = 80$ and $a_2 = 12$, which are positive and therefore feasible.

Having introduced these artificial variables into the problem, we need to be able to eliminate them from the final solution. This is achieved by writing them into the objective function:

$$F = 2x + y + ma_1 + ma_2$$

where the coefficient m is a very large positive number. When this function is minimized, the term $ma_1 + ma_2$ takes a low value, and this requires that a_1 and a_2 will tend to zero and therefore disappear.

The remaining steps are identical to those used in the maximization problem, except that the largest *negative* value in the $C - Z$ row identifies the pivotal column. The solution tables are laid out below.

The equations which must be inserted in the first table are:

Objective function: $F = 2x + y + ma_1 + ma_2$

First constraint: $10x + 8y - s_1 + a_1 = 80$

Second constraint: $3x + y - s_2 + a_2 = 12$

The initial solution is, as we have seen, $a_1 = 80$ and $a_2 = 12$, and so the row headings in the first table are a_1, a_2. As in the maximization problem, the numbers in the C row and the C column are the coefficients of the relevant variables in the objective function, the numbers in the a_1 row are the coefficients in the first constraint equation, and the numbers in the a_2 row are the coefficients in the second constraint equation.

The $C - Z$ row has the largest negative number in the x column (m is a large positive number, and therefore $2 - 13m$ is the largest negative number in the row), and so the x column is pivotal. Dividing the solution column by the x column to obtain the solution $\div x$ column, we see that the row with the smallest positive value is a_2, and so this is pivotal.

C		2	1	0	0	m	m	First	Solution
		x	y	s_1	s_2	a_1	a_2	solution	$\div x$
m	a_1	10	8	-1	0	1	0	80	8
m	a_2	③	1	0	-1	0	1	12	4 ←
	Z	$13m$	$9m$	$-m$	$-m$	m	m	$92m$	
	$C-Z$	$2-13m$	$1-9m$	m	m	0	0		
Incoming row	x	1	$\frac{1}{3}$	0	$-\frac{1}{3}$	0	$\frac{1}{3}$		

The new a_1 row—which must have a zero in the x column—is obtained by multiplying the incoming x row by 10 and subtracting the result from the existing a_1 row.

C		2	1	0	0	m	m	Second	Solution
		x	y	s_1	s_2	a_1	a_2	solution	$\div x$
m	a_1	0	$4\frac{2}{3}$	-1	$3\frac{1}{3}$	1	$-3\frac{1}{3}$	40	8.57 ←
2	x	1	$\frac{1}{3}$	0	$-\frac{1}{3}$	0	$\frac{1}{3}$	4	12
	Z	2	$4\frac{2}{3}m+\frac{2}{3}$	$-m$	$3\frac{1}{3}m-\frac{2}{3}$	m	$-3\frac{1}{3}m+\frac{2}{3}$	$40m+8$	
	$C-Z$	0	$\frac{1}{3}-4\frac{2}{3}m$	m	$\frac{2}{3}-3\frac{1}{3}m$	0	$2\frac{1}{3}m-\frac{2}{3}$		
Incoming row	y	0	1	$-\frac{3}{14}$	$\frac{5}{7}$	$\frac{3}{14}$	$-\frac{5}{7}$		

The new x row—which must have a zero in the y column—is obtained by dividing the incoming y row by 3 and subtracting the result from the existing x row.

C		2	1	0	0	m	m	*Third*
		x	y	s_1	s_2	a_1	a_2	*solution*
1	y	0	1	$-\frac{3}{14}$	$\frac{5}{7}$	$\frac{3}{14}$	$-\frac{5}{7}$	8.57
2	x	1	0	$\frac{1}{14}$	$-\frac{4}{7}$	$-\frac{1}{14}$	$\frac{4}{7}$	1.14
	Z	2	1	$-\frac{1}{14}$	$-\frac{3}{7}$	$\frac{1}{14}$	$\frac{3}{7}$	10.85
	$C-Z$	0	0	$\frac{1}{14}$	$\frac{3}{7}$	$m-\frac{1}{14}$	$m-\frac{3}{7}$	

There are no negative values in the $C-Z$ row, and hence the optimum solution has been reached. This is $x = 1.14$ and $y = 8.57$. So to minimize his expenditure, the man should consume 1.14 oz of corned beef and 8.57 oz of sardines. The cost will be 10.85 coupons per day.

EXERCISES

1. An eastern potentate wishes to have a harem, and in order to house it he orders the construction of a building with 4000 square metres of living accommodation. Being desirous of variety, he decides to include both fat and slim women in his harem. He has available £20,000 for the purchase of these women, and he estimates that he will have available £600 per day from oil revenues to feed and clothe them. His chief buyer informs him that fat women cost £200 each to buy, £12 per day to feed and clothe, and require on average 73 m² of living accommodation each, whereas slim women cost £400 each to buy, £7 per day to feed and clothe, and require on average 66 m² of living accommodation. Calling the number of fat women purchased x, and the number of slim women y, relate these facts about women to the resources available by means of algebraic inequalities, and draw a linear programming graph. What is the maximum number of women the potentate can have in his harem?

2. A furniture factory makes two products: chairs and tables. The products pass through three manufacturing stages: woodworking, assembly, and finishing. The woodworking shop can make 12 chairs an hour or 6 tables an hour, the assembly shop can assemble 8 chairs or 10 tables an hour, and the finishing shop can finish 9 chairs or 7 tables an hour. The workshops are operating for 8 hours per day. If the contribution to profits from each chair is £4 and from each table is £5, determine by (a) the graphical method, and (b) the simplex method, the numbers of chairs and tables that should be produced per day to maximize profits.

3. An investment company wishes to purchase property for commercial and private letting. It estimates that rents from commercial property will give a return of 12% p.a. on capital invested, and that rents from private lettings will give a return of 6% on capital invested. Commerical property is expected to appreciate in value by 8% p.a., whereas property for private lettings is expected to appreciate by 12% p.a. The company wishes to have an income from lettings of at least £60,000 p.a., and wants the value of its investments to increase by at least £75,000 in the first year. Determine by the graphical method the minimum amount that must be invested in the two types of property.

4. Kemico Ltd has devised a process for making three products simultaneously from low-grade oil. The products are marketed under the names 'Kleeno', 'Waxo', and 'Shino'. The company has

two experimental plants operating the process, and the hourly outputs of the plants, together with their hourly costs, are as follows:

	Kleeno	Waxo	Shino	Costs (£/hour)
Plant A	250 kg	300 kg	250 kg	75
Plant B	125 kg	350 kg	625 kg	120

Kemico Ltd has orders in hand for 5000 kg of Kleeno, 10,500 kg of Waxo, and 12,500 kg of Shino. Determine by (a) the graphical method, and (b) the simplex method, the number of hours each plant should be run to provide sufficient quantities of the products at minimum cost.

Sixteen

Calculus

The methods of calculus were discovered by Isaac Newton, who used them for solving problems involving the motion of planets. Calculus is not, however, limited in its application to the physical sciences; the methods can be applied in almost any situation involving variables which can be modelled by means of equations.

There are two aspects to calculus: differential calculus, which is concerned with the technique of differentiation, and integral calculus, which is concerned with the reverse technique of integration. To grasp the meanings of these terms, imagine that an equation is plotted on a graph. *Differentiation* gives the slope of the curve at any point (this shows the rate of change at that point), *integration* gives the area under the curve over any interval (this shows the total accumulated over that interval).

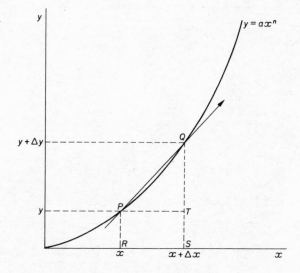

Figure 16.1 *Graph of the equation* $y = ax^n$, *with straight line through the points P, Q*

THE DIFFERENTIATION AND INTEGRATION FORMULAE

We shall briefly indicate here how the formulae are derived for the equation $y = ax^n$ (a and n being constants). We shall then show how, by extending these formulae, it is possible to differentiate or integrate any equation encountered on this course.

The graph of $y = ax^n$ is sketched in Figure 16.1, with two points P and Q marked on it. A straight line has been drawn through these

two points, and the slope of this line is the vertical distance between P and Q (which we denote Δy) divided by the horizontal distance between P and Q (which we denote Δx):

$$\text{slope} = \frac{\Delta y}{\Delta x}$$

(Δ – the Greek letter delta — is equivalent to the English 'D'.)

If we call the x- and y-values of P simply x and y, then the x- and y-values of Q are $x + \Delta x$ and $y + \Delta y$. Now the equation of the curve is $y = ax^n$, and so the y-value of P is

ax^n, and the y-value of Q is $a(x + \Delta x)^n$. It follows that Δy (which is the difference between these two y-values) equals $a(x + \Delta x)^n - ax^n$, and hence that the slope of the straight line PQ is

$$\frac{\Delta y}{\Delta x} = \frac{a(x + \Delta x)^n - ax^n}{\Delta x}$$

$$= anx^{n-1} + \tfrac{1}{2}an(n-1)x^{n-2}(\Delta x) + \dots$$

$$+ a(\Delta x)^{n-1}$$

(The second line of this formula is derived from the first by expanding the $(x + \Delta x)^n$ term, subtracting the ax^n term from the result, and dividing through by Δx. The power of x in each successive term is 1 less than its predecessor, the power of Δx is 1 more.)

If we now move the point Q closer and closer to the point P, then Δx and Δy become very small, the straight line PQ becomes increasingly tangential to the curve (that is, it touches the curve at a tangent rather than crossing it), and the slope of this line approaches the slope of the curve at the point P. As this process reaches the limit, Δx and Δy become vanishingly small, and the above expression for the slope becomes

anx^{n-1} + vanishingly small terms

It is conventional to replace the symbol $\Delta y/\Delta x$ by dy/dx to indicate that we are at this limit, and the formula for the slope of the curve at any point P can then be written

$$\frac{dy}{dx} = anx^{n-1}$$

This, then, is the differentiation formula for the equation $y = ax^n$. When we apply this formula, we are 'differentiating y with respect to x', or 'finding dy by dx'. The formula is an instruction to carry out the following two steps: first, multiply the coefficient (a) by the power of x (n), and secondly, reduce the power of x by 1.

The integration formula is derived by considering the area below the section of the curve PQ in Figure 16.1 (we denote this area by the symbol ΔA), that is the area of the rectangle $PRST$ plus the area PQT. If the point Q is close to P, then the section of the curve PQ approximates to a straight line, and PQT approximates to a triangle. Now the area of the rectangle $PRST$ equals $y\Delta x$ (height × breadth), the area of the triangle PQT equals $\tfrac{1}{2}\Delta x\Delta y$ ($\tfrac{1}{2}$ base × height), and so

$$\Delta A = y\Delta x + \tfrac{1}{2}\Delta x\Delta y$$

Dividing each term by Δx, we obtain

$$\frac{\Delta A}{\Delta x} = y + \tfrac{1}{2}\Delta y$$

If Q moves closer and closer to P, then $\Delta A/\Delta x$ becomes dA/dx, and the term $\tfrac{1}{2}\Delta y$ becomes vanishingly small. Hence $dA/dx = y$, and since $y = ax^n$, it follows that $dA/dx = ax^n$. It follows that A must be that quantity which, when differentiated, becomes ax^n, and so

$$A = \frac{a}{n+1}x^{n+1} + c,$$

where c is a constant. (Confirm that this is so by differentiating A with respect to x.)

Integration is therefore the reverse of differentiation. Areas under a curve represent totals or sums (recall that the area under the normal frequency curve represents total frequency over the specified interval), and so the symbol used for integration is $\int$, the old English 's'. The integration formula for the equation $y = ax^n$ can therefore be written

$$\int y\, dx = \frac{a}{n+1}x^{n+1} + c$$

When we apply this formula, we are 'integrating y with respect to x'.

EXAMPLE

For the equation $y = 3x^2 + 5x + 2$ find: (a) the slope at the point $x = 2$; and (b) the area under the curve over the interval $x = 1$ to $x = 2$.

ANSWER

(a) The differentiation formula is applied to each term of the equation. The first term is $3x^2$, and for this $a = 3$ and $n = 2$, and so

$$\frac{dy}{dx} = 3(2x^{2-1})$$

$$= 6x$$

For the second term $a = 5$ and $n = 1$ (since $x = x^1$), and so

$$\frac{dy}{dx} = 5x^0$$

$$= 5 \quad \text{(since } x^0 = 1\text{)}$$

The third term is the constant 2. The slope of the line $y = 2$ is zero (since this line is parallel to the x-axis), and so

$$\frac{dy}{dx} = 0$$

for this term (note that $dy/dx = 0$ for any constant). Hence for this equation

$$\frac{dy}{dx} = 6x + 5$$

Substituting $x = 2$, the required slope is

$$6 \times 2 + 5 = 17$$

(b) The x-values of the interval over which the area is to be determined are written at the bottom and top of the integration symbol. The area up to $x = 2$ is calculated (by substituting $x = 2$ into $\int y \, dx$), then the area up to $x = 1$, and the difference gives the area over the interval $x = 1$ to $x = 2$. As with differentiation, each term is integrated separately (the first term is $3x^2$, and the integral of this is

$$\frac{3}{2+1} \, x^{2+1} = x^3 \text{ and so on):}$$

$$\int_1^2 y \, dx = [x^3 + \tfrac{5}{2}x^2 + 2x + c]_1^2$$

$$= (2^3 + \tfrac{5}{2}2^2 + 2 \times 2 + c) -$$

$$(1^3 + \tfrac{5}{2}1^2 + 2 \times 1 + c)$$

$$= (8 + 10 + 4 + c) -$$

$$(1 + 2.5 + 2 + c)$$

$$= (22 + c) - (5.5 + c) = 16.5$$

FURTHER NOTES ON DIFFERENTIATION AND INTEGRATION

The differentiation and integration formulae given above can be applied to most of the equations on this course. To differentiate or integrate $y = 1/x^2$, for example, the method is to rewrite this as $y = x^{-2}$, and then apply the formulae in the usual way:

$$\frac{dy}{dx} = -2x^{-2-1}$$

$$= -2x^{-3}$$

$$= -\frac{2}{x^3}$$

$$\int y \, dx = -x^{-1} + c$$

$$= -\frac{1}{x} + c$$

The exponential constant e (= 2.71828) has special properties with regard to differentiation and integration. If $y = e^x$, then $dy/dx = e^x$ (that is, the slope at any point on the graph is equal to the value of y at that point). The following results should be noted:

1. If $y = e^{nx}$, then $dy/dx = ne^{nx}$.

2. If $y = 1/x$, then $\int y \, dx = \log_e x + c$ (i.e. the logarithm to the base e of x).

The interpretation of an area obtained by integration is obtained by multiplying the units of the dependent variable by the units of the independent variable (since area = height × length). For example, if y represents the number of units of electricity demanded per hour (i.e. units/hour), and x represents the passage of time (in hours), then the area represents: (number of units/hour) × (number of hours) = total number of units demanded during the specified passage of time. Again, if *y* represents marginal costs (i.e. the addition to total costs resulting from a unit increase in output), and *x* represents the number of units of output, then the area represents: (addition to costs/unit) × (number of units) = total costs.

In the case of a frequency curve, *y* represents the frequency density (i.e. frequency/interval), *x* represents the interval, and so the area represents: (frequency/interval) × (interval) = frequency. The equation of the standard normal curve, for example, is

$$y = \frac{1}{\sqrt{2\pi}} \, e^{-1/2x^2}$$

and relative frequencies (or probabilities) for normally distributed variables are determined by integrating this equation and calculating the relevant areas. It is these areas that are given in Appendix I.

APPLICATION OF CALCULUS TO MAXIMIZATION AND MINIMIZATION PROBLEMS

The main business application of the differential calculus is to optimization problems, that is problems which require the determination of *x*- and *y*-values for which (for example) profits are maximized or costs are minimized. As shown below, maximum or minimum points can be determined simply by setting d*y*/d*x* equal to zero.

The slope of a curve at a point, given by the value of d*y*/d*x* at that point, shows the rate of change of *y* relative to *x*. For example, the slope of $y = 3x^2 + 5x + 2$ at the point $x = 2$ was found to be 17 (page 160), indicating that a small increase in *x* at this point will be accompanied by an increase in *y* 17 times as large. If we consider the point *A* in Figure 16.2, the slope at this point is indicated by the steepness of the tangent (that is, the

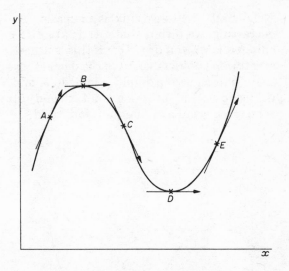

Figure 16.2 Graph showing slopes at maximum and minimum points

straight line which touches the curve at *A*). The tangent slopes steeply upwards from left to right, showing that the slope has a large positive value — a small increase in *x* at this point will be accompanied by a much larger increase in *y*. As we move along the curve towards the maximum point (at *B*), the slope decreases in value until at *B* itself it becomes zero — a very small increase in *x* has no effect on the value of *y*. Moving beyond *B* towards the point *C*, the tangent begins to slope downwards from left to right, indicating that the slope is now negative — an increase in the value of *x* results in a decrease in *y*.

So for *x*-values immediately to the left of *B*, d*y*/d*x* > 0, to the right of *B*, d*y*/d*x* < 0, and at *B* itself d*y*/d*x* = 0. By a similar reasoning it can be seen that for *x*-values immediately to the left of the minimum point *C*, d*y*/d*x* < 0, to the right of *C*, d*y*/d*x* > 0, and at *C* itself, d*y*/d*x* = 0. It is clear, therefore, that in order to determine maximum and minimum points (the 'turning points') it is necessary to locate the *x*-values for which d*y*/d*x* = 0. If at such an *x*-value d*y*/d*x* is *decreasing* in value (from positive to negative), we have a maximum, if it is *increasing* (from negative to positive), we have a minimum.

To find whether dy/dx is increasing or decreasing, we differentiate it. dy/dx differentiated is written d^2y/dx^2; if this is negative at a turning point, then dy/dx is decreasing at that point and a maximum is indicated, and if it is positive at a turning point, then dy/dx is increasing and a minimum is indicated.

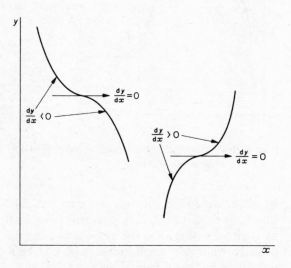

Figure 16.3 Graphs showing points of inflection

(Note that if $d^2y/dx^2 = 0$ in the above test, then an inflectionary point (illustrated in Figure 16.3) is indicated. Points for which $dy/dx = 0$, whether maxima, minima, or inflectionary, are referred to as 'stationary points'.)

For the equation $y = 3x^2 + 5x + 2$ considered previously

$$\frac{dy}{dx} = 6x + 5$$

and so

$$\frac{dy}{dx} = 0 \text{ when } 6x + 5 = 0$$

i.e. $x = -5/6$

To determine whether the stationary point at $x = -5/6$ is a maximum, minimum, or point of inflection, differentiate again:

$$d^2y/dx^2 = 6$$

which is positive for all values of x, including $x = -5/6$. Hence there is a minimum at $x = -5/6$.

EXAMPLE

It is found that the number of shoppers queueing at any given time in a certain supermarket can be approximately represented by the equation $y = x^3 - 14x^2 + 50x$ over the range $0 \leqslant x \leqslant 8.5$, where y is the number queueing and x is the time in hours after the store opens at 9 a.m. (so that, for example 10.30 a.m. is $x = 1.5$, and 5.30 p.m. — when the store closes — is $x = 8.5$). Calculate:

1. The time when the greatest number of shoppers are queueing, and the number queueing at that time

2. The total number of man-hours spent per day by shoppers queueing.

ANSWER

1. $\dfrac{dy}{dx} = 3x^2 - 28x + 50$

At the stationary points

$$\frac{dy}{dx} = 0$$

i.e.

$$3x^2 - 28x + 50 = 0$$

Applying the formula for solving quadratic equations, it follows that

$$x = \frac{28 \pm \sqrt{(28^2 - 4 \times 3 \times 50)}}{6}$$

$$= 2.41 \text{ or } 6.93$$

To determine the type of stationary point, evaluate d^2y/dx^2:

$$\frac{d^2y}{dx^2} = 6x - 28$$

and this is less than 0 when $x = 2.41$ (and so there is a maximum at this point), and greater than 0 when $x = 6.93$ (and so there is a minimum at this point). The graph of this equation would in fact be similar to the graph shown in Figure 16.2.

The value of y when $x = 2.41$ is

$$y = 2.41^3 - 14 \times 2.41^2 + 50 \times 2.41$$

$$= 53$$

The number queueing at the maximum point $x = 2.41$ is not necessarily the greatest number queueing. A glance at Figure 16.2 will convince the student that the number queueing at x-values to the right of the graph may well exceed 53. Maximum and minimum points should normally be regarded as 'local' maxima and minima, giving maximum or minimum values of y for x-values in the immediate vicinity of the turning points.

It is necessary, therefore, to check the value of y at the extreme right-hand part of the graph, namely at $x = 8.5$ (closing time):

$$y = 8.5^3 - 14 \times 8.5^2 + 50 \times 8.5$$

$$\simeq 28$$

This is less than 53, and so the time when the greatest number of shoppers are queueing is given by $x = 2.41$ (i.e. 11.25 a.m.), and the number queueing at this time is 53.

2. To find the total man-hours spent queueing it is necessary to integrate the equation (since area under the curve = (number queueing) x (number of hours) = man-hours queueing):

$$\int_0^{8.5} (x^3 - 14x^2 + 50x) \, dx$$

$$= [\tfrac{1}{4}x^4 - \tfrac{14}{3}x^3 + 25x^2 + c]_0^{8.5}$$

$$= (\tfrac{1}{4} \times 8.5^4 - \tfrac{14}{3} \times 8.5^3 + 25 \times 8.5^2 + c) - (c)$$

$$= 245 \text{ man-hours per day}$$

APPLICATION OF CALCULUS TO COST AND REVENUE EQUATIONS

'Theory of the firm' problems in economics (for example, the determination of the profit-maximization output) can be easily solved using calculus. Provided that just one cost equation is known (that is, either the marginal cost equation, or the average cost equation, or the total cost equation), and provided that just one revenue equation is known (that is, either the marginal revenue equation, or the average revenue (= price) equation, or the total revenue equation), then all the remaining cost and revenue equations can be determined, together with any maxima or minima required.

As indicated in the section dealing with the interpretation of integrals, if the marginal cost equation is known, then its integral is the total cost equation. Conversely, if the total cost equation is known, the marginal cost equation is found by differentiation (since marginal revenue

= increase in revenue/increase in output
= gradient of the total revenue curve, which is determined by differentiating the total revenue equation).
The average cost equation can be found by dividing the total cost equation by x (since average costs = total costs/output).

Similarly the total revenue equation can be found by integrating the marginal revenue equation (or the marginal revenue equation found by differentiating the total revenue equation), and the average revenue (= price) equation is found by dividing the total revenue equation by the output (x).

To illustrate this application of calculus we shall consider the following example. An electronics firm carries out a small-scale test launch of a new low-price pocket calculator. It estimates from this test that if it went into full-scale production it would sell between 1000 and 2500 calculators a month, and that its monthly revenue in thousands of pounds over this range of sales could be represented by the equation

$$R = -x^2 + 5x$$

where x is the monthly output in thousands of calculators (it is assumed that it sells its entire output). From its experience of calculator production, the firm estimates that its marginal costs in thousands of pounds could be represented by the equation

$$M.C. = x^2 - x + 2$$

and that its fixed costs will be £500 per month.

In this example we are given the marginal cost equation and the total revenue equation, and from these we can determine all aspects of the costs, revenue, and profit. We begin by determining the total cost and average cost equations, then we determine the marginal revenue and average revenue equations, and finally we determine the profit equation, the profit-maximizing output, the price that should be charged to maximize profit, and how much each calculator will then cost to make.

1. Total cost $(T.C.)$ = integral of marginal cost equation

$$= \int (x^2 - x + 2)\,dx$$

$$= \tfrac{1}{3}x^3 - \tfrac{1}{2}x^2 + 2x + c$$

When $x = 0$ (i.e. when there is no output) the total costs = the fixed costs = £500, i.e. 0.5 (since costs are measured in £000s). So substituting $x = 0$ in the total cost equation, it can be seen that $c = 0.5$. Hence

$$T.C. = \tfrac{1}{3}x^3 - \tfrac{1}{2}x^2 + 2x + 0.5$$

2. Average cost $(A.C.)$ = $\dfrac{\text{total cost}}{\text{output}}$

$$= \frac{(\tfrac{1}{3}x^3 - \tfrac{1}{2}x^2 + 2x + 0.5)}{x}$$

$$= \tfrac{1}{3}x^2 - \tfrac{1}{2}x + 2 + \frac{1}{2x}$$

3. Marginal revenue $(M.R.)$ = revenue equation differentiated

$$= \frac{d}{dx}(-x^2 + 5x)$$

$$= -2x + 5$$

4. Average revenue $(A.R.)$ = $\dfrac{\text{revenue}}{\text{output}}$

$$= \frac{-x^2 + 5x}{x}$$

$$= -x + 5$$

5. Profit (P) = revenue − costs

$$= (-x^2 + 5x) - (\tfrac{1}{3}x^3 - \tfrac{1}{2}x^2 + 2x + \tfrac{1}{2})$$

$$= -\tfrac{1}{3}x^3 - \tfrac{1}{2}x^2 + 3x - \tfrac{1}{2}$$

6. To determine the output which maximizes profit, differentiate the profit equation:

$$\frac{dP}{dx} = -x^2 - x + 3$$

At the stationary points, $dP/dx = 0$, i.e. $-x^2 - x + 3 = 0$, i.e.

$$x = \frac{1 \pm \sqrt{(1 + 12)}}{-2}$$

$$= \frac{1 \pm 3.6}{-2}$$

$$= 1.3 \text{ or } -2.3$$

The negative x-value can be ignored — the equations are only valid over the range $x = 1$ to $x = 2.5$ (i.e. 1000 to 2500 calculators per month), and so the only relevant stationary point is at $x = 1.3$. To determine which type of stationary point this is, differentiate again:

$$d^2P/dx^2 = -2x - 1$$

$$= -3.6 \text{ at } x = 1.3$$

The stationary point at $x = 1.3$ is therefore a maximum, and so profit is maximized at an output of 1300 calculators a month.

7. To determine the profit, price, and average cost at the profit-maximizing output, substitute $x = 1.3$ in the relevant equations:
   (a) $x = 1.3$ in the profit equation gives

   $$P = -0.732 - 0.845 + 3.9 - 0.5$$

   $$\simeq 1.8$$

   Hence maximum profit = £1800 per month.
   (b) $x = 1.3$ in the average revenue equation gives

   $$A.R. = -1.3 + 5$$

   $$= 3.7$$

   Now costs, revenue, etc., in this example are expressed in £000s, and the output (x) is in 000s, and so the average revenue is £3700 per thousand calculators. Hence the price is £3.70 per calculator.
   (c) $x = 1.3$ in the average cost equation gives

   $$A.C. = 0.563 - 0.65 + 2 + 0.385$$

   $$= 2.3$$

   Hence the average cost is £2300 per thousand calculators, or £2.30 per calculator.

EXERCISES

1. Differentiate and integrate the following equations:
   (a) $y = 3x + 2$
   (b) $y = 4x^2 - 6x + 12$
   (c) $y = \sqrt{x}$ (hint: $\sqrt{x} = x^{1/2}$)
   (d) $y = \dfrac{1}{x}$ (hint: $\dfrac{1}{x} = x^{-1}$)
   (e) $y = \dfrac{1}{\sqrt{x}}$
   (f) $y = \left(\dfrac{1}{\sqrt{x}}\right)^3$
   (g) $y = \dfrac{1}{x^2}$
   (h) $y = 4e^{2x}$

2. For the following equations, determine:
   (a) the stationary points; and (b) the area over the interval $x = 1$ to $x = 3$.
   (i) $y = x^3 - 6x^2 + 9x + 4$
   (ii) $y = x^4 - 2x^2 + 1$
   (iii) $y = 6x^5 - 45x^4 + 80x^3 + 14$

3. Malaria eradication programmes require the analysis of blood samples, which take the form of blood smears on microscope slides. In a certain tropical country the rate of analysing slides by the laboratory staff varies during the day (due partly to eye-fatigue), and this rate can be approximately represented by the equation

   $$y = x^3 - 15x^2 + 27x + 243$$

   over the range $0 \leqslant x \leqslant 4$ and $6 \leqslant x \leqslant 9$, where x is the time in hours after work commences at 8 a.m. (there is a midday break from 12 a.m. to 2 p.m.) and y is the number of slides analysed per hour. Work finishes at 5 p.m.
   (a) At what time is the laboratory working at maximum efficiency (i.e. when is the rate of analysing slides greatest)?
   (b) What is the rate of analysing slides at the time of lowest efficiency?
   (c) What is the total number of slides analysed during a working day?

4. A chemical company is planning to launch a new fertilizer and carries out a market-research survey in order to determine the likely demand. The survey indicates that the company can expect to sell between 1000 and 2000 tons per month, and that the relationship between price charged and quantity demanded will be as follows:

Price (£000s per thousand tons):	16	15	14	13	12
Monthly demand in thousand tons:	1.00	1.25	1.50	1.75	2.00

The company estimates that the variable costs (in £000s) of producing the fertilizer can be represented by the equation

$$y = \tfrac{2}{3}x^3 - \tfrac{1}{2}x^2 + 5x$$

where x is the monthly output in thousands of tons. The fixed costs will be £1000 per month. Assume in this problem that the company matches output to demand.

(a) Determine the (linear) equation relating selling price (in £000s) to x, the monthly quantity demanded (in thousand tons). (The technique is explained in Chapter 2.)

(b) Using (a) deduce the revenue equation.

(c) From (b) determine the marginal-revenue equation.

(d) Write down the total-cost equation and differentiate this to determine the marginal-cost equation.

(e) Profit is maximized when marginal revenue = marginal cost. Use this fact to determine the profit-maximizing output.

(f) Confirm the answer to (e) by writing down the profit equation and determining the maximum by differentiating.

(g) Determine the revenue and the profit at the profit-maximizing output.

(h) Differentiate the revenue equation and so determine the revenue-maximizing output.

(i) Determine the revenue and the profit at the revenue-maximizing output, and compare with the answer to (g).

5. A company manufactures a certain component which it sells in lots of 100. Its demand function is given by the equation

$$p = 26 - \tfrac{1}{2}x$$

where x is the number of lots produced per month, and p is the price per lot in £hundreds (assume that all of its monthly output is sold). Its marginal costs are given by the equation

$$y = 3x^2 - 12x + 22$$

where x is as above, and y is in £hundreds. Its fixed costs are £2000 per month. Determine:

(a) The total cost equation
(b) The revenue equation
(c) The profit equation
(d) The maximum profit that can be achieved
(e) The maximum revenue that can be achieved
(f) The profit at the revenue-maximizing output.

Part Four

Probabilistic Methods

Seventeen

Expectation and Decision Trees

The growth, linear programming, and other mathematical models included in Part III are called 'deterministic', for they take no account of any indeterminism or uncertainty which may exist in the situation modelled. In this, the final part of the text, we deal with 'probabilistic' models, that is models which incorporate probabilities in an attempt to take account of uncertainty.

EXPECTATION

To introduce the application of 'expectation' (or 'expected values') to decision-making we shall use the simple example of a removal firm which has received an order to remove the contents of a house situated 200 miles from its offices. The firm operates two sizes of removal van, medium and large and, from a description of the contents of the house, the manager is 80% confident that a medium van is sufficiently large for the job (that is, he assigns a probability of 0.8 to the event 'the load is medium'). If he sends a medium van and the load is in fact medium, the cost of the job will be £110; if, however, the load is 'large', then the van will have to make a double journey, in which case an additional cost of £40 will be incurred. To avoid the possibility of a double journey, a large van could be sent, in which case the cost will be £120. The customer has been quoted a price of £145 for the job.

The manager has to choose between two alternative acts, 'send a medium van' and 'send a large van', and when faced with a choice of this sort the procedure is to calculate the expected monetary value of each act and choose the one with the highest expected value. The expected value formula is

$$E.V. = \Sigma px$$

where x represents values of the variable under consideration (in this case x represents 'removal costs'), and p represents the associated probabilities (see the section on probability in Chapter 8).

As usual when carrying out a summation calculation, it is helpful to present the information in tabular form (see Table 17.1). The resulting display is called a 'pay-off table'. The formula $E.V. = \Sigma px$ dictates the design, the probabilities and x-values being listed vertically, with the $E.V.$ column alongside. The explanation of the table is as follows.

There are two possible events: either the load is 'medium', or it is 'large'. These are listed in the 'event' column, with the associated probabilities alongside. There are two possible 'acts' open to the firm: either 'send a medium van' or 'send a large van'. These alternatives are written at the top of the table to form the headings of the columns below.

If a medium van is sent, the value of the event 'medium load' equals the price charged for the job (£145) minus the cost of carrying out the job with the medium van (£110), i.e.

Table 17.1 Pay-off table for the removal firm example

EVENT	PROBABILITY (p)	ACTS			
		Send medium van		Send large van	
		C.V. (x)	E.V. (px)	C.V. (x)	E.V. (px)
Medium load	0.8	35	28	25	20
Large load	0.2	−5	−1	25	5
	Totals		27		25

£35. This amount is entered in the x-column. It is called the 'conditional value' (C.V.) of the event — it is the profit accruing on condition that the event occurs. The conditional value of the event 'large load' equals the price charged for the job (£145) minus the cost of sending the medium van which has to make a double journey (£150), i.e. −£5 (the negative sign indicating a loss to the firm). The amounts entered in the E.V. column are obtained by multiplying these conditional values by the associated probabilities: 0.8 in the case of the event 'medium load', and $1 − 0.8 = 0.2$ in the case of the event 'large load'.

If a large van is sent, the conditional value is $£145 − £120 = £25$ for both events, and this figure is entered against both events in the 'Send large van' x-column, the E.V. entries being calculated as before.

Finally, Σpx is calculated for both acts, and it can be seen from the table that the expected monetary value of sending a medium van is £27, whereas that of sending a large van is only £25. A medium van should therefore be used for the job.

As a result of this decision the firm may make a loss of £5, but it is much more likely to make a profit of £35. It is the high probability of this relatively large profit that makes this alternative a better choice than the 'safe' option of sending a large van with a guaranteed (but lower) profit of £25.

THE RELEVANCE OF EXPECTED MONETARY VALUES

Expected monetary values should not be used indiscriminately in the evaluation of alterna-tives, for monetary return is not always the only factor to be considered. A man may choose one job in preference to another more highly paid job because of the job satisfaction obtained. A businessman insures his business because his entire livelihood is at stake. The expected value of an insurance policy always favours the insurance company rather than the policy-holder (since insurance companies exist to make a profit), but no one refuses to take out insurance on that account.

When expected monetary values cannot be used to decide between alternatives, a scale of non-monetary values, called 'utilities', must be constructed. The expected utilities of the alternatives are calculated, and the alternative with the highest expected utility chosen. (This subject is beyond the scope of this text.)

For many business decisions, however, monetary return is the sole criterion and, provided the outcome of the decision cannot jeopardize the existence of the business, expected monetary values can be usefully employed.

EXAMPLE

A baker's speciality is a cake containing fresh cream. Between 25 and 30 of these cakes are demanded each day by customers, the frequency distribution of the daily numbers demanded over the last 100 days being as follows:

Number demanded per day:	25	26	27	28	29	30
Number of days with this demand:	10	15	25	30	15	5

The cakes are made in the morning before the shop opens. Each cake costs £1.00 to produce and sells for £1.80. Any not sold by the end of the day are given to the staff.

How many of these cakes should the baker produce each day to maximize his profit?

ANSWER

A pay-off table is drawn up as shown in Table 17.2, and from this it can be seen that the baker should produce 27 cakes each day to maximize his profit (which will then average £20.97 per day). The explanation of the table is as follows. The possible outcomes of each day's trading (demand 25, or 26, or 27, etc.) are listed in the event column, with the associated probabilities alongside. These probabilities are assessed from the baker's records by calculating relative frequencies (see Chapter 8): P (demand 25) = 10/100 = 0.10, P (demand 26) = 15/100 = 0.15, etc. The alternative production policies facing the baker are listed across the top of the table ('produce 25', 'produce 26', etc.), and the expected values calculated.

To show how these $E.V.$s are obtained, consider the 'produce 26' column. The first possible event is 'demand 25', and the takings resulting from this are 25 × £1.80 = £45. The profit is therefore £45 − £26 = £19, and this is entered as the conditional value of this event. The probability of this is 0.10, and so

the amount to be entered under the $E.V.$ heading is 0.10 × £19 = £1.90.

The second possible event is 'demand 26', and in this case the takings are 26 × £1.80 = £46.80, the cost is £26, and so the profit figure to be entered in the $C.V.$ column is £20.80. The probability of this is 0.15, and so the $E.V.$ is 0.15 × £20.80 = £3.12. The third possible event is 'demand 27', but the baker can only sell 26 (since this is the number produced), and so the $C.V.$ is, again, £20.80, and the $E.V.$ is 0.25 × £20.80 = £5.20. The $C.V.$s for 'demand 28, 29, and 30' will also be £20.80, and the respective $E.V.$s are obtained by multiplying by the associated probabilities (0.30, 0.15, and 0.05). The sum of the amounts entered in the $E.V.$ column is £20.62, and this is the expected value of the 'produce 26' alternative.

TREE DIAGRAMS

A simple tree diagram illustrating the furniture removal example is shown in Figure 17.1. There are two consecutive stages to this example, with two alternatives at each stage: (a) either a medium or a large van can be sent; (b) upon arrival at the house, either a medium or a large load will be found. The stages are shown in sequence from left to right in the figure, with the alternatives 'branching out' at each stage to give a tree-like appearance.

Table 17.2 Pay-off table for cream cake example

Event	Probability	Cream cake production alternatives											
		25		26		27		28		29		30	
		C.V.	E.V.	C.V.	E.V.	C.V.	E.V.	C.V.	E.V.	C.V.	E.V.	C.V.	E.V.
25	0.10	20	2.00	19.00	1.90	18.00	1.80	17.00	1.70	16.00	1.60	15.00	1.50
26	0.15	20	3.00	20.80	3.12	19.80	2.97	18.80	2.82	17.80	2.67	16.80	2.52
27	0.25	20	5.00	20.80	5.20	21.60	5.40	20.60	5.15	19.60	4.90	18.60	4.65
28	0.30	20	6.00	20.80	6.24	21.60	6.48	22.40	6.72	21.40	6.42	20.40	6.12
29	0.15	20	3.00	20.80	3.12	21.60	3.24	22.40	3.36	23.20	3.48	22.40	3.33
30	0.05	20	1.00	20.80	1.04	21.60	1.08	22.40	1.12	23.20	1.16	24.00	1.20
	Totals	20.00		20.62		20.97		20.87		20.23		19.32	

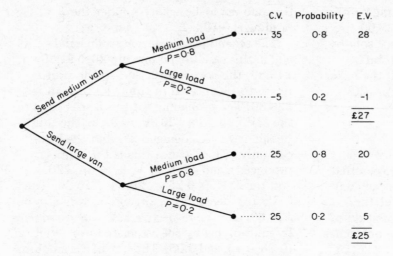

Figure 17.1 Decision tree — which van should be sent?

The probabilities associated with the alternatives 'medium load' and 'large load' are written under the relevant branches. (For a slightly more complex tree, see the answer given to question 3 (page 214).) If desired, the *C.V.*s and *E.V.*s can be shown at the right of the tree, as has been done in this figure (a tree diagram such as this, which is constructed to determine expected values for decision-making purposes, is called a 'decision tree').

Tree diagrams are particularly useful for determining probabilities when there are several consecutive stages to the process being evaluated, with mutually exclusive outcomes at each stage. As an example, suppose that the manager of the furniture removal firm considers the possibility of asking Joe, an employee who is about to make a journey in the general direction of the house in question, to make a detour and call at the house to estimate the size of load. The cost of this detour will be £1.50. The manager has not got a great deal of faith in Joe, however, and he is only 70% confident that Joe will estimate the size of load correctly — in other words, he reckons that the probability that Joe will estimate a medium load, given that the load is medium, is 0.7, and the probability that Joe will estimate a large load, given that the load is large, is 0.7.

The tree diagram showing the full range of possibilities is shown in Figure 17.2. From this the probability of an event can be calculated by multiplying the probabilities associated

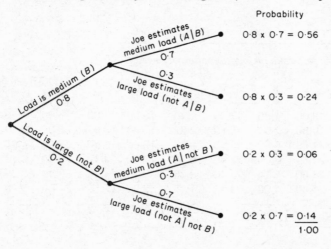

Figure 17.2 Tree diagram showing result of sending Joe for additional information

with successive relevant branches of the tree. For example, the probability that the load is medium *and* Joe estimates that the load is medium is $0.8 \times 0.7 = 0.56$.

CONDITIONAL PROBABILITY

In this example we have encountered for the first time the concept of 'conditional probability', that is the probability that an event A will occur given that (or 'on condition' that) another event B has occurred. The probability of A given the occurrence of B is written:

$$P(A \mid B)$$

Using this notation the probability that Joe estimates a medium load given that the load is medium is written:

P(Joe estimates medium load | load is medium)

At the end of the last section we calculated the probability that the load is medium *and* that Joe estimates that the load is medium by multiplying the probabilities of the two events. In doing this we were extending the multiplication law of probability given in Chapter 3 to conditional probabilities:

P(load is medium *and* Joe estimates a medium load)

$= P$(load is medium) $\times P$(Joe estimates a medium load | load is medium)

$= 0.8 \times 0.7$

$= 0.56$

Using the symbols A and B instead of 'Joe estimates a medium load' and 'load is medium', the multiplication law for conditional probabilities can be seen to be:

$$P(A \text{ and } B) = P(A \mid B)P(B)$$

Note that A and B are interchangeable in this formula:

$$P(A \text{ and } B) = P(B \text{ and } A)$$
$$= P(B \mid A)P(A)$$

THE EFFECT OF ADDITIONAL INFORMATION ON DECISION-MAKING

Any increase in the amount of relevant information at the decision-maker's disposal will tend to improve the quality of the decision made, and this will result in an increased expected value. However, the procurement of additional information costs money, and to avoid uneconomic information-gathering the decision-maker must compare the cost of obtaining the information with the increase in the expected value that will result from that information.

If the additional information is 'perfect', that is, not subject to uncertainty, the comparison is easy to make. Suppose that in the cream cake example the baker has perfect knowledge of each day's demand prior to baking, so that he is always able to match the number of cakes produced with the number demanded. On the 10% of days when only 25 are demanded, he makes £20 profit; on the 15% of days when 26 are demanded, he makes £20.80 profit; and so on. The expected value of cream cake production if the baker is always able to match production to demand in this way is therefore

$$0.10 \times 20 + 0.15 \times 20.80 + \ldots = 2.00 + 3.12$$
$$+ \ldots \text{ (all the underlined } E.V.\text{s in Table}$$
$$17.2) = \text{£21.92}$$

We found that the baker's best policy under uncertainty was to produce 27 cakes each day, when the expected value was £20.97. The value of perfect information to the baker is therefore £21.92 − £20.97 = £0.95 each day. If the cost of obtaining perfect information exceeds this amount, the baker should not obtain it.

If the additional information is subject to uncertainty (as is the case with Joe's estimates in the furniture removal example), then the calculations are more complicated. The first task is to reassess the various probabilities — for if, in the removal example, Joe *is* sent for the additional information, then that information will cause the manager to revise his original probability estimates. If Joe estimates a medium load, then the manager will be more confident than he was before that the load is in fact medium, and the probability that he will assign to this event will be higher than his original figure of 0.8. If Joe estimates a large load, then the manager will be less confident than he was before that the load is medium, and the probability that he will assign to this event will be less than 0.8.

Using the notation of the last section, i.e. A is the event 'Joe estimates a medium load', B is the event 'the load is medium' (and therefore 'not A' is the event 'Joe estimates a large load' and 'not B' is the event 'the load is large'), it can be seen from Figure 17.2 that

$P(A)$ = sum of first and third probabilities listed

= $P(B)P(A|B) + P(\text{not } B)P(A|\text{not } B)$

= 0.56 + 0.06

= 0.62.

Similarly:

$P(\text{not } A)$ = sum of second and fourth probabilities listed

= $P(B)P(\text{not } A|B) +$

$P(\text{not } B)P(\text{not } A|\text{not } B)$

= 0.24 + 0.14

= 0.38

Now the probability that the load is medium *and* Joe then estimates a medium load is $P(B)P(A|B) = 0.56$ (from Figure 17.2), and it is now fairly obvious from the figure that if Joe does estimate a medium load, then the probability that the load is in fact medium is this probability of 0.56 divided by $P(A)$:

$\dfrac{0.56}{0.62} = 0.9032$

Similarly, if Joe estimates a large load, then the probability that the load is medium is $P(B)P(\text{not } A|B)$ divided by $P(\text{not } A)$

$= \dfrac{0.24}{0.38}$

= 0.6316

A more formal method of reassessing probabilities is to use Bayes' formula. This is derived from the multiplication law for conditional probabilities:

$P(B \text{ and } A) = P(B|A)P(A)$

$\therefore \; P(B|A) = \dfrac{P(B \text{ and } A)}{P(A)}$

$= \dfrac{P(A \text{ and } B)}{P(A)}$

$= \dfrac{P(A|B)P(B)}{P(A)}$

Now we have already seen that

$P(A) = P(B)P(A|B) + P(\text{not } B)P(A|\text{not } B)$

i.e.

$P(A) = P(A|B)P(B) + P(A|\text{not } B)P(\text{not } B)$

and substituting this result in the above formula for $P(B|A)$, we obtain the formula:

$P(B|A) = \dfrac{P(A|B)P(B)}{P(A|B)P(B) + P(A|\text{not } B)P(\text{not } B)}$

Using Bayes' formula, it can be seen that

$P(\text{load is large} | \text{Joe estimates a medium load})$

$= \dfrac{0.3 \times 0.2}{0.3 \times 0.2 + 0.7 \times 0.8}$

= 0.0968

(in this case A = 'Joe estimates a medium load' and B = 'load is large'), and

$P(\text{load is large} | \text{Joe estimates a large load})$

$= \dfrac{0.7 \times 0.2}{0.7 \times 0.2 + 0.3 \times 0.8}$

= 0.3684

So our revised probabilities are as follows:

If Joe estimates a medium load,

P(load is medium) = 0.9032

P(load is large) = 0.0968
_____

1.0000

If Joe estimates a large load,

P(load is medium) = 0.6316

P(load is large) = 0.3684
_____

1.0000

The next task is to construct decision trees incorporating these probabilities. The tree in Figure 17.3 shows the *E.V.* calculation if Joe estimates a large load, and it can be seen that the expected value in this case of sending a medium van is £20.27, whereas that of sending a large van is £25.00. If Joe returns with an estimate for a large load, the manager should therefore reverse his original decision to send a medium van and send instead a large van, as this now has the highest *E.V.* (If it was found as a result of this calculation that the manager should *not* reverse his decision, then there would be no point in sending Joe, for the additional information obtained would be of no value.)

As an exercise the student should construct a decision tree giving the *E.V.* calculation if Joe estimates a medium load. The *E.V.* of

sending a medium van is in this case £31.13, whereas that of sending a large van is, again, £25. The manager will obviously send a medium van in this case.

So if Joe estimates a medium load (and the probability of this estimate has been found to be 0.62 (see page 174)), then a medium van should be sent, and the *E.V.* is £31.13. If Joe estimates a large load (and the probability of this is 0.38), then a large van should be sent, and the *E.V.* is £25. These results are set out in the decision tree in Figure 17.4, and from this the expected value of the job if the additional information is obtained can be determined. As the calculation at the right of the figure shows, this *E.V.* equals £28.80.

Now the *E.V.* of the job calculated on the basis of the manager's original probability estimates in Figure 17.1 was £27, which is £1.80 less than the *E.V.* if Joe obtains the additional information. The manager should therefore pay up to £1.80 for this information, and since the cost of sending Joe on the detour is only £1.50, the information should be obtained.

To summarize, the procedure for deciding whether or not to purchase additional information, when that information is not perfect is:

1. Determine the *E.V.* of each alternative if additional information is not obtained, and select the most favourable.

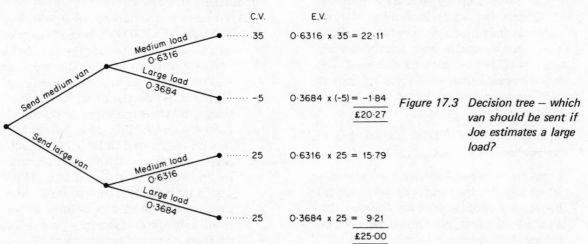

	C.V.	E.V.
Medium load 0·6316	 35	0·6316 × 35 = 22·11
Large load 0·3684	.... −5	0·3684 × (−5) = −1·84
		£20·27
Medium load 0·6316	 25	0·6316 × 25 = 15·79
Large load 0·3684	 25	0·3684 × 25 = 9·21
		£25·00

Send medium van / Send large van

Figure 17.3 Decision tree − which van should be sent if Joe estimates a large load?

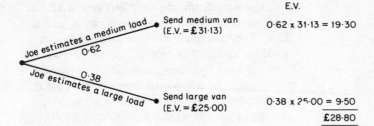

E.V.

Send medium van
(E.V. = £31·13)   0·62 × 31·13 = 19·30

Figure 17.4   Tree diagram — ex-pected value of job if Joe obtains additional information

Send large van
(E.V. = £25·00)   0·38 × 25·00 = 9·50

£28·80

2. For each possible outcome of obtaining the additional information, revise the previously established probabilities, re-compute the *E.V.*s, and select the most favourable alternative.

3. Multiply the probability of each outcome by the *E.V.* of the most favourable alternative given that outcome, and add the results to obtain the expected value if additional information is obtained. The difference between this and the *E.V.* obtained in (1) gives the value to the decision-maker of the additional information.

EXERCISES

1. A charity is about to launch an appeal and has to choose between the following fund-raising strategies:

    Strategy (a), which involves an initial appeal outlay of £4000 and administrative costs of 5p for each £1 collected. Strategy (b), which has no initial outlay but instead involves an extensive door-to-door campaign with administrative costs of 30p for each £1 collected.

    It is estimated that, whichever strategy is used, the amount collected will be as follows:

Amount (£):	5000	10,000	15,000	20,000
Probability:	0.2	0.4	0.3	0.1

    Construct a pay-off table and so determine which strategy the charity should adopt. If the charity could accurately forecast the amount collected, how much would this information be worth to it?

2. Jim has found that the probability of tossing a head with a certain bent coin is 0.6. He proposes the following wager to his friend Fred. The coin is tossed three times: if the result is 'three heads', he will pay Fred £2; if the result is 'two heads and a tail' (in any order), he will pay Fred £2; if the result is 'less than two heads', Fred will pay him £3.
   (a) Represent this by a decision tree, and show whether the wager is fair. (Note: a wager is fair if its expected value is zero.) What should Fred pay Jim to make it fair if no heads are tossed?
   (b) Fred accepts the wager and wins. What is the probability that the first toss was a head?

3. A British food company has developed an enzyme process for manufacturing synthetic meat from vegetable waste. It wishes to market the product in the U.K., and must choose one of three alternative marketing strategies:
   (a) To carry out a market research survey at a cost of £100,000. If the results of this survey indicate that the product is unlikely to be successful, the process will be sold to an American company for £3m. If, on the other hand, the results of the survey are favourable (and the probability of a favourable result is estimated to be 0.7), a small-scale test-launch of the product will be undertaken at a cost of £2m. If the test-launch result is unfavourable, the process will be sold as before; if the result is favourable (and the probability of this, given a favourable market-

research result, is estimated to be 0.8), then the company will go into full-scale production. The net present value of full-scale production, given a favourable test-launch result, is estimated to be:

£10m with a probability of 0.2

£20m with a probability of 0.5

£30m with a probability of 0.3

(b) The second strategy involves omitting the test-launch, and instead proceeding direct from a favourable market-research result to full-scale production. In this case the company will be less confident of success, and it estimates the net present value of full-scale production to be:

£NIL with a probability of 0.1

£10m with a probability of 0.5

£20m with a probability of 0.4

(c) To omit the market-research survey and commence with the test-launch. The probability that the test-launch will yield a favourable result in the absence of market-research information is estimated to be 0.6. On the basis of the test-launch result, the company will either sell the process or go into full-scale production with N.P.V.s as in (a).

You are required to represent these alternatives by decision trees and so determine which one the company should adopt.

4. The existing water supply to a remote township has to be replaced, and the water authority has to decide between laying a pipe from the nearest lake at a cost of £1,000,000 or drilling for artesian water in the vicinity of the town at a cost of £800,000. The probability that the artesian supply will prove adequate for the town's needs is estimated to be 0.6. If it proves inadequate, then it will have to be supplemented by laying a narrow pipe to the lake at an additional cost of £700,000.

By carrying out a series of test drills at a cost of £50,000 the authority can get a better idea as to whether or not the artesian supply will be adequate. If it is adequate, then the authority knows from past experience that the probabilities of the various outcomes of the test-drilling programme are as follows:

test drills indicate supply adequate 0.7

test drills indicate supply inadequate. . . . 0.1

test drills give ambiguous result 0.2

If the artesian supply is inadequate, the probabilities of the various outcomes of the test-drilling programme are:

test drills indicate supply adequate . . . . . .Nil

test drills indicate supply inadequate. . . . 0.7

test drills give ambiguous result 0.3

Should the authority carry out the test drills?

Eighteen

Probability Distributions and Queueing Theory

In the section of this text dealing with frequency distributions it was seen that if a variable is normally distributed, then its behaviour can be described in a mathematically exact manner by applying the table of normal curve areas. Many variables are not normally distributed, and the assignment of probabilities using normal curve areas cannot then be applied. In the bakery example given in the last chapter the probabilities were determined by calculating relative frequencies from past records; in the furniture removal example, the probabilities were determined on the basis of the experience and judgement of the manager involved. In this chapter we examine variables which are not normally distributed but whose behaviour can nevertheless be described mathematically, using one or other of three related probability distributions: the binomial, the Poisson, and the exponential distributions.

PERMUTATIONS AND COMBINATIONS

Before discussing these distributions it is necessary to touch upon the subject of permutations and combinations. We shall use in this section the example of a pack of 52 playing cards, which is shuffled, and from which are dealt three cards.

We begin by considering the question, how many arrangements of three cards dealt in this way are possible? (It is assumed that the order in which the cards are dealt is relevant, so that the arrangement: king of hearts followed by queen of hearts followed by jack of hearts is different from the arrangement: jack of hearts followed by queen of hearts followed by king of hearts.)

The first card dealt can be any of 52 cards, the second card can be any of the remaining 51 cards, and the third card can be any of the remaining 50 cards. The number of possible arrangements of cards is therefore

$$52 \times 51 \times 50 = 132,600$$

By extending this reasoning it can be seen that if r cards are dealt from a pack, then the number of possible arrangements is

$$52 \times 51 \times 50 \times 49 \times \ldots \times (52 - (r-2)) \times$$
$$(52 - (r-1))$$

and this is equal to

$$\frac{52 \times 51 \times 50 \times \ldots \times 3 \times 2 \times 1}{(52-r)(52-(r+1))(52-(r+2)) \times \ldots \times 3 \times 2 \times 1}$$

(To prove this equality, cancel the terms in the denominator with those in the numerator.)

Generally, if r objects are selected from n objects, and if the order of selection is relevant, then the number of possible arrangements (or 'permutations') is

$$\frac{n(n-1)(n-2) \ldots 3 \times 2 \times 1}{(n-r)(n-(r+1)) \ldots 3 \times 2 \times 1}$$

The mathematic shorthand for $n(n-1)$

$(n-2) \ldots 3 \times 2 \times 1$ is $n!$ (called 'factorial n').
The above fraction can therefore be written

$$\frac{n!}{(n-r)!}$$

The symbol $_nP_r$ is used to denote the number of possible permutations of r objects selected from n objects. So the permutation formula is:

$$_nP_r = \frac{n!}{(n-r)!}$$

Let us now consider the question, how many arrangements of the three cards are possible if order is *irrelevant* (so that, for example, the arrangement: king of hearts followed by queen of hearts followed by jack of hearts is considered to be identical to the arrangement: jack of hearts followed by queen of hearts followed by king of hearts).

We have seen that the number of permutations is $52 \times 51 \times 50$. Many of these permutations are now, however, considered to be identical: they consist of the same cards arranged in a different order. How many possible orders of three cards are there? If we consider the king, queen and jack of hearts, the king can take any one of three positions (for it can be dealt first, second or third), the queen can take any one of the remaining two positions, and the jack must occupy the third remaining position. The number of possible orders of the three cards is therefore $3 \times 2 \times 1 = 6$. (The six orders are: KQJ, KJQ, QKJ, QJK, JKQ, JQK).

It follows that each possible set of three cards dealt from the pack can be ordered in six ways, and so only one-sixth of the $51 \times 52 \times 50$ permutations consist of different sets of cards. Hence the number of ways in which three cards can be dealt from a pack if the order in which they are dealt is irrelevant is

$$\frac{52 \times 51 \times 50}{3 \times 2 \times 1} \quad (= 22{,}100)$$

A moment's thought will convince the student that this fraction can be rewritten

$$\frac{52!}{(52-3)!\,3!}, \text{ i.e. } \frac{52!}{49!\,3!}$$

Generally, if r objects are selected from n objects, and if the order of selection is irrelevant, then the number of possible selections (or 'combinations') is

$$\frac{n!}{(n-r)!\,r!}$$

This fraction is denoted by the symbol $_nC_r$.

EXAMPLE

A team of 6 students is to be selected from a class of 20. In how many ways can this be done?

ANSWER

The order of selection is not relevant, and so the number of ways is

$$_{20}C_6 = \frac{20!}{(20-6)!\,6!}$$

$$= \frac{20!}{14!\,6!}$$

$$= \frac{20 \times 19 \times 18 \times 17 \times 16 \times 15}{6 \times 5 \times 4 \times 3 \times 2 \times 1}$$

$$= 155{,}040$$

THE BINOMIAL DISTRIBUTION

Many processes consist of a number of actions or trials each of which can result in one of two possible events. Examples include: a machine producing components which are either satisfactory or defective: a sample of viewers who either watched or did not watch a particular programme; a drug which either cures or does not cure a patient.

It is conventional to refer to one of the two events as 'success' and the other as 'failure'. (The event 'success' is not, however, necessarily to be preferred to the event 'failure'. These are simply convenient labels, like x and y.)

Such a process is a binomial process if it satisfies the following conditions:

1. The events are independent, so that there is no pattern to the way in which successes and failures occur

2. The probability of the event 'success' remains constant from one action to another, so that the probability of 'success' on a future action can be known with certainty.

Suppose a trial consists of shuffling a pack of cards, selecting a card, and replacing it in the pack, and the event 'success' is 'select a heart' ('failure' being 'select a diamond, spade or club'). This is a binomial trial, for the probability that the card selected will be a heart is known with certainty (it is $\frac{1}{4}$), and the result of one trial will not affect the results of subsequent trials, since the card is replaced and the pack reshuffled.

If, however, the card is discarded after it has been selected, then the process is not binomial, since the result of one trial will affect the results of subsequent trials. For example, if the first card selected is a heart, then there are 51 cards left in the pack of which 12 are hearts. The probability that the next card will be a heart is therefore not 1/4 but 12/51.

Another example of a binomial trial is the throw of a die. If the event 'success' is 'throw a six', then, if the die is fair, $P(\text{success}) = 1/6$, and $P(\text{failure}) = $ probability of throwing any number other than a six $= 5/6$.

Suppose the die is thrown 10 times. What is the probability that just 2 of the throws will be sixes? The 10 throws can result in many possible combinations of sixes and non-sixes, and to answer this question we must first determine the probability that any given combination is 2 sixes and 8 non-sixes. By the multiplication rule this probability is

$$\tfrac{1}{6} \times \tfrac{1}{6} \times \tfrac{5}{6} \times \tfrac{5}{6} \times \tfrac{5}{6} \times \tfrac{5}{6} \times \tfrac{5}{6} \times \tfrac{5}{6} \times \tfrac{5}{6} \times \tfrac{5}{6}$$

$$= (\tfrac{1}{6})^2 (\tfrac{5}{6})^8$$

$$= 0.00646$$

Secondly, we must determine how many combinations containing just 2 sixes are possible. It is helpful to look at this problem in the following manner: in how many ways can the 2 sixes be allocated to the 10 positions in the run of throws? The order of the 2 sixes among themselves is irrelevant — it does not matter which six is thrown first and which second — and so we have a combination problem. The number of ways in which 2 positions can be selected out of 10 without regard to order is

$$_{10}C_2 = \frac{10!}{8! \; 2!}$$

$$= 45$$

There are therefore 45 combinations containing 2 sixes, and each of these has a probability of 0.00646. The probability of obtaining just 2 sixes in a run of 10 throws is therefore $45 \times 0.00646 = 0.2907$.

The probability of obtaining r sixes in n throws of the die is determined in the same way. The probability that a run of n throws contains r sixes and $n - r$ non-sixes is

$$(\tfrac{1}{6})^r (\tfrac{5}{6})^{n-r}$$

The number of ways in which r sixes can occur in a run of n throws is

$$\frac{n!}{(n-r)! \, r!}$$

Hence the required probability is

$$\frac{n!}{(n-r)! \, r!} \, (\tfrac{1}{6})^r (\tfrac{5}{6})^{n-r}$$

The formula for the binomial distribution is obtained by generalizing this argument. If a trial is binomial, and $P(\text{success}) = p$ (so that $P(\text{failure}) = 1 - p = q$), then the probability of r successes in n trials is

$$\frac{n!}{(n-r)! \, r!} \, p^r \, q^{n-r}$$

$p = 0.2$
$q = 0.8$
$n = 5$

EXAMPLE

20% of the components produced by a machine are defective. Five components are selected at random. What is the probability that 0, 1, 2, 3, 4, 5 of these components will be defective?

ANSWER

In this example $p = 0.2$, $q = 0.8$, and $n = 5$. Applying the formula for the binomial distribution, the required probabilities are as follows:

Number defective		Probability
$r = 0$	$\dfrac{5!}{5!0!}\,0.2^2 0.8^5 = 0.8^5$	$= 0.32768^*$
$r = 1$	$\dfrac{5!}{4!1!}\,0.2^1 0.8^4 = 5 \times 0.2 \times 0.8^4$	$= 0.4096$
$r = 2$	$\dfrac{5!}{3!2!}\,0.2^2 0.8^3 =$	0.2048
$r = 3$	$\dfrac{5!}{2!3!}\,0.2^3 0.8^2 =$	0.0512
$r = 4$	$\dfrac{5!}{1!4!}\,0.2^4 0.8^1 =$	0.0064
$r = 5$	$\dfrac{5!}{0!5!}\,0.2^5 0.8^0 =$	0.00032^*
		1.00000

(*0! is defined to equal 1)

THE NORMAL APPROXIMATION TO THE BINOMIAL DISTRIBUTION

The probabilities listed in the above defective components example form a probability distribution, and the histogram of this distribution is shown in Figure 18.1. It can be seen from this figure that the distribution has a pronounced positive skew. However, as the value of n increases, the degree of skewness in a binomial distribution decreases, and in the above example the histogram is virtually

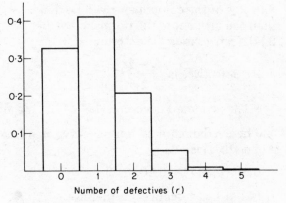

Figure 18.1   Histogram of binomial distribution $(n = 5, p = 0.2)$

symmetrical for $n \geqslant 25$. As an exercise, the student should calculate the probabilities for the above example if the sample is of size 25, over the range 0 to 10 defectives, and plot the results on a histogram.

The binomial distribution in fact approaches the normal distribution if the value of n is sufficiently large, and it is then possible to use the table of normal curve areas to estimate binomial probabilities. This avoids the need to carry out the rather arduous calculations of the type listed above. The rule is that the normal approximation can be used provided that $np > 5$ for $p \leqslant 0.5$ (or $nq > 5$ if $p > 0.5$).

In order to use the table of normal curve areas, the mean and the standard deviation of the distribution must be determined. (Since we are dealing with probabilities we should, strictly, use the term 'expectation' rather than 'mean'). Expectation = Σ(probability multiplied by x-value), and by substituting the formula for binomial probabilities into this expression and manipulating the terms it is quite easy to show that the expectation equals np. The standard deviation can also be shown to equal $\sqrt{npq}$.

In the exercise given above, in which $n = 25$ and $p = 0.2$, the mean $= np = 25 \times 0.2 = 5$, and the standard deviation $= \sqrt{npq} = \sqrt{25 \times 0.2 \times 0.8} = 2$. If it is required to determine the probability that, for instance,

2 or less of the components will be defective, then the area under the normal curve below $2\frac{1}{2}$ defectives must be determined.

$2\frac{1}{2}$ defectives is $\dfrac{5 - 2\frac{1}{2}}{2}$

= 1.25 standard deviations below the mean

and hence the required normal curve area (see Appendix I) is

0.5 − 0.3944 = 0.1056.

$P(2$ or less defectives) is therefore 0.1056, and this result can be compared with that obtained by computing the probabilities from the binomial formula. Using that formula,

$$P(0) = \frac{25!}{25!\,0!}\ 0.2^0\ 0.8^{25} = 0.0038$$

$$P(1) = \frac{25!}{24!\,1!}\ 0.2^1\ 0.8^{24} = 0.0236$$

$$P(2) = \frac{25!}{23!\,2!}\ 0.2^2\ 0.8^{23} = 0.0708$$

and so

$$P(2 \text{ or less}) = P(0) + P(1) + P(2) = 0.0982$$

which is fairly close to the result obtained by the use of the normal approximation. As the value of n increases, so the binomial distribution more closely resembles the normal distribution, and the agreement between the two results improves.

The normal approximation to the binomial distribution was used in Chapter 10 in estimating population proportions from sample data. If np is the expected number of 'successes' in a sample, then

$$\frac{np}{n} = p$$

is the expected proportion of successes, and the standard deviation of this proportion is

$$\frac{\sqrt{npq}}{n} = \sqrt{\frac{pq}{n}}$$

The application of these formulae is given in Chapter 10.

THE POISSON DISTRIBUTION

The binomial distribution discussed in the last section is used to determine the probability of r successes in n trials. In this section we discuss the Poisson distribution, which is used to determine the probability of r successes in a given space or time period.

Consider the example of a machine producing magnetic tape with occasional minute defects in the magnetic coating. It is found that there are, on average, m defects in every 5 metres of tape. Imagine that a 5-metre length of this tape is taken, and that it is cut into 100 lengths each of 5 cm. We now make two assumptions about these short lengths:

1. No more than one defect occurs in each short length

2. There is no pattern in the way in which the defects occur, so that the number of defects in one length is independent of the number of defects in other lengths.

For each short length there are therefore two possible events: 'one defect' or 'no defects'. The probability of one defect in a 5-cm length is clearly $m/100$, and the probability of no defects is therefore $1 − m/100$. In view of the second assumption, the number of defects in the 100 short lengths follows the binomial distribution (it is assumed in this example that the characteristics of the machine do not alter, so that the average number of defects per 5 metres remains equal to m), and the probability of r defects in the 100 short lengths is therefore

$$P(r) = \frac{100!}{(100 - r)!\,r!}\ \left(\frac{m}{100}\right)^r\ \left(1 - \frac{m}{100}\right)^{100 - r}$$

The first assumption is, however, not realistic, since there might sometimes be more than 1 defect in a 5-cm length. We should instead assume that the 5-metre length is cut into n short equal lengths, where n is a very large number. Under this assumption the probability of r defects becomes

$$P(r) = \frac{n!}{(n-r)!r!} \left(\frac{m}{n}\right)^r \left(1 - \frac{m}{n}\right)^{n-r}$$

$$= \frac{n(n-1)(n-2)\ldots(n-r+1)m^r}{r!\, n^r} \times \frac{(1-m/n)^n}{(1-m/n)^r}$$

$$= \frac{1(1-1/n)(1-2/n)\ldots(1-(r-1)/n)m^r(1-m/n)^n}{r!\,(1-m/n)^r}$$

Since n is assumed to be a very large number, the terms $(1 - 1/n)$, $(1 - 2/n)$, etc., all approach 1, and the term $(1 - m/n)^r$ also approaches 1 (these terms approach 1 because $1/n$, $2/n$, $\ldots$ m/n all approach zero). In Chapter 14 it was shown that the term $(1 + i/n)^n$ approaches e^i as n increases, where e is the exponential constant 2.71828. Replacing i by $-m$, it follows that $(1 - m/n)^n = e^{-m}$. Substituting all these results in the formula for $P(r)$, it follows that

$$P(r) = \frac{1 \times 1 \times 1 \ldots \times 1 \times m^r \times e^{-m}}{r! \times 1}$$

$$= \frac{e^{-m}\, m^r}{r!}$$

This is the formula for the Poisson probability distribution. It is the limiting case of the binomial distribution, with n becoming very large and $p = m/n$ becoming very small. It is subject to similar conditions to those applying to the binomial distribution, namely that the occurrence of the event 'success' at one point in space or time does not affect the probability of 'success' at any other point in space or time, and the probability of 'success' remains constant from point to point.

Referring to the above example, if the average number of defects in 5 m of tape is $m = 2$, then the probability of 0, 1, 2, 3, 4, 5, etc., defects in a 5 m length is:

$$P(0) = \frac{e^{-2}\, 2^0}{0!} = e^{-2} = \frac{1}{2.71828^2} = 0.1353$$

$$P(1) = \frac{e^{-2}\, 2^1}{1!} = 2P(0) \qquad = 0.2707$$

$$P(2) = \frac{e^{-2}\, 2^2}{2!} = P(1) \qquad = 0.2707$$

$$P(3) = \frac{e^{-2}\, 2^3}{3!} = \tfrac{2}{3}P(2) \qquad = 0.1804$$

$$P(4) = \frac{e^{-2}\, 2^4}{4!} = \tfrac{1}{2}P(3) \qquad = 0.0902$$

$$P(5) = \frac{e^{-2}\, 2^5}{5!} = \tfrac{2}{5}P(4) \qquad = 0.0361$$

etc.

EXAMPLE

During the afternoon the average number of cars passing a certain point on a quiet country road is 1 car every 2 minutes. What is the probability that over a 10-minute period there will be (a) 0, (b) 1, (c) 2, (d) at least 3 cars passing the point?

ANSWER

The requirements of the Poisson distribution are satisfied, for the average number of 'successes' (i.e. cars passing) remains constant, and the passage of a car at one instant does not affect the probability of the passage of a car at another instant — so that there is no pattern to the passage of cars. (Note that if the road were busy the second requirement would not be satisfied, since the cars would tend to 'bunch' behind slow-moving vehicles, and a definite pattern would then emerge.)

The average number of cars passing every 10 minutes is $m = 5$ (since 1 passes every 2 minutes), and so

$$P(0) = \frac{e^{-5}\, 5^0}{0!} = \frac{1}{2.71828^5} = 0.0067$$

$$P(1) = \frac{e^{-5}\, 5^1}{1!} = 5P(0) \qquad = 0.0337$$

$$P(2) = \frac{e^{-5}\, 5^2}{2!} = \tfrac{5}{2}P(1) \qquad = 0.0842$$

$P(\text{at least } 3) = 1 - (P(0) + P(1) + P(2))$
$$= 0.8753$$

THE NORMAL APPROXIMATION TO THE POISSON DISTRIBUTION

Just as the binomial distribution approaches the normal distribution under certain conditions, so too does its limiting case, the Poisson distribution. The mean of the binomial distribution is np, and the standard deviation is $\sqrt{npq}$; it follows that the mean of the Poisson distribution is $np = m$ (since $p = m/n$), and the standard deviation is

$$\sqrt{npq} = \sqrt{np(1-p)}$$
$$\simeq \sqrt{np}$$
$$= \sqrt{m}$$

(since $1 - p \simeq 1$ when p is very small).

The condition for the binomial distribution to approximate to the normal distribution is that $np > 5$; since $np = m$, it follows that the condition for the Poisson distribution to approximate to the normal distribution is $m > 5$.

Referring to the previous example, to find the probability that at least 3 cars pass the point in a 10-minute period, the normal curve area required is that lying above $2\frac{1}{2}$ cars. The mean $= m = 5$, the standard deviation $= \sqrt{m} = \sqrt{5} = 2.236$, and so the standard normal value corresponding to $2\frac{1}{2}$ cars is

$$z = \frac{2\frac{1}{2} - 5}{2.236} = -1.118$$

(i.e. $2\frac{1}{2}$ cars is 1.118 S.D.s below the mean). From Appendix I the required area is $0.5 + 0.3682 = 0.8682$, and this is the probability that at least 3 cars will pass the point in a 10-minute period. This figure accords well with the probability calculated using the formula for the Poisson distribution in the example (0.8753).

The accuracy of probability estimates using the normal approximation improves as the value of m increases.

THE EXPONENTIAL DISTRIBUTION

In this section we return to the example of the machine producing magnetic tape with minute defects along its length, and the problem we now consider is, what is the probability that a given length x of tape has no defects?

The average number of defects per 5-metre length was m. Hence in x metres the average will be $mx/5$. The number of defects in x metres will therefore follow the Poisson distribution with mean $= mx/5$, and hence the probability of no defects in this length is

$$P(0) = \frac{e^{-mx/5} \, (mx/5)^0}{0!} = e^{-mx/5}$$

Now $m/5$ is the average number of defects per unit length (the unit in this case being 1 metre), and it is conventional to denote this quantity by the Greek letter λ (lambda). So $P(0) = e^{-\lambda x}$.

The probability that the length x has no defects is clearly the probability that the length of tape between two successive defects exceeds x. It follows that the probability that the length between successive defects is less than x is $1 - e^{-\lambda x}$.

What, then, is the probability $P(x)$ that the length between successive defects is exactly x? From our knowledge of calculus it is clear that the probability that this length takes any value between 0 and x is $\int P(x) \, dx$. This probability was shown in the previous paragraph to be equal to $1 - e^{-\lambda x}$, and it therefore follows that

$$1 - e^{-\lambda x} = \int P(x) \, dx$$

$P(x)$ therefore equals $\dfrac{d}{dx} (1 - e^{-\lambda x})$

$$= \lambda e^{-\lambda x}$$

Hence the probability that the interval between successive defects (or other 'successes' or 'events' which satisfy the requirements of the Poisson distribution) is equal to x is

$$P(x) = \lambda e^{-\lambda x}$$

where λ is the mean number of events per unit interval of space or time. This is the formula for the exponential distribution.

It should be noted that since there are, on average, λ events per unit interval, then the average interval between successive events is $1/\lambda$.

EXAMPLE

The bushes on a certain type of electric motor wear down and have to be replaced after an average of 800 hours running. What is the probability that a set of bushes will last more than 1000 hours?

ANSWER

The average length of running time between successive replacements is $1/\lambda = 800$ hours. Hence $\lambda = 1/800$. The probability that the interval between replacements is less than $x = 1000$ hours is

$$1 - e^{-\lambda x} = 1 - e^{-1000/800}$$
$$= 1 - 1/e^{1.25} = 0.7135$$

The probability that the interval exceeds 1000 hours is therefore

$$1 - 0.7135 = 0.2865$$

QUEUEING THEORY

Queues are an important feature of modern societies. Shoppers queue at supermarket checkouts, machines queue for servicing, orders queue for processing, and so on. Queues develop in a system because customers arrive in an irregular manner, and at times the rate at which they arrive exceeds the rate at which they can be serviced. The only way to eliminate queues is to increase the servicing facilities to such an extent that all arrivals into the system can be dealt with without delay, but the result would be that for most of the time the servicing facilities would be under-utilized. There is clearly some optimum

level of servicing facilities for any system, which on the one hand does not allow queues to become excessively long, and on the other, ensures a reasonably high utilization of servicing facilities. Queueing theory is concerned with describing such systems by means of mathematical models, and determining from these models the optimum level and arrangement of servicing facilities.

We shall limit the discussion to deriving and applying the formulae for 'simple queues', that is one-channel queues passing through a single service point (an example being the queue in a self-service store with a single checkout). Similar principles apply to queues passing through a number of servicing points (these are discussed briefly at the end of the chapter), but the formulae for these are very complex.

It is assumed that customers arrive into the system in an irregular, pattern-free manner, and that the average number of arrivals per unit of time (designated by the symbol λ) remains constant. Under these two conditions the number of arrivals per unit of time can be described by the Poisson distribution.

It is also assumed that the time taken to service customers varies in an irregular manner, and that the average number of customers dealt with by the service point per unit of time (designated by the symbol μ) remains constant. (In calculating this average any idle time caused by lack of customers is excluded.) Under these conditions the service times can be described by the exponential distribution. Note that the average time taken to service one customer is $1/\mu$.

An important measure used in queueing theory is the 'traffic intensity', designated by the symbol ρ (the Greek letter 'rho'):

$$\rho = \frac{\text{average number of customers arriving per unit of time}}{\text{average number of customers serviced per unit of time}}$$

$$= \lambda/\mu$$

The value of ρ must never exceed 1, otherwise λ exceeds μ, and customers arrive faster than they can be serviced, the queue growing indefinitely long.

The various formulae required for handling problems involving simple queues can be very easily derived, as we show below.

1. During one unit of time an average of λ customers arrive, and since the average time taken to service each one is $1/\mu$, the length of time that the service point is in use during that time unit is

$$\lambda \frac{1}{\mu} = \rho$$

ρ therefore represents the proportion of the time that the service point is in use, and $1 - \rho$ is the proportion of time that it is not in use (and when, therefore, there are no customers in the system). It follows that the probability that, on arrival, a customer finds the service point in use is ρ, and the probability he finds it not in use is $1 - \rho$.

2. From the above it is clear that the probability that a customer can be serviced without having to queue is $1 - \rho$. The probability that another customer arrives and has to wait because the previous customer is still being serviced is $(1 - \rho)\rho$. The probability that a customer arrives and has to wait because the first customer is being serviced and another is waiting is $((1 - \rho)\rho)\rho = (1 - \rho)\rho^2$. Extending this argument, it can be seen that the probability that at any time there are n people in the system (i.e. 1 being serviced and $n - 1$ queueing) is

$$(1 - \rho)\rho^n$$

3. The expected (or average) number of customers in a system is

$\Sigma(\text{probability} \times \text{number})$

$= \Sigma(1 - \rho)\rho^n \, n$

$= \Sigma \, n\rho^n - \Sigma \, n\rho^{n+1}$

$= (\rho + 2\rho^2 + 3\rho^2 + 4\rho^4 + \ldots) - $
$(\rho^2 + 2\rho^3 + 3\rho^4 + \ldots)$

$= \rho + \rho^2 + \rho^3 + \rho^4 + \ldots$

This is a geometric progression with first term $= \rho$ and common ratio $= \rho$. The sum to m terms is, by the formula given in Chapter 14

$$\frac{\rho(1 - \rho^m)}{1 - \rho}$$

Since m, the number of terms in this G.P., is indefinitely large, and since $\rho < 1$, it follows that ρ^m is infinitesimally small. Hence the sum of this G.P. is

$$\frac{\rho}{1 - \rho}$$

4. The average time spent by a customer in the queue = (average number in the system when he arrives) × (average servicing time)

$$= \frac{\rho}{1 - \rho} \times \frac{1}{\mu}$$

$$= \frac{\lambda}{\mu(\mu - \lambda)}$$

5. The average time spent by a customer in the system (queueing and being serviced) = average queueing time + average servicing time

$$= \frac{\lambda}{\mu(\mu - \lambda)} + \frac{1}{\mu}$$

$$= \frac{\lambda + (\mu - \lambda)}{\mu(\mu - \lambda)}$$

$$= \frac{1}{\mu - \lambda}$$

The average time spent queueing in a simple queue system is proportional to

$$\frac{\rho}{1 - \rho}$$

(from formula (4)); this fraction is in fact the ratio of the time spent queueing to the time spent being serviced. The values that this fraction takes for various values of ρ are:

ρ = 0.2 0.3 0.4 0.5 0.6 0.7 0.8 0.9 1.0

$\dfrac{\rho}{1-\rho}$ = 0.25 0.43 0.67 1.00 1.50 2.33 4.00 9.00 ∞

It is clear from this that queueing time will not be excessive provided that ρ is less than 0.7 or 0.8. At $\rho = 0.8$ the time spent queueing is, on average, four times as great as the time spent being serviced. As ρ approaches 1, the queueing time becomes very large indeed. In certain systems a value of ρ in excess of 0.8 may be acceptable (for example, non-urgent paperwork queueing for processing), but in systems involving high delay costs, or where people are queueing, ρ should normally be less than 0.8.

Since the proportion of time that the service point is in use is equal to ρ, it follows that in a large number of simple queue situations the service point must be less than 80% utilized.

If the number of service points is increased (so that the system no longer consists of a simple one-channel queue + one service point), the value of ρ can rise above 0.8 without excessive queues forming. If, for example, two service points are used, $\rho = 0.9$ will result in an average queueing time four times as great as the average servicing time, and $\rho = 0.8$ will result in the average queueing time being less than twice the servicing time.

The reduction in queueing time and the higher utilization of servicing facilities that results from increasing the number of servicing points is one reason why pooled stores, typing, and other facilities are normally more efficient than small dispersed units.

EXAMPLE

To illustrate the application of the above formulae, we shall consider the example of a busy launderette with one coin-operated dry-cleaning machine. The cycle time of the machine is thermostatically controlled and varies with the size of load, the mean time being 30 minutes (including loading and unloading). The rate at which customers arrive to use the machine follows the Poisson distribution with a mean of one customer every 40 minutes. For simplicity it is assumed that each customer brings just one machine-load of cleaning.

If 1 hour is our unit of time, then customers arrive at a mean hourly rate of $\lambda = 1.5$. μ is the average number of machine-loads that can be processed per hour (excluding machine idle time), and this equals 2. So

$$\rho = \frac{1.5}{2} = 0.75$$

The proportion of time that the machine remains idle is $1 - \rho = 0.25$, and the probability that a customer will be able to use the machine immediately on arrival is also $1 - \rho = 0.25$. The probability that a customer will have to wait is $\rho = 0.75$.

The expected number of customers in the system (i.e. queueing or using the machine) is

$$\frac{\rho}{1-\rho} = \frac{0.75}{0.25}$$

$$= 3$$

The average time that a customer has to spend queueing is

$$\frac{\lambda}{\mu(\mu - \lambda)} = \frac{1.5}{2(2 - 1.5)}$$

$$= 1.5 \text{ hours}$$

Although the drycleaner is idle for 25% of the time, the proprietor should obviously consider installing a second machine. Let us suppose that the costs of a drycleaning machine average out at 20p per hour (fixed costs) plus 30p per load (variable costs). Let us suppose further that the loss of goodwill caused by the long waiting time is causing customers to look elsewhere for drycleaning facilities, and the proprietor estimates that this loss can be valued at 50p per hour of queueing time. Each customer has to queue for an average of 1.5 hours, and so the queueing time cost per customer = 1.5 × 50p = 75p.

1.5 customers arrive per hour, so the total hourly costs = (machine costs: 20p + 1.5 × 30p = 65p) + (customer queueing costs: 1.5 × 75p = 112.5p) = 177.5p.

If a second machine is installed, then

$$\rho = \lambda/2\mu$$

$$= \frac{1.5}{4}$$

$$= 0.375$$

The formulae we have derived must be modified for two service points, and the average time spent queueing can be shown to be

$$\frac{\rho^2}{(1-\rho)(1+\rho^2)\mu} = \frac{0.375^2}{(1-0.375)(1+0.375^2)2}$$

$$\simeq 0.1 \text{ hours}$$

The queueing costs per customer are therefore

$$0.1 \times 50p = 5p$$

The total hourly costs for two machines = (machine costs: 2 × 20p + 1.5 × 30p = 85p) + (customer queueing costs: 1.5 × 5p = 7.5p) = 92.5p.

The proprietor should therefore install a second machine, as this will result in a reduction in the queueing time to an average of 0.1 hours (i.e. 6 minutes) per customer, and the total hourly costs will be almost halved.

Other Queueing Systems

Several types of non-simple queues are possible. For example, in busy launderettes customers form a single queue and leave it to take the first available machine; in supermarkets a number of queues form, one behind each checkout. The mathematics of these systems can be extremely complex, and they are often more easily analysed using simulation methods.

Simulation of queues involves using random numbers to produce a frequency table which models arrivals of customers on the basis of a known frequency table of arrivals, and calculating from this model the average queueing time and any other measures required. (The method is explained in Appendix IV, assignment C4). Besides avoiding the need to use complex mathematics, simulation methods have the advantage that they do not require a Poisson distribution of arrivals, since any arrival pattern can be modelled simply by adjusting the number of random numbers assigned to each class of the frequency table.

EXERCISES

1. Only 60% of melon seeds of a certain type will germinate. If 10 of the seeds are planted in a row, what is the probability that: (i) 5, (ii) 6, (iii) 7 will germinate? If 7 of the seeds germinate, leaving 3 gaps in the row, how many arrangements of the gaps are possible?

2. (a) A certain drug is found to be effective in 80% of cases. A doctor treats 5 of his patients with the drug. What is the probability that it will be effective for: (i) none (ii) 1, (iii) 2, (iv) 3, (v) 4, (vi) all 5 of them? Show the results on a histogram.

   (b) If 100 patients are treated with the drug, find, using the normal approximation to the binomial distribution, the probability that it will be effective for at least 75 of them.

3. No. 13 buses arrive at a certain bus-stop in a completely irregular manner. The company intends to do nothing to rectify the situation, because the average interval between arrivals is only 10 minutes, and it claims that buses are 'rarely' more than 15 minutes apart. To test this claim, a member of a local consumers' organization turns up one morning at the bus-stop to observe the arrival of 10 successive buses.

(a) Find the probability that: (i) 0, (ii) 1, (iii) 2, (iv) 3, (v) 4, (vi) 5, (vii) 6 buses all arrive in the first 30 minutes of observation, and show the results on a histogram.

(b) Using the normal approximation to the Poisson distribution, determine the probability that the 10 buses all arrive within the space of one hour. (Hint: find the probability that 10 or more buses arrive in a one-hour period.)

(c) What is the probability that the interval between the first two buses is less than 15 minutes?

(d) What is the probability that for all 10 buses the interval between successive buses in no case exceeds 15 minutes? (Note that there are *nine* intervals involved.)

4. A lorry driver has a choice of two routes into a certain small country. The customs post on each route can only process one lorry at a time. The number of lorries arriving at the posts follows the Poisson distribution, the mean arrival rate at the route A post being 2 lorries per hour, the rate at the route B post being 4 lorries per hour. At each post the lorry-processing times follow the exponential distribution, with the mean time for the route A post being 21 minutes, and that for the route B post being 12 minutes.

Calculate for each customs post:

(a) The traffic intensity

(b) The probability that the driver will not have to queue on arrival

(c) The expected number of lorries queueing or being processed when he arrives

(d) The length of time he can expect to spend queueing and being processed.

Appendices

Appendix I

Normal Curve Areas

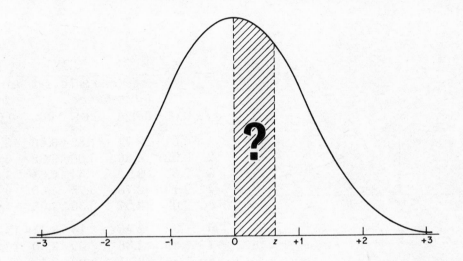

z is measured in standard normal units, i.e.

$$z = \frac{x - \overline{x}}{\text{S.D.}}$$

The following z-values are commonly used:

z	Area
1.64	0.450
1.96	0.475
2.33	0.490
2.58	0.495
3.09	0.499

To determine areas for intermediate z-values from the table, use linear interpolation. For example, z = 1.01 is 0.01/0.05 = 1/5 of the way between z = 1.00 and z = 1.05 hence the required area equals 0.3413 + 1/5 × (0.3531 − 0.3413) ≃ 0.3437.

z	0.00	0.05	z	0.00	0.05
0.0	0.0000	0.0199	1.5	0.4332	0.4394
0.1	0.0398	0.0596	1.6	0.4452	0.4505
0.2	0.0793	0.0987	1.7	0.4554	0.4599
0.3	0.1179	0.1368	1.8	0.4641	0.4678
0.4	0.1554	0.1736	1.9	0.4713	0.4744
0.5	0.1915	0.2088	2.0	0.4772	0.4798
0.6	0.2257	0.2422	2.1	0.4821	0.4842
0.7	0.2580	0.2734	2.2	0.4861	0.4878
0.8	0.2881	0.3023	2.3	0.4893	0.4906
0.9	0.3159	0.3289	2.4	0.4918	0.4929
1.0	0.3413	0.3531	2.5	0.4938	0.4946
1.1	0.3643	0.3749	2.6	0.4953	0.4960
1.2	0.3849	0.3944	2.7	0.4965	0.4970
1.3	0.4032	0.4115	2.8	0.4974	0.4978
1.4	0.4192	0.4265	2.9	0.4981	0.4984
			3.0	0.4987	0.4989

Critical Values of t and of χ^2

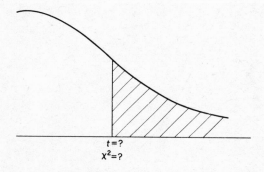

$t = ?$
$\chi^2 = ?$

The area under the tail gives the probability that sampling errors alone cause the value of t or χ^2 given in the table to be exceeded. For example, for 10 degrees of freedom:

(a) t-distribution:

  (i) 95% confidence limits: the area under each tail equals 0.025, so $t = -2.23$ and $+2.23$

  (ii) Two-tailed test at the 1% significance level: area under each tail equals 0.005, so critical value of t is 3.17

  (iii) One-tailed test at the 1% significance level: area under one tail equals 0.01, so critical value of t is 2.76.

(b) χ^2 distribution:
The calculated value of χ^2 is significant at the 1% level if it exceeds 23.21.

	Area under one tail of the t-distribution				Area under tail of χ^2	
d.f.	0.05	0.025	0.01	0.005	0.05	0.01
1	6.31	12.71	31.82	63.66	3.84	6.63
2	2.92	4.30	6.96	9.92	5.99	9.21
3	2.35	3.18	4.54	5.84	7.81	11.34
4	2.13	2.78	3.75	4.60	9.49	13.28
5	2.02	2.57	3.36	4.03	11.07	15.09
6	1.94	2.45	3.14	3.71	12.59	16.81
7	1.89	2.36	3.00	3.50	14.07	18.48
8	1.86	2.31	2.90	3.36	15.51	20.09
9	1.83	2.26	2.82	3.25	16.92	21.67
10	1.81	2.23	2.76	3.17	18.31	23.21
11	1.80	2.20	2.72	3.12	19.68	24.73
12	1.78	2.18	2.68	3.05	21.03	26.22
13	1.77	2.16	2.65	3.01	22.36	27.69
14	1.76	2.14	2.62	2.98	23.68	29.14
15	1.75	2.13	2.60	2.95	25.00	30.58
16	1.75	2.12	2.58	2.92	26.30	32.00
17	1.74	2.11	2.57	2.90	27.59	33.41
18	1.73	2.10	2.55	2.88	28.87	34.81
19	1.73	2.09	2.54	2.86	30.14	36.19
20	1.72	2.09	2.53	2.85	31.41	37.57
22	1.72	2.07	2.51	2.82	33.92	40.29
24	1.71	2.06	2.49	2.80	36.42	42.98
26	1.71	2.06	2.48	2.78	38.89	45.64
28	1.70	2.05	2.47	2.76	41.34	48.28
30	1.70	2.04	2.46	2.75	43.77	50.89

Appendix III

Table of Random Numbers

2349	4069	6382	0351	7060	2537	7699	4216
7696	2686	9714	0752	7579	8959	3537	3858
1342	7683	0229	3351	7806	1707	4820	0606
2465	4471	7762	7500	9907	3018	9349	1311
8671	1122	3646	5564	6864	1627	0675	7691
5124	7258	9004	5249	4273	8874	6244	4997
2396	4336	7549	6383	3143	3431	8099	1195
2942	7473	2984	5472	3139	1137	9686	7237
8543	6039	4258	3108	1487	5917	2213	7985
4172	3257	7888	1904	3998	5857	0271	5650
8568	6327	0213	9428	3157	7587	7050	1438
1540	3871	3533	7970	3863	8570	4976	2537
8785	6511	4213	3962	7716	6650	9830	0352
8123	5022	9481	0671	9910	2949	6658	8832
5563	4484	4858	4677	8355	3502	8067	4768
3287	6426	2711	6731	7869	6415	9705	9315
7123	7146	6354	0932	3535	3102	6816	6926
5327	6320	0167	8114	9696	0655	0266	1340
8110	2237	9813	4182	9357	8998	3586	5736
3644	2114	1750	8904	9892	8179	2578	6474
7618	8541	5468	9767	1274	4325	6743	0366
8110	6571	9731	1739	7603	5877	5390	1331
1170	4744	4886	8002	8804	6968	0783	6606
2319	2153	6974	2174	4348	1221	2888	8009
8062	7433	3620	8084	0790	6440	9728	3595
6072	3962	6939	3417	0591	3141	9497	9451
0184	1669	7001	5196	3161	9546	1451	6910
8777	9091	3695	1211	0998	3641	9842	8723
0292	9826	7498	2049	9606	5974	1052	7479
7300	8961	3728	2340	8851	7911	2131	7769
8514	6520	2667	2288	3408	6163	6289	1238
8625	2969	6139	9243	1671	4623	4892	2060
7629	0598	8182	2718	8043	6706	8869	7631
8143	9445	7320	1737	9202	8339	3686	5406
5108	5680	1134	2137	1187	1595	6108	3024

Appendix IV

Assignments and Simulations

Practical work involving the statistical and other techniques covered on this course stimulates an interest in the subject and enables the student to relate it to his other studies. Some of the assignments suggested below involve practical work in planning investigations, collecting or simulating data, and analysing and presenting data in a report. Assignments undertaken by students on BEC courses can range from simple tasks (such as answering an end-of-chapter question) to the more complex investigations outlined in this Appendix, some of which can last for several weeks.

A.   Assignments Based upon Data collected from Sample Surveys, Shops, and other Sources External to the College

1. At the Buckinghamshire College of Higher Education a number of research projects involving BEC students are being planned in association with the Wycombe District Council Department of Planning and Architecture. These include a town centre shopper survey, the purpose of which is to obtain and analyse data on the catchment area, modes of transport used, frequencies of visit, types of goods purchased, and attitudes towards High Wycombe as a shopping centre. The questionnaire form to be used (see Figure IV) was designed by the

Department of Planning and Architecture to meet its planning information requirements, and it will use the results of the survey to review, for example, public transport arrangements, car parking provision, and the need to encourage the establishment of additional stores. It is anticipated that a sample of 1,000 shoppers will be interviewed, and the results will be analysed using the College's computing facility. It will be noted that most of the possible responses to the questionnaire have been coded, so that the interviewer has merely to ring the appropriate number — this facilitates the subsequent analysis. A pilot survey has been carried out, and this indicates that one student can interview about 10 shoppers an hour. If two or three classes are involved in the survey work, no student will have to spend more than two hours interviewing. The sample will be selected by the systematic method — the tenth person passing the interviewer after the conclusion of the previous interview is chosen.

Other projects which it is hoped to undertake include a survey of local shopping parades with particular reference to social factors (such as their role as social centres, and the availability of public transport to the town centre), and a survey of pedestrian flows in the town centre.

2. Obtain monthly sales and wages figures for a run of several years for the departments

HIGH WYCOMBE TOWN CENTRE SHOPPER SURVEY

Date . . . .   Time . . . .   Reference . . . .

Location of Interview   1.   2.   3.   4.   5.   6.   7.   8.

Are you in High Wycombe Town Centre to do any shopping?

Yes   No   (if NO, terminate interview)
1   2

Q.1 (a) Where have you come from to do your shopping?

Home   Work   Elsewhere
1   2   3

Q.1 (b) Where is that?   . . . .
        (Specify location)

Q.2 How did you travel to the Town Centre?

1. Walking   4. Train
2. Car/Van   5. Motor Cycle/Bicycle
3. Bus/Coach   6. Other (Specify. . . . .)

Q.3 Are you here for anything other than shopping?

Yes   No   (if YES, ask what is that?)
1   2
1. Business   3. Services (e.g. hairdressers, bank)
2. Leisure (e.g. cinema,
        social visit)   4. Other (Specify. . . . .)

Q.4 Which goods are you shopping here for?

1. Food   5. Clothing/footwear
2. Furniture   6. Just looking
3. Household goods   7. Other items (Specify . . . .)
4. Electrical goods

Q.5 Which of the following advantages do you think applies to shopping in
    High Wycombe Town Centre?
    (Show card)

1.   2.   3.   4.   5.   6.   7.   (None)

Anything else (Specify   . . . .

. . . .)

Figure IV

Figure IV-continued

Q.6 Which of the following disadvantages do you think applies to shopping in
High Wycombe Town Centre?
(Show card)

1.   2.   3.   4.   5.   6.   (None)

Anything else (Specify ....

....)

Q.7 What improvements to shopping in High Wycombe Town Centre would you like to see?

None   (Specify...
  1

....

....)

Q.8 What other Shopping Centres have you visited for your more important
shopping requirements in the last six months?

01. Central London	06. Slough	11. Princes Risborough
02. Remainder of London	07. Luton	12. Marlow
03. Reading	08. Aylesbury	13. Other (Specify.................)
04. Oxford	09. Maidenhead	14. None
05. Watford	10. Windsor	

Q.9 How often do you come here to shop?

1. Daily	4. Irregularly
2. Weekly/several times a week	5. First time
3. Monthly/ 2/3 times a month	

By Observation: (Select main spokesperson if a group)

Sex: Male   Female
                               1   2

Age: Up to 25   26–40   41–64   65+
             1   2   3   4

Shopping Group: Adults   Males   1   2   3   4+
                                           Females   1   2   3   4+
                             Children   1   2   3   4+

of a department store (most stores are willing to release data of this sort, provided the figures required do not relate to the current or the previous year's trading). Construct appropriate tables and charts (including a Z-chart), adjust the figures to compensate for inflation, and comment on the trends revealed. Calculate relevant ratios, for example the ratio of departmental sales to floor area, and compare these with ratios for similar stores by referring to published statistics (for example the Report on the Census of Distribution in the Business Monitor Series).

B.   Assignments Based upon Published Statistics

1. Obtain data from Population Trends on the population figures for India and Japan for 1951, 1961, 1966, 1971, and 1976. Plot on natural scale graph paper and on semi-logarithmic graph paper and comment. Determine the (exponential) equations describing the growth in the two populations, and predict from these the population figures for a number of future years. Determine the annual growth rates for both populations.

     A similar exercise can be carried out on the number of branches of the Abbey National and Halifax Building Societies for the period 1968 onwards.

2. By referring to the appropriate tables in the Annual Abstract of Statistics, carry out the exercises given below for each of the following industries: (i) mining and quarrying; (ii) chemicals and allied industries; (iii) metal manufacture; (iv) textiles.
   (a) Examine and describe changes in the number of employees and in the output (as measured by the production index) over the 10-year period covered by the tables.
   (b) Show these changes by a suitable chart or graph.
   (c) Explain why these changes have occurred.

(d) On the basis of the information given and the reasons you have put forward in (c), estimate what the employment figures and the production index will be for the current year. Give reasons for your answer.

C.   Assignments Based upon Data Collected in the Classroom

1. Carry out a series of dice-throwing runs, each run consisting of 60 throws. Record the number of sixes thrown on each run, and construct a frequency table and a histogram. Find the mean and standard deviation, and check that the binomial formulae hold. Compare the frequencies with which different numbers of sixes occur with the expected frequencies (calculate these using the normal approximation to the binomial distribution). The results of the runs can be divided into groups of e.g. 6 or 12 throws to show the effect of reducing the sample size. As an alternative to throwing dice, toss coins.

2. Purchase or make a set of 1,000 cards (about 1 inch by $\frac{1}{2}$ inch) suitably numbered to simulate the values taken by a normally distributed variable. The cards should be kept in a container, and when required an appropriate quantity extracted to simulate random sampling from a normally distributed population. Uses to which the cards can be put include:
   (a) Illustration of the teaching given in Chapter 4 on random sampling, sampling errors, and the effect of increasing the sample size.
   (b) Construction of sampling distributions to demonstrate the results of the central limit theorem (Chapter 10).
   (c) Simulation of a quality control exercise.

3. The following exercise can be used to investigate the effects of rounding and truncation of data. Take a sample of size 30 (e.g. of the cards referred to above), and calculate the mean and standard deviation.

Round the data and recalculate $\bar{x}$ and S.D. Truncate the data and recalculate. Construct a frequency distribution and again calculate $\bar{x}$ and S.D. Double the class interval and recalculate. Compare all the results.

4. A queueing situation can be simulated as follows. Suppose that the number of arrivals per minute in a queueing system has been found to be as shown in the first two columns of the table below (note that other frequency distributions of numbers of arrivals can be simulated, if desired, using the Poisson distribution — see Chapter 18).

Table IV.1

Number of arrivals per minute interval	Frequency	Cumulative %	Random number limits
0	10	5	0–4
1	40	25	5–24
2	50	50	25–49
3	40	70	50–69
4	30	85	70–84
5	20	95	85–94
6	10	100	95–99
	200		

Calculate the cumulative percentages (see column 3), and from these percentages assign random number limits (column 4). Using the table of random numbers in Appendix III, simulate the number of arrivals over a given period of time in the following way. Starting at the top of the table (although any other place in the table would serve equally well as a starting point) and proceeding horizontally, the first two-digit number is 23. This lies within the limits 5 and 24, and so there is one arrival in the first minute. The next two-digit number is 49, which lies within the limits 25 and 49, and so there are two arrivals in the second minute. Proceeding in this way, the numbers of arrivals in successive one-minute intervals are as shown below. From this one can investigate the effect that

altering the number of servicing points has on queue length and on waiting time, as well as the effect of altering the type of queue from e.g. single channel to multi-channel.

Minute number: 1 2 3 4 5 6 7 8 9 10 11 etc.
Number of
  arrivals: 1 2 2 3 4 0 3 4 3 2 2
Queue length at
  end of minute*:1 2 3 5 8 7 9 12 14 15 16

(*If one customer is processed per minute and there is one service point.)

D.   A Multi-part Assignment

[Using most of the statistical techniques covered in this text (suitable for use as a single embracing BEC National Award assignment to be done in stages during the course)]

A trades union wishes to recruit employees of a non-unionized company. In order to determine what strategy to adopt the union officials carry out a survey of a random sample of 67 employees. The results of this survey are shown in Table IV.2.

1. By constructing suitable charts show how attitudes to the union vary with the sex, salary, and number of years service of employees in the sample. Give reasons for your choice of charts and state what they show (see Chapter 5).

2. For the salaries of the female employees in the sample determine the mean, median, standard deviation, quartile deviation, and coefficient of skewness. State what the results of your calculations show (Chapter 6).

3. Construct a frequency table of the salaries of the male employees in the sample using not less than 8 classes, and from this table construct a histogram and a cumulative frequency curve. Determine the mean, median, mode, standard deviation, quartile

Table IV.2

Sex of employee	Monthly salary (£)	Number of years service	Attitude to union	Sex of employee	Monthly salary (£)	Number of years service	Attitude to union
Male	398	8	Undecided	Male	346	8	For
Female	258	3	For	Male	245	2	For
Female	446	33	Against	Male	409	24	Against
Male	493	18	Undecided	Female	369	21	Against
Male	358	9	Against	Female	315	7	For
Male	346	12	Against	Male	328	4	For
Female	328	12	Undecided	Female	374	16	Against
Male	574	21	Undecided	Male	428	22	Against
Female	334	2	Undecided	Male	294	3	For
Male	380	6	For	Female	541	17	Against
Male	446	19	Against	Male	352	2	For
Female	430	20	Against	Male	302	5	Against
Female	245	1	For	Male	315	6	Undecided
Male	374	12	Against	Male	473	29	Against
Male	374	11	Undecided	Female	346	14	Undecided
Male	387	3	For	Male	428	9	Undecided
Female	263	8	Undecided	Female	398	13	Against
Male	387	10	For	Female	511	25	Against
Male	592	35	Against	Male	339	10	For
Male	276	2	For	Male	415	18	For
Female	315	4	For	Female	282	7	Undecided
Female	346	13	Undecided	Male	339	10	For
Male	339	7	Against	Male	446	15	Against
Female	430	20	Against	Male	525	30	Against
Female	245	4	Undecided	Female	474	18	For
Male	358	13	For	Male	398	19	Against
Male	294	1	For	Male	315	9	Undecided
Female	328	6	Undecided	Male	352	1	Undecided
Female	421	9	Undecided	Female	387	12	Against
Male	480	24	Against	Male	415	17	For
Female	282	1	For	Male	358	7	Undecided
Female	374	10	For	Female	346	14	For
Male	387	11	Against	Male	358	9	For
Female	315	5	Undecided				

deviation, and coefficient of skewness. Using these measures and those obtained in

(2) above comment on the differences between the salaries of male and female employees (Chapter 8).

By calculating a weighted average determine the mean salary of all the employees in the sample (Chapter 7).

4. (a) Determine the z-value of a salary of £300 for (i) the female distribution and

(ii) the male distribution (Chapter 9).

(b) Determine the 95% confidence interval of the mean salary of female employees, and the 99% confidence interval of the mean salary of male employees (Chapter 10).

5. (a) The management of the company claims that there is no significant difference between the mean salaries of male and female employees. Test this claim at

the 5% significance level.

(b) The management claims that only 20% of all employees are in favour of joining the union. Test this claim at the 1% significance level (Chapter 11).

6. The management claims that there is a strong association between the number of years worked by female employees and their salary.

(a) Construct a scattergraph showing number of years worked against monthly salary for the female employees of the sample.

(b) Determine the correlation coefficient for these two variables and test its significance. Explain your result.

(c) By determining the appropriate regression equation predict the monthly salary of a female employee who has been with the company for 10 years (Chapter 12).

Answers

CHAPTER 1

1. The missing figures are as follows:
   (a) 20, 25, 20
   (b) 120, 30, 25
   (c) 150, 180, $16\frac{2}{3}$
   (d) 140, 14.3, 160
   (e) 33.33, $33\frac{1}{3}$, 133.33
   (f) 60.87, 9.13, 13.

2. (a) A: £8750, B: £5000, C: £6250.
   (b) A: £7350, B: £4200, C: £5250, D: £6300

3. $\frac{1}{16}$

5. (a) 1.3286
   (b) $\log(2.462^{1.357}) = 1.357 \times$
   $$0.39129 = 0.53098+$$
   $\log(0.5678^{0.36}) = 0.36 \times \overline{1}.75420$
   $= -0.36 + 0.27151$
   $= -1 + 0.64 + 0.27151 = \overline{1}.91151$
   $$0.44249-$$
   $\log(248^{1.08}) = 1.08 \times 2.39445 = 2.58601$
   $$\overline{3}.85648$$
   antilog $\overline{3}.85648 = 0.0071859$

6. -117.80

7. 59,850

8. (b) 268 metres
   (c) 739 metres^2
   (d) (i) New length
   $= 2(\Sigma(x-a)) + 2\Sigma y = 2(\Sigma x - na)$
   $\quad + 2\Sigma y$
   $= 2\Sigma x + 2\Sigma y - 2na$
   $= 268 - 2 \times 6 \times 1.5$
   $= 250$ m
   (ii) New area $= 739 - 1.5 \times 53 =$
   659.5 m^2.

9. (a) Number of cabbages $= 10 \times 80 \pm 10\%$
   (the maximum error in the number of rows is 0%, since this figure is known exactly)
   $$= 800 \pm 10\% = 800 \pm 80$$
   Number of lettuces $= 15 \times 140 \pm 10\%$
   $$= 2100 \pm 10\% = 2100 \pm 210$$
   Number of cauliflowers $= 5 \times 65 \pm 5\%$
   $$= 325 \pm 5\% = \underline{325 \pm 16}$$
   So total number of
   plants $\qquad = \underline{3225 \pm 306}$

   The maximum error rounded to 1 significant figure = 300, and the approximate number to the same accuracy (i.e. to the nearest 100) = 3200.
   (b) The approximate value of the plants is £470, and the maximum error is £100.

CHAPTER 2

1. Two points on the line of best fit are (0, 22) and (7, 53). Substituting these values in the equation $y = a + bx$ and solving gives $a = 22$ and $b = 4.43$. Substituting $x = 9$ in $y = 22 + 4.43x$ gives the estimated profit for 1979 to be £62,000.

2. Annual motorbike costs (in £s) = $60 + 0.02x$, annual public transport costs = $0.05x$. The two are equal when $x = 2000$. If $x = 1400$, Jim will save £18 a year using public transport.

3. (a) £6211.70
   (b) £6414.27

4. Two points are (0, 200) and (8, 410). Substituting these in the equation $\log y = \log a + x \log b$ gives $a = 200$ and $b =$ antilog $0.03897 = 1.094$

5. Company B catches up with Company A when $100{,}000\,(1.1^x) = 50{,}000\,(1.2^x)$, i.e. $2 = 1.0909^x$. Hence

   $$x = \frac{\log 2}{\log 1.0909} = 7.97$$

   (end of year 7).

6. (a) Roots are -4 and -2.5, turning point is at $(-3.25, -1.125)$
   (b) Roots are -3 and 2, turning point is at $(-0.5, 6.25)$.

7. Call the quantity sold x. Then price = $3.6 - 0.001x$, revenue = $3.6x - 0.001x^2$ Turning point is at $x = 1800$, when revenue = £3240. Total costs = $800 + 1.2x$, profit = $-800 + 2.4x$. Turning point is at $x = 1200$, when profit = £640.

CHAPTER 3

1. $\{0, 1, 2\}, \{0, 1, 3\}, \{1, 2, 3\}, \{0, 1\},$ $\{1, 2\}, \{1, 3\}, \{1\}$.

2. 55 male employees are not shift-workers.

3. 1 boy dated Mary and Jane but not Susan.

4. The outcomes are H,H,H H,H,T H,T,H H,T,T
   T,H,H   T,H,T T,T,H T,T,T
   The event A contains the outcomes H,H,H and H,H,T. $P(A) = \frac{1}{4}$. The event B contains the outcomes H,H,H, H,T,H, T,H,H, and T,T,H. $P(B) = \frac{1}{2}$.

   $$P(A \text{ or } B) = P(A) + P(B) - P(A)P(B)$$
   $$= \frac{1}{4} + \frac{1}{2} - \frac{1}{4} \times \frac{1}{2}$$
   $$= \frac{5}{8}$$

5. (a) $\frac{5}{20} \times \frac{5}{20} = \frac{1}{16}$
   (b) $\frac{10}{20} \times \frac{5}{20} = \frac{1}{8}$
   (c) $\frac{15}{20} \times \frac{15}{20} = \frac{9}{16}$
   (d) $\frac{10}{20} + \frac{10}{20} - \frac{10}{20} \times \frac{10}{20} = \frac{3}{4}$
   (e) $\frac{5}{20} \times (1 - \frac{5}{20}) = \frac{3}{16}$

6. (a) $\frac{1}{4} \times \frac{1}{4} \times \frac{1}{4} \times \frac{1}{4} = \frac{1}{256}$
   (b) $\frac{3}{4} \times \frac{3}{4} \times \frac{3}{4} \times \frac{3}{4} = \frac{81}{256}$
   (c) $1 - \frac{81}{256} = \frac{175}{256}$
   (d) $\frac{1}{4} \times \frac{3}{4} \times \frac{3}{4} \times \frac{3}{4} = \frac{27}{256}$
   (e) $\frac{27}{256} + \frac{27}{256} + \frac{27}{256} + \frac{27}{256} = \frac{27}{64}$
   (f) P (at least two have petrol) = $1 - P$ (none have petrol) $- P$ (just one has petrol) = $1 - \frac{81}{256} - \frac{108}{256} = \frac{67}{256}$

7. $1 - P$ (none germinate) = $1 - \frac{1}{2} \times \frac{1}{2} \times \frac{1}{2} = \frac{7}{8}$

CHAPTER 6

1. $\Sigma X = 8, \Sigma X^2 = 40, n = 8,$ so $\bar{x} = 13 + \frac{8}{8} \times 3 = 16$ hours, S.D. = $3 \times \sqrt{\frac{40}{8} - (\frac{8}{8})^2} = 6$ hours.

2. (a) (i) For males, mode = 40, median = 45, range = 35, Q.D. = $\frac{1}{2}(58.75 - 40) = 9.375$. For females, mode =

median = 36, range = 12, Q.D. = $\frac{1}{2}(38.5 - 31.75) = 3.375$.

(ii) A suitable transformation for the male wages is: subtract 40 from each and divide the remainders by 5. Then $\Sigma X = 18$, $\Sigma X^2 = 88$, and $\overline{x} = 47.5$, S.D. = 11.3. For females, transform the wages by subtracting 36 from each. Then $\Sigma X = -3$, $\Sigma X^2 = 111$, and $\overline{x} \simeq 35.6$, S.D. $\simeq 3.7$.

(iii) For males, coeff. var. = 23.8, and Sk = + 0.7. For females, coeff. var. = 10.4 and Sk = −0.3.

3. For males, a suitable transformation is: subtract 43 from each and divide the remainders by 4. $\overline{x} = 55$, S.D. = 13.3, median = 55, coeff. var. = 24.2, Sk = 0. For females, subtract 48 from each and divide the remainders by 5. $\overline{x} = 51.75$, S.D. = 11.1, median = 48, coeff. var. = 21.5, Sk = +1.0.

4. (a) $\overline{x} = 13$, S.D. = 3.1.
   (b) Quartile coefficient of dispersion = 27.8, $Sk_q = + 0.4$.

CHAPTER 7

1. (a) The price relatives are:

	1975	1976	1977
Butter	112	147	129
Milk	112	125	137
Cheese	125	135	156

(b) The weighted averages are:

1975	1976	1977
$\frac{799}{7} = 114.1$	$\frac{927}{7} = 132.4$	$\frac{964}{7} = 137.7$

(c) The chain index numbers are:

	1975	1976	1977
	114.1	116.0	104.0

(d) The rebased numbers are:

1974	1975	1976	1977
72.6	82.9	96.2	100.0

2. The required summations are: $\Sigma p_0 q_0 = 280.6$, $\Sigma p_1 q_0 = 391.7$, $\Sigma p_2 q_0 = 492.3$, $\Sigma p_3 q_0 = 587.95$, $\Sigma p_0 q_1 = 363.9$, $\Sigma p_0 q_2 = 291.44$, $\Sigma p_0 q_3 = 260.54$, where p_0, p_1, etc., represent the hourly rates for 1972, 1974, etc., and q_0, q_1, etc., represent the numbers employed.

(a) Laspeyre wages index for 1974, 1976, 1978 is: 139.6, 175.4 and 209.5.

(b) Laspeyre quantity index for these years is: 129.7, 103.9 and 92.9.

3.

Year:	1968	1969	1970	1971	1972
(a) Rebased index:	65.3	67.1	69.8	73.3	80.1
(b) Chain index:		102.7	104.1	104.9	109.3
Year:	1973	1974	1975	1976	1977
	101.4	96.2	100.0	103.9	108.9
	126.6	94.9	104.0	103.9	104.8

5. The required index numbers for 1976, 1977, and 1978 are:

(a) (i) 124.9, 159.9, 174.0
    (ii) 125.0, 160.2, 174.2
(b)   125.0, 128.0, 108.6.

CHAPTER 8

1. The frequencies are: 6, 10, 14, 6, 4. $\Sigma fx = 78$, $\Sigma fx^2 = 241$, $\overline{x} = 1.95$, S.D. = 1.49.

2. (a) The probabilities are: $\frac{13}{60}$, $\frac{6}{60}$, $\frac{7}{60}$, $\frac{11}{60}$, $\frac{12}{60}$, $\frac{11}{60}$

(b) Expected value = $\Sigma px = \frac{216}{60} = 3.6$. Most likely score = 1.

(c) For an unbiased die each score has probability = $\frac{1}{6}$. Expected value in this case = 3.5. The biased die has a higher expected value, and is therefore biased towards the high scores.

3. Possible classes are $29\frac{1}{2} - 34\frac{1}{2}$, $34\frac{1}{2} - 39\frac{1}{2}$, etc. Frequencies are then: 1, 2, 5, 4, 10, 14, 6, 5, 2, 1.

(a) $\overline{x} = 55.0$, S.D. = 9.5.

(b) Median = 55.6, Q_1 = 50, Q_3 = 61.17, quartile dev. = 5.6.

(c) 20% = 10 students, so 11th student and above must pass. Pass mark = 48.

(d) 10% = 5 students, so 46th student and above should gain distinctions. Distinction mark = 68.

4. (a) For calculation purposes and for drawing the histograms the class intervals should be $54\frac{1}{2} - 64\frac{1}{2}$, $64\frac{1}{2} - 74\frac{1}{2}$, etc. To transform the x-values (i.e. the class midpoints) in the 'before change' distribution, subtract the assumed mean (say 97) and divide the remainders by 2.5. Then $\overline{x}$ = 97 forms, and S.D. = 10.6 forms. The x-values of the 'after change' distributions can be transformed in the usual way, and for this $\overline{x}$ = 110.1, S.D. = 8.0. The modes of the two distributions are 102 and 111, and the coefficients of skewness are −0.5 and −0.1.

(b) (i) 0.125
    (ii) 0.13
    (iii) 0.05.

5. Before change: median = 99.0, Q_1 = 92.6, Q_3 = 104.1. After change: median = 110.25, Q_1 = 104.5, Q_3 = 115.7.

6. Cumulative % number of incomes: 19, 62, 88, 95, 98, 99, 99.5, 100, 100, 100. Cumulative % total income: 8, 40, 71, 82, 89, 92, 94, 98, 99, 100. There is little difference between the two Lorenz curves, indicating that the lower incomes have received approximately the same percentage increase as the upper incomes, with little change in the distribution of total personal income.

CHAPTER 9

1. (a) (i) 96
       (ii) 341
       (iii) 11
       (iv) 68

(b) (i) 0.13%
    (ii) 13.59%

(c) (i) 0.8413
    (ii) 0.9332
    (iii) 0.0094

2. (a) The relative frequencies are: 0.0049, 0.0166, 0.0440, 0.0919, 0.1498, 0.1915, 0.1915, 0.1498, 0.0919, 0.0440, 0.0166, 0.0049.

3. (a) Exam marks are discrete. Students who fail have marks in the class 'less than 39.5'. 39.5 corresponds to z = 1.5, so the relevant standard normal curve area is 0.5−0.4332 = 0.0668. Hence percentage = 6.68.

(b) 5% of the area under the standard normal curve lies above z = 1.64. Hence the required mark is 51.5 + 1.64 × 8.0 = 64.6, i.e. above 64.

(c) Median = mean = 51.5. 25% of marks lie between Q_1 and the median, hence the relevant area = 0.25. Hence Q_1 lies approximately 0.7 S.D.s below the mean = 51.5 − 0.7 × 8 = 45.9. Q_3 = 51.5 + 0.7 × 8 = 57.1.

CHAPTER 10

1. (a) S.E. = 0.002 cm. The 95% confidence interval is 4.108 − 1.96 × 0.002 to 4.108 + 1.96 × 0.002, i.e. 4.104 to 4.112 cm. The 99% confidence interval is 4.108 − 2.58 × 0.002 to 4.108 + 2.58 × 0.002, i.e. 4.103 to 4.113 cm.

(b) Make the transformation: subtract 4.10 from each x-value, and multiply the remainders by 100. Then ΣX = 18 and ΣX^2 = 72, and

$$\overline{x} = 4.10 + \frac{18}{10} \times \frac{1}{100}$$
$$= 4.118$$

$$s = \frac{1}{100} \sqrt{\left(\frac{72}{9} - \frac{18^2}{10 \times 9} \right)}$$
$$= 0.021$$

S.E. = 0.0066, number of d.f. = 9, 95% of the area under the *t*-distribution lies between $t = -2.26$ and $t = +2.26$, 99% of the area lies between $t = -3.25$ and $t = +3.25$. The 95% confidence interval is $4.118 - 2.26 \times 0.0066$ to $4.118 + 2.26 \times 0.066$, i.e. 4.103 to 4.133. The 99% confidence interval is 4.097 to 4.139.

2. (a) 24.96 to 24.98
    (b) 15.98 to 16.06
    (c) 111.87 to 116.13
    (d) 7.845 to 10.155.

3. (a) $p = 0.46$, $q = 1 - 0.46 = 0.54$

    $$\text{S.E.} = \sqrt{\frac{0.46 \times 0.54}{500}}$$

    $$= 0.0223$$

    The 99% confidence interval is $0.46 - 2.58 \times 0.0223$ to $0.46 + 2.58 \times 0.0223$, i.e. 0.402 to 0.518.
    (b) 0.214 to 0.300.
    (c) 0.156 to 0.544.

4. (a) (i) S.E. = 0.85, confidence interval is £34.25 to £39.35;
         (ii) S.E. = 0.03, the interval is 0.01 to 0.19.
    (b) If the width of the confidence interval for μ is reduced to £1, then the $99\frac{3}{4}\%$ confidence limits must lie £0.50 from $\bar{x}$. Hence

    $$\text{S.E.} = \frac{0.5}{3}$$

    $$= 0.167$$

    So

    $$\frac{8.50}{\sqrt{n}} = 0.167$$

    and therefore

    $$\sqrt{n} = \frac{8.50}{0.167}$$

    $$= 51$$

Hence

$$n = 51^2$$

$$= 2600$$

If the width of the confidence interval for π is reduced to 0.06, then the 99% limits must lie 0.03 from p. Hence

$$\text{S.E.} = \frac{0.03}{3}$$

$$= 0.01$$

and therefore

$$\frac{0.09}{n} = 0.01^2$$

$$= 0.0001$$

Hence

$$n = \frac{0.09}{0.0001}$$

$$= 900$$

CHAPTER 11

1. (a) S.E. = 0.005, $\bar{x} - \mu = 2.0$ S.E.s, so reject N.H. at 5% level
    (b) S.E. = 0.00714, $\bar{x} - \mu = 2.8$ S.E.s, so reject N.H.
    (c) Critical value of *t* at 5% level with 15 df is 2.13
        S.E. = 2, $\bar{x} - \mu = 2$ S.E.s, so accept N.H.
    (d) Critical value of *t* at 5% level with 8 df is 2.31. S.E. = 0.05, $\bar{x} - \mu = 2$ S.E.s, so accept N.H.

2. (a) For one-tailed test at 1% level, the critical number of S.E.s is 2.33. So reject N.H.
    (b) Reject N.H.
    (c) Critical value of *t* is 2.60, so accept N.H.
    (d) Critical value of *t* is 2.90, so accept N.H.

3. (i) S.E. = 0.0175, $p - \pi$ = 2.29 (a) Reject N.H. at 5% level, accept at 1% level
    (b) Reject N.H. at 5% level, accept at 1% level.
    (ii) S.E. = 0.0512, $p - \pi$ = 1.95 S.E.s
    (a) Accept N.H. at 5% and 1% levels
    (b) Reject N.H. at 5% level, accept at 1% level.
    (iii) S.E. = 0.03, $p - \pi$ = 2 S.E.s (a) Reject N.H. at 5% level, accept at 1% level
    (b) Reject N.H. at 5% level, accept at 1% level.

4. (a) S.E.$_{\text{diff}}$ = 0.04614, $p_1 - p_2$ = 2.17 S.E.s, so reject N.H. at 5% level, accept at 1% level
    (b) S.E.$_{\text{diff}}$ = 0.05, $p_1 - p_2$ = 2.0 S.E.s, so reject N.H. at 5% level, accept at 1% level
    (c) S.E.$_{\text{diff}}$ = 0.0829, $p_1 - p_2$ = 3.02 S.E.s, so reject N.H. at 5% and 1% level.

5. For this distribution $\bar{x}$ = 97.0, S.D. = 10.6. For no E-value to be less than 5, the following classes should be used: under $84\frac{1}{2}$, $84\frac{1}{2}$-$89\frac{1}{2}$, $89\frac{1}{2}$-$94\frac{1}{2}$, $94\frac{1}{2}$-$99\frac{1}{2}$, $99\frac{1}{2}$-$104\frac{1}{2}$, $104\frac{1}{2}$-$109\frac{1}{2}$, over $109\frac{1}{2}$. The E-values for these classes are: 11.7, 12.2, 16.6, 19.0, 16.6, 12.2, 11.7. χ^2 = 0.247 + 2.216 + 0.781 + 0.474 + 4.251 + 2.757 + 3.837 = 14.563. The critical value of χ^2 with 4 df at the 1% level is 13.277. Hence reject N.H. — the distribution is not normal.

6. χ^2 = 1.043 + 1.405 + 0.110 + 3.207 + 2.519 + 0.008 + 0.331 + 0.050 + 0.074 = 8.747. The critical value of χ^2 with 4 df at the 5% level is 9.488, so accept N.H. — we cannot conclude that a relationship exists.

7. χ^2 = 0.667 + 0.667 + 0.400 + 0.400 = 2.134. The critical value of χ^2 with 1 df at the 1% level is 6.635, so the difference is not significant at this level.

CHAPTER 12

1. (b) Making the transformation $Y = y/40$, $\Sigma x = 48$, $\Sigma Y = 40$, $\Sigma xY = 373$, $\Sigma x^2 = 474$, $\Sigma Y^2 = 330$, $n = 5$
    (c) $r = -0.96$, indicating strong negative correlation
    (d) $Y = 16 - \frac{5}{6}x$, so $y/40 = 16 - \frac{5}{6}x$, hence $y = 640 - 33\frac{1}{3}x$
    (e) If $x = 10$, $y = 307$ pints
    (f) $x = 18.4 - 1.1Y = 18.4 - 1.1y/40 = 18.4 - 0.0275y$
    (g) If $y = 400$, $x = 7.4$, i.e. $7\frac{1}{2}$p.
    (h) Main causes of uncertainty include: small value of n; untypical months (for example, December) in sample; regression line (which represents the demand function) is unlikely to be linear
    (j) $\Sigma d^2 = 38.5$, $r' = -0.925$.

2. $r = 0.8$. Regression line of x on y is $x = 1.5 + 0.004y$. When $y = 100$, $x = £1.90$ per hour.

3. (b) y on x line is $y = 12(x - 1970) + 136$. When $x = 1978$, $y = 232$.
    (c) The scattergraph indicates that the national income is subject to cyclical fluctuations (see Chapter 13) which could push the value above £232m in 1978. In addition, the small value of n makes the prediction unreliable.

4. (a) $r = -0.50$,
    $$t = \sqrt{\frac{(-0.50)^2(15 - 2)}{1 - (-0.50)^2}} = 2.08.$$
    Applying the two-tailed test at the 0.05 significance level, the critical value of t with 13 df is 2.16, and since the calculated value is less than this it cannot be concluded that correlation exists.
    (b) y on x line is $y = 7.0 - 1.8x$. When $x = 0$, $y = 7.0$. Since correlation has

not been established, no reliance can be placed on this result.

5. (a) $\Sigma x = 36$, $\Sigma \log y = 22.05133$, $\Sigma x \log y = 90.42391$, $\Sigma x^2 = 204$, $\Sigma(\log y)^2 = 54.12134$, $n = 9$.

(b) $r = \dfrac{n\Sigma x \log y - \Sigma x \Sigma \log y}{\sqrt{\{(n\Sigma x^2 - (\Sigma x)^2)(n\Sigma \log y)^2 - (\Sigma \log y)^2)\}}}$

$= \dfrac{19.96731}{\sqrt{(540 \times 0.83091)}}$

$= 0.94$

(c) Regression equation of $\log y$ on x is $\log y = \log a + x \log b$.

$\log b = \dfrac{n\Sigma x \log y - \Sigma x \Sigma \log y}{n\Sigma x^2 - (\Sigma x)^2}$

$= \dfrac{19.96731}{540}$

$= 0.0369754$

$\log a = \dfrac{\Sigma \log y - b\Sigma x}{n}$

$= 2.3022462$

Hence $\log y = 2.3022462 + 0.0369754x$
Taking antilogs, $y = 200.56 \times 1.0889^x$
i.e. $y = 200 \times 1.09^x$.

CHAPTER 13

1. (b)

Quarter		Quarterly figures	M.A.T.	Moving averages	Trend	Variation from trend	Seasonal variation	Residual fluctuation
1974	3	110.5						
	4	81.7						
				101.15				
1975	1	116.0			100.79	15.21	15.16	0.05
				100.425				
	2	96.4	404.6		98.78	−2.38	2.47	4.85
				97.125				
	3	107.6	401.7		97.04	10.56	6.15	4.41
				96.95				
	4	68.5	388.5		98.61	−30.11	−23.78	−6.33
				100.275				
1976	1	115.3	387.8		100.15	15.15	15.16	−0.01
				100.025				
	2	109.7	401.1		102.35	7.35	2.47	4.88
				104.675				
	3	106.6	400.1		104.82	1.78	6.15	−4.37
				104.975				
	4	87.1	418.7		104.52	−17.42	−23.78	6.36
				104.075				
1977	1	116.5	419.9					
	2	106.1	416.3					

Seasonal variations:

Year	1	2	3	4	
		Quarter			
1975	15.21	−2.38	10.56	−30.11	
1976	15.15	7.35	1.78	−17.42	
Totals	30.36	4.97	12.34	−47.53	
Averages	15.18	2.485	6.17	−23.765	(sum = 0.07)
Correcting factor	−0.0175	−0.0175	−0.0175	− 0.0175	
Seasonal variations	15.16	2.47	6.15	−23.78	

(c) The deseasonalized figures are: 110.5 − 6.15 = 104.35, 105.5, 100.8, 93.9, 101.4, 92.3, 100.1, 107.2, 100.4, 109.9, 131.7, 108.6.

(d) Forecast for the 3rd quarter of 1977 is: $A = T + S = 108 + 6.15 = 114$. Error from residual fluctuations is ±7.

2. (b)

Year (x)	$X = x$-1967	Index (y)	Xy	X^2	Trend	Actual trend	Cyclical fluctuations	Residual fluctuations
1961	−6	76.7	−460.2	36	76.72	1.000	0.992	1.008
1962	−5	77.4	−387.0	25	79.34	0.976	0.978	0.998
1963	−4	79.7	−318.8	16	81.96	0.972	1.002	0.970
1964	−3	86.5	−259.5	9	84.58	1.023	1.021	1.002
1965	−2	89.1	−178.2	4	87.20	1.022	1.007	1.015
1966	−1	90.6	− 90.6	1	89.81	1.009	0.992	1.017
1967	0	91.7	0	0	92.43	0.992	0.978	1.014
1968	1	97.2	97.2	1	95.05	1.023	1.002	1.021
1969	2	99.9	199.8	4	97.67	1.023	1.021	1.002
1970	3	100.0	300.0	9	100.28	0.997	1.007	0.990
1971	4	100.3	401.2	16	102.90	0.975	0.992	0.983
1972	5	102.5	512.5	25	105.52	0.971	0.978	0.993
1973	6	110.0	660.0	36	108.14	1.017	1.002	1.015
Totals	0	1201.6	476.4	182				

$$a = \frac{\Sigma y}{n}$$

$$= \frac{1201.6}{13}$$

$$= 92.431$$

$$b = \frac{\Sigma Xy}{\Sigma X^2}$$

$$= \frac{476.4}{182}$$

$$= 2.6176$$

Hence the equation of the trend line is

$$y = 92.431 + 2.6176X$$

$$= 92.431 + 2.6176(x - 1967)$$

Cyclical fluctuations:

	1	2	3	4	5
	1.000	0.976	0.972	1.023	1.022
	1.009	0.992	1.023	1.023	0.997
	0.975	0.971	1.017		
Totals	2.984	2.939	3.012	2.046	2.019
Averages	0.995	0.980	1.004	1.023	1.010
Averages × $\frac{5}{5.012}$	0.992	0.978	1.002	1.021	1.007

(Sum = 5.012)

(c) For 1960, trend = 92.431 + 2.6176 (1960–1967)

$$= 74.108$$

cyclical fluctuations = 1.007

estimate = $T \times C$

$$= 74.108 \times 1.007$$

$$= 74.6$$

error from residual fluctuations = ± 3%.

This estimate accords well with the actual index for 1960 of 75.8.

CHAPTER 14

1. (a) 5, 9, 13, 17, 21
    (b) 20, 10, 0, −10, −20
    (c) 10, 20, 40, 80, 160
    (d) 2, −6, 18, −54, 162.

2. (a) A.P. with $a = 10$, $d = 4$
    20th term = 10 + 19 × 4
    $$= 86$$
    $S = \frac{20}{2}(2 \times 10 + 19 \times 4)$
    $$= 960$$
    (b) −37, −170
    (c) 524, 288, 1,048, 575
    (d) 20th term = $\dfrac{2700}{3^{19}}$

    $$= 0.000002323$$

    $S = \dfrac{2700[1 - (\frac{1}{3})^{20}]}{1 - \frac{1}{3}}$

    ($(\frac{1}{3})^{20}$ is negligibly small and can be ignored)

3. $P = 25,000$, $i = 0.15$.
    Profit in eighth year = $25,000(1.15)^8$
    $$= £76,476$$

    Total profit = $\dfrac{25,000(1 - 1.15)^8}{1 - 1.15}$

    $$= £343,170$$

4. The opening balances of successive quarters are: 10,000, 9750, 9500, 9250, ... This is an A.P. consisting of 40 terms with $a = 10,000$ and $d = -250$. $S = 205,000$. Quarterly rate of interest = 0.1/4 = 0.025, so total amount of interest paid = 10,000 × 0.025 + 9750 × 0.025 + 9500 × 0.025 + ... = 205,000 × 0.025 = £5125.

5. (a) £684.28, £686.39, £688.39
    (b) 8.16%, 8.24%, 8.33%.

6. (a) (i)   £nil
        (ii) £1638.40

(b) $389 = 5000 (1 + i)^5$, so

$$1 + i = \left(\frac{389}{5000}\right)^{1/5}$$

$$= 0.6 \text{ (by logs)}$$

Hence $i = -0.4$, so rate = 40%.

7. (a) £391.76
    (b) £28301.

8. N.P.V. of existing launderette =
    $$-8000 + \frac{4500}{1.11} + \frac{4700}{1.11^2} + \ldots = £10,176.$$
    N.P.V. of new launderette = £12,520, so should choose this.

9. N.P.V. =
    $$-2000 - \frac{25,000}{1 + i} + \frac{10,000}{(1 + i)^2} + \frac{30,000}{(1 + i)^3} + \frac{30,000}{(1 + i)^4}$$
    $$+ \frac{15,000}{(1 + i)^5}$$
    By trial and error, i is found to be 0.2388, so rate = 23.88%.

10. Present value =
    $$\frac{1000}{1.08} + \frac{1000}{1.08^2} + \ldots + \frac{1000}{1.08^5} = \frac{1000}{0.08}\left(1 - \frac{1}{1.08^5}\right)$$
    = £3993. There is little to choose between the two methods.

CHAPTER 15

1. The three constraints are:

    $200x + 400y \leqslant 20,000$, i.e. $x + 2y \leqslant 100$
    $12x + 7y \leqslant 600$
    $73x + 66y \leqslant 4000$

    The objective function is $F = x + y$.
    The maximum number is 17 fat women, 41 slim women.

2. Call the number of chairs produced per day x, and the number of tables y. The woodworking shop spends $\frac{1}{12}$ hours on each chair and $\frac{1}{6}$ hours on each table. It

therefore spends $x/12 + y/6$ hours on x chairs and y tables, and this number cannot exceed 8. Hence the first constraint is

$$\frac{x}{12} + \frac{y}{6} \leqslant 8, \text{ i.e. } x + 2y \leqslant 96.$$

Similarly the other two constraints are:

$5x + 4y \leqslant 320$

$7x + 9y \leqslant 504$

The objective function is $F = 4x + 5y$.
51 chairs and 16 tables should be produced.

3. Call the number of £s invested in commercial property x, and the number invested in property for private letting y. Then the two constraints are:

    $$\frac{12}{100}x + \frac{6}{100}y \geqslant 60,000, \text{ i.e. } 2x + y \geqslant 1,000,000$$

    $8x + 12y \geqslant 7,500,000$

    The objective function is $F = x + y$.
    The minimum investment is £562,500 on commercial property, £437,500 on private.

4. Call the number of hours run by plant A x, and the number run by plant B y. The constraints are:

    $2x + y \geqslant 40$

    $6x + 7y \geqslant 210$

    $2x + 5y \geqslant 100$

    The objective function is $F = 75x + 120y$.
    To minimize costs, plant A should be run for 21.875 hours, plant B should be run for 11.25 hours.

CHAPTER 16

1. (a) $dy/dx = 3$; $\int y \, dx = \frac{3}{2}x^2 + 2x + c$
    (b) $8x - 6$; $\frac{4}{3}x^3 - 3x^2 + 12x + c$
    (c) $1/2\sqrt{x}$; $\frac{2}{3}x^{3/2} + c$
    (d) $-1/x^2$; $\log_e x + c$

(e) $-\frac{1}{2}x^{-3/2}$; $2\sqrt{x} + c$

(f) $-\frac{3}{2}x^{-5/2}$; $-2/\sqrt{x} + c$

(g) $-2/x^3$; $-1/x + c$

(h) $8e^{2x}$; $2e^{2x} + c$.

2. (i) Max at $x = 1$, min at $x = 3$, area = 12.

(ii) Min at $x = -1$, max at $x = 0$, min at $x = +1$, area = 33.07.

(iii) Inflectionary point at $x = 0$, max at $x = 2$, min at $x = 4$, area = 178.

3. (a) $x = 1$, i.e. 9 a.m.

(b) 0

(c) 1020.

4. (a) Price = $20 - 4x$

(b) Revenue $(R) = 20x - 4x^2$

(c) $M.R. = 20 - 8x$

(d) Total costs = $\frac{2}{3}x^3 - \frac{1}{2}x^2 + 5x + 1$, and so $M.C. = 2x^2 - x + 5$

(e) $M.R. = M.C.$, so

$$20 - 8x = 2x^2 - x + 5$$

and therefore

$$2x^2 + 7x - 15 = 0$$

Hence

$$x = -5 \text{ or } +1\tfrac{1}{2}$$

Negative values are impossible, so profit maximized at $x = 1\frac{1}{2}$

(f) Profit $(P) = (20x - 4x^2) -$
$$(\tfrac{2}{3}x^3 - \tfrac{1}{2}x^2 + 5x + 1)$$
$$= -\tfrac{2}{3}x^3 - 3\tfrac{1}{2}x^2 + 15x - 1$$

$\dfrac{dP}{dx} = -2x^2 - 7x + 15$, and this is zero when $x = -5$ or $+1\frac{1}{2}$.

$\dfrac{d^2P}{dx^2} = -4x - 7$, which is less than 0 when $x = 1\frac{1}{2}$.

Hence profit is maximized at $x = 1\frac{1}{2}$.

(g) At $x = 1\frac{1}{2}$, $R = 21$, hence revenue = £21,000. At $x = 1\frac{1}{2}$, $P = 11.375$, hence profit = £11,375.

(h) $\dfrac{dR}{dx} = 20 - 8x$, so stationary point is at

$x = 2\frac{1}{2}$.

$\dfrac{d^2R}{dx^2} = -8$, hence stationary point is a maximum.

(i) At $x = 2\frac{1}{2}$, revenue = £25,000 and profit = £5458.

5. (a) $T.C. = x^3 - 6x^2 + 22x + 20$

(b) $R = 26x - \frac{1}{2}x^2$

(c) $P = -x^3 + 5.5x^2 + 4x - 20$

(d) Max at $x = 4$ (min at $x = -\frac{1}{3}$). Profit is then £2000 per month.

(e) Max revenue at $x = 20$, when $R = £32,000$ per month.

(f) At revenue-maximizing output there is a loss of £574,000 per month.

CHAPTER 17

1. For strategy (a), $E.V. = £6925$; for strategy (b), $E.V. = £8050$. Choose (b). The $E.V.$ under perfect information is $700 + 2800 + 3150 + 1500 = £8150$. Value of perfect information = $8150 - 8050 = £100$.

2. The expected value of the wager to Fred is:

Event	Probability	C.V.	E.V.
HHH	$0.6 \times 0.6 \times 0.6 = 0.216$	+2p	+0.432p
HHT	$0.6 \times 0.6 \times 0.4 = 0.144$	+1	+0.144
HTH	$0.6 \times 0.4 \times 0.6 = 0.144$	+1	+0.144
HTT	$0.6 \times 0.4 \times 0.4 = 0.096$	−3	−0.288
THH	$0.4 \times 0.6 \times 0.6 = 0.144$	+1	+0.144
THT	$0.4 \times 0.6 \times 0.4 = 0.096$	−3	−0.288
TTH	$0.4 \times 0.4 \times 0.6 = 0.096$	−3	−0.288
TTT	$0.4 \times 0.4 \times 0.4 = 0.064$	−3	−0.192
			−0.192

The wager favours Jim. To make it fair (so that $E.V. = 0$), Fred should pay nothing when no heads are tossed.

3. The accompanying figure shows the tree diagrams and the $E.V.$ calculations. The company should choose alternative (a).

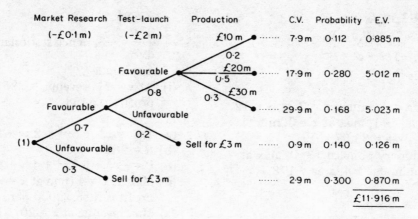

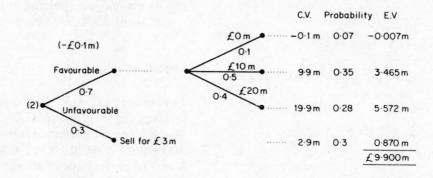

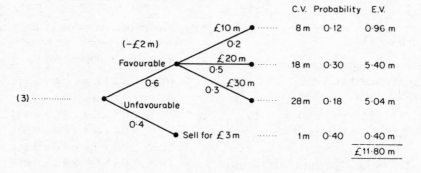

4. (The decision trees required for this answer are not included.)

If test drills are not made, expected cost of artesian supply = £1,080,000, so the authority should lay a pipe to the lake at a cost of £1,000,000.

If test drills are made, the revised probabilities are:

P(artesian supply adequate | test drills indicate supply adequate)

$$= \frac{0.6 \times 0.7}{0.6 \times 0.7 + 0.4 \times 0}$$

$$= 1$$

P(artesian supply adequate | test drills indicate supply inadequate)

$$= \frac{0.6 \times 0.1}{0.6 \times 0.1 + 0.4 \times 0.7}$$

$$= 0.1765$$

P(supply adequate | test drills give ambiguous result)

$$= \frac{0.6 \times 0.2}{0.6 \times 0.2 + 0.4 \times 0.3}$$

$$= 0.5$$

If the test drills indicate that the supply is adequate, then the optimum decision is to supply the town by artesian water, the expected cost being $1 \times 800{,}000 = £800{,}000$.

If the test drills indicate that the supply is inadequate, then the expected cost of supplying the town by artesian well is £1,376,470, and so the optimum decision is to lay the pipe to the lake at a cost of £1,000,000.

If the test drills give an ambiguous result, then the expected cost of supply by artesian well is £1,250,000, and again the optimum decision is to lay the pipe to the lake at a cost of £1,000,000.

P(test drills indicate supply adequate)
   $= 0.42$
P(test drills indicate supply inadequate)
   $= 0.06 + 0.28$
   $= 0.34$
P(test drills indicate ambiguous result)
   $= 0.12 + 0.12$
   $= 0.24$

So the expected cost if test drills are made is $0.42 \times 800{,}000 + 0.34 \times 1{,}000{,}000 + 0.24 \times 1{,}000{,}000 = £916{,}000$.

The value of the test drill information is therefore $£1{,}000{,}000 - £916{,}000 = £84{,}000$. The conclusion is that the authority should undertake test drills, since the cost of doing so is only £50,000, which is £34,000 less than the value of the information obtained.

CHAPTER 18

1. (i) $\dfrac{10!}{5!5!}\, 0.6^5\, 0.4^5 = 0.201$
    (ii) 0.251
    (iii) 0.215.

    Number of arrangements $= \dfrac{10!}{7!3!} = 120$.

2. (a) (i) $\dfrac{5!}{5!0!}\, 0.8^0\, 0.2^5 = 0.2^5 = 0.00032$
        (ii) 0.0064
        (iii) 0.0512
        (iv) 0.2048
        (v) 0.4096
        (vi) 0.32768.
    (b) Mean $= 80$, S.D. $= 4$, $z = (80 - 74.5)/4$
         $= 1.375$ so area $= 0.9155$.

3. (a) (i) $\dfrac{e^{-3}\, 3^0}{0!} = \dfrac{1}{e^3} = 0.050$
        (ii) 0.150
        (iii) 0.224
        (iv) 0.224
        (v) 0.168
        (vi) 0.101
        (vii) 0.050.
    (b) $m = 6$, S.D. $= 2.4495$,
         $z = (9.5 - 6)/2.4495 = 1.43$. Area $=$
         $0.5 - 0.4236 = 0.0764$.
    (c) If unit of time $= 1$ minute, $1/\lambda = 10$, so $\lambda = 0.1$. Probability that interval is less than $x = 15$ minutes is

    $$1 - e^{-1.5} = 1 - \frac{1}{\sqrt{e^3}}$$

    $$= 0.77687$$
    (d) $0.77687^9 = 0.1031$.

4. If 1 hour is the unit of time, then for post A $\lambda = 2$ and $\mu = 60/21$ and for post B $\lambda = 4$ and $\mu = 5$.
    (a) For A, $\rho = \lambda/\mu = 0.7$, and for B $\rho = 0.8$.
    (b) $1 - \rho = 0.3$ for A and 0.2 for B.
    (c) $\rho/(1-\rho) = 2\frac{1}{3}$ lorries for A and 4 lorries for B.
    (d) $\rho/(1-\rho) \times 1/\mu = 49$ minutes for A and 48 minutes for B.

Index

Also from Heinemann

Management and the Organization
Shaun Gregson and Frank Livesey

Specifically designed for BTEC Higher National Awards courses, this book combines the principles of management with an analysis of the problems occurring in an organization. Examples and assignments are included to give students a real-life glimpse of the business environment, furnish the text. Special attention is given to communication, planning, and decision-making, and their implications for the main management functions. The book is intended as a central text for business studies and professional management courses. It will be especially useful to BTEC students and those preparing for DMS, NEBSS, and professional examinations.

Contents

The Pressures and Challenges of Management · Management and the Manager · Organizations in The Private and Public Sectors · Communications in Principle · Communications in Action · The Planning Function · Decision Making · Organizing · Leading and Directing · Controlling · The Finance Function · The Marketing Function · The Production Function · The Purchasing Function · The Personnel Function · Management Services · Managment in the Office · The Future.

Business Organization
R. J. Williamson

This basic topic is given a clear and comprehensive treatment with a wealth of examples from current business situations. Theory and practice are so linked that the modern business techniques presented can be applied as well as understood. Aspects of the subject covered include the manager's role, communications, control, business law, finance, purchasing, production, human resources, industrial relations, marketing, and change. The revision exercises on each chapter will be especially helpful to students preparing for examinations. Designed to meet the needs of students working for the Institute of Marketing Certificate and the examinations of the CAM Foundation, this book will also be of value to BTEC students at National and Higher National Awards levels and to professional and degree students following courses in business studies and marketing, leading up to the examinations of the ICA, ACA, ICMA and IMC.

Business Administration:
A Textbook for the Computer Age
Roger Carter

'This is a first-class volume, opening up some of the possibilities of the future and examining the equipment and technology appropriate to its needs.'
Times Educational Supplement

Contents include:

The Organization of Production; The System Approach to Organization and Control; Designing the Organization; Information for Decision-Making; The Work of the Office; Office Systems – The Equipment and the Emerging Technology of the Integrated Office; The Well-Controlled Business; The Well-Organized Job; The Well-Planned Office; The Well-Managed Worker. Written to meet the needs of students on the BTEC 'Administration in Business' course and those on the BTEC computer studies module 'Information in Organizations' at National Awards level, *Business Administration* will also be useful to students on professional courses who wish to acquire an understanding of administration in the age of the intelligent office machine.

Management Techniques and Quantitative Methods
Robert Ball

This book will provide students with a basic knowledge and understanding of management techniques and quantitative methods. It assumes only basic numeracy rather than sophisticated mathematical skills. Whilst the book concentrates on the practical applications of techniques there is sufficient treatment of the underlying concepts and theory to make it readily intelligible. Student exercises form an important part of the text and are introduced at regular intervals in each chapter.

Contents

The quantitative approach to Management · Descriptive Statistics · Statistical Methods 1 · Statistical Methods 2 · Forecasting · Optimisation Techniques · Linear Programming · Making Decisions · Production Planning · Stock Control · Planning and Control · Queuing and Congestion Problems · Simulation.
Management Techniques and Quantitative Methods will be essential reading for all students taking degrees in Management Science or Business Studies, and of considerable interest to students of Economics, Finance and Engineering.